Operational Gaming

An International Approach

Edited by

INGOLF STÅHL

International Institute for Applied Systems Analysis
Laxenburg, Austria

PERGAMON PRESS

OXFORD · NEW YORK · TORONTO · SYDNEY · PARIS · FRANKFURT

7142-4581

MATH.-STAT.

U.K.	Pergamon Press Ltd., Headington Hill Hall, Oxford OX3 0BW, England
U.S.A.	Pergamon Press Inc., Maxwell House, Fairview Park, Elmsford, New York 10523, U.S.A.
CANADA	Pergamon Press Canada Ltd., Suite 104, 150 Consumers Road, Willowdale, Ontario M2J 1P9, Canada
AUSTRALIA	Pergamon Press (Aust.) Pty. Ltd., P.O. Box 544, Potts Point, N.S.W. 2011, Australia
FRANCE	Pergamon Press SARL, 24 rue des Ecoles, 75240 Paris, Cedex 05, France
FEDERAL REPUBLIC OF GERMANY	Pergamon Press GmbH, Hammerweg 6, D-6242 Kronberg-Taunus, Federal Republic of Germany

Library of Congress Cataloging in Publication Data

Main entry under title:
Operational gaming.
(Frontiers of operational research and applied systems analysis ; v. 3) (Pergamon international library of science, technology, engineering, and social studies)
Includes bibliographical references.
1. Game theory — Addresses, essays, lectures.
I. Ståhl, Ingolf, 1940-   . II. International Institute for Applied Systems Analysis. III. Series.
IV. Series: Pergamon international library of science, technology, engineering, and social studies.
QA269.O64 1983   519.3   83-17399
ISBN 0-08-030836-8 (Hardcover)
ISBN 0-08-030870-8 (Flexicover)

In order to make this volume available as economically and as rapidly as possible the authors' typescripts have been reproduced in their original forms. This method unfortunately has its typographical limitations but it is hoped that they in no way distract the reader.

Printed and bound in Great Britain by William Clowes Limited, Beccles and London

GENERAL PREFACE

Operational Gaming is one of the oldest techniques available for assisting   policy advisors in exploring the consequences of possible future actions. The technique has indeed always been a major tool in connection with military strategy, but its transfer to the civilian decision-making area has been slow and largely directed towards management training rather than policy formulation. Clearly its potential is very great.

One of the reasons for the scant use of operational gaming must be the paucity of the literature - particularly in the form of books. It was because of this that I recruited Ingolf Stahl to work at the International Institute of Applied Systems Analysis for the prime purpose of ensuring that a thorough review of the field was undertaken and that the resulting knowledge was made generally available. We were particularly fortunate in being able to recruit Isak Assa from Bulgaria to work with him on this, so that the review covered both east and west experience of the subject.

This work is therefore unique in the review it provides of the practice and potential for operational gaming as an aid to civilian decision-making and policy formulation. Its international character appears in two forms. In the first place it compares and contrasts experience in gaming from many different countries. Secondly, it discusses some of the problems associated with the gaming of international situations.

It is hoped that this book will enable practitioners and decision-makers with a chart to explore more effectively one of the lesser-known frontiers of the subject.

Rolfe Tomlinson
General Editor

PREFACE

This book on operational gaming is the result of research carried out at, or in collaboration with, the International Institute for Applied Systems Analysis (IIASA), which is situated at Laxenburg (near Vienna), Austria.

IIASA is an international research institute with scientific academies and similar nongovernmental bodies from 17 countries as its national member organizations. The fact that IIASA's membership includes organizations from both East and West gives the Institute a unique character.

The work of the Institute has been applied in the sense that research has focused on practical problems of importance, such as energy, food, water, etc. At the same time, IIASA work has also dealt with the development and appraisal of systems-analytical methods that appear helpful in analyzing practical problems. Since the ultimate aim of much of IIASA's research is to aid decision making and policy implementation, there has been constant concern about the ways in which systems analysis can make a more effective impact on decision-making processes. Being very much involved in the development of models, a natural question for IIASA has been how to ensure that these models are of real practical value. It is widely recognized that one major difficulty preventing the integration of analytical ideas into the decision-making process is the fact that we are still unable to adequately model the decision process to which the analysis is to be applied. One of the few tools that can help to close this gap is operational gaming, in which several people interact in a simulation of a real-world problem.

Apart from some work on a specific global economy game by Olaf Helmer, gaming activity at IIASA really started with a workshop in August 1978. This workshop, at which gaming experts from most of IIASA's national member organization countries participated, was initiated by Rolfe Tomlinson, then Chairman of the Management and Technology Area of IIASA. The workshop focused on the question of the most suitable way for IIASA to contribute to the new methodology of operational gaming. It was recognized by the workshop participants that IIASA's international character, and particularly its unique East-West contacts, made it especially suitable for dealing with international aspects of operational gaming. It was generally agreed that one important topic was to report on the development of operational gaming in the socialist countries, and in particular on how the method has been used for planning in industry and government. Other topics of interest were the international transfer of games and the development of certain methodological aspects of gaming. The publication of a monograph, which could partly serve as a handbook in introducing systems analysts to certain aspects of gaming, was considered to be an essential goal.

The editor of this volume, who was the Swedish delegate at the 1978 workshop, was invited by Rolfe Tomlinson and Peter de Janosi, then Chairman of the System and Decision Sciences Area at IIASA, to come to the Institute to draw up a plan for IIASA research on gaming during 1980 and 1981. This research plan proposed the collection of information suitable for the type of monograph discussed at the workshop as well as independent research using relatively small games, for example in the fields of natural resources and the environment.

The plan also envisaged an active ongoing role for IIASA in establishing international contacts between gamers by organizing occasional meetings. A small advisory group meeting was held in the fall of 1980, followed by a larger task force meeting at the end of 1981. Papers were invited from selected authors specifically to become chapters in the planned monograph, which later developed into the present volume.

This book also describes in-house research done by the editor and by Isak Assa (Bulgaria), who spent six months working on gaming at IIASA, and by Vadim Marshev (USSR), Hans Gernert (GDR), and Ryszard Wasniowski (Poland) who visited IIASA for several short periods. Klaus Niemeyer (FRG), Laszlo Mozes (Hungary), and Myron Uretsky (USA) also contributed in an advisory capacity to the gaming task, particularly during its formative stages.

In conclusion, I would like to thank Tim Devenport for his careful editorial work, Noël Blackwell and Rhonda Starnes for keyboarding and formatting the book on IIASA's computerized text-processing system, and all the others who have helped in the book's production.

Ingolf Stahl
Editor

CONTENTS

PART I

INTRODUCTION

Chapter I

INTRODUCTION

Ingolf Stahl
*International Institute for Applied Systems Analysis,
Laxenburg (Austria)*

Operational gaming is regarded by many as a new and promising method within systems analysis. It involves a number of people interacting in a simulation of a real-world problem for the purpose of aiding decision making, planning, or policy implementation. Operational gaming focuses on the interdependence between decision makers and can serve as an interface between model construction and implementation in the solution of complex problems.

Operational gaming has a long tradition in the military sphere,[1] but its use in the civilian sector is much more recent.[2] Although it is difficult to find any comprehensive overview in the existing literature in the extent to which operational gaming is used in practice, we have reason to believe that there is substantial use of gaming in the civilian sector, not least in the socialist countries, as described later in this book.

In connection with the IIASA gaming project, Richard Duke of the University of Michigan and myself recently sent out questionnaires to survey the uses of operational gaming in practice. Although we have probably been able to reach only a fraction of all the scientists in the gaming field, the approximately 50 answers we received indicate that operational gaming is used fairly widely in the civilian sector and that many interesting applications of gaming have not been documented at all for an outside audience. From the completed questionnaires we gathered answers to three general questions:

Q: Who are the clients of operational gaming?

A: International organizations like UNESCO, UNEP, WHO; state governments: central government departments like the US Department of Energy (DOE); national health services; regional administrative bodies; corporations and industrial enterprises (particularly in the socialist countries); to mention just a few examples.

Q: What areas are covered?

A: Agriculture, construction, disaster planning, educational systems, energy, environment, financial policy, garbage disposal, health care, location policy, management information systems, marketing strategy in industry, and tourism, among many others.

Q: For what purposes is operational gaming used?

A: Changing attitudes, dress rehearsals, forecasting, improving communications, generating new alternatives, planning, testing decision aids, testing personnel, training for specific tasks, and numerous other purposes.[3]

These answers show that gaming is used at various levels in different organizations, in a great many different fields, and for a great many purposes.

However, it is our belief that the use of operational gaming could be considerably extended if information about the possibilities, and the limitations, of the method was more systematically and widely available. At the 1978 IIASA workshop dissatisfaction was expressed with the existing literature on gaming. It was suggested that a "handbook" should be produced whose purpose would be to help scientists entering the field of gaming. The gaming research task at IIASA started by examining the feasibility of such a handbook and this monograph, *Operational Gaming: An International Approach*, is the ultimate result of these efforts.

In surveying the existing literature on gaming, the broadness of the field and the variety of backgrounds of the game constructors is striking. It is very difficult to get a good overview of the whole field. One starting point appeared to be a search for suitable bibliographies on the subject. In fact there are many such bibliographies, some not in printed form but stored in computer systems. We thought it would be possible to locate a few standard bibliographies, but even here the diversity within the gaming field is very obvious. At the end of this introduction we list a few valuable sources, but it should be stressed that the selection has been somewhat random and may have missed several interesting bibliographies.

The gaming literature is growing rapidly, while at the same time some of the earlier literature, particularly on computer-supported gaming, is rapidly becoming outdated. Therefore, it seems that the ideal method of keeping a gaming bibliography is to have it on a computer where it can be updated easily. To our knowledge, the most comprehensive up-to-date computerized bibliography covering the literature in English is the one kept by Richard Duke, University of Michigan, on APPLE II disks. Updated files on gaming in the socialist countries are kept in the GDR; here the contact person is Hans Gernert of Humboldt University, Berlin. Some other gaming files are mentioned in the references.

Against this background it did not appear sensible to focus our "handbook" activities on providing some type of bibliography on gaming. Furthermore, the results of our literature search emphasized the pitfalls of trying to write any kind of general handbook that hoped to cover broad areas of gaming. Gaming is very much a "moving target"; it is constantly developing, so any detailed state-of-the-art survey would rapidly become obsolete.

Gaming is also very diverse as regards the professional backgrounds its developers require. Complex computer games require a knowledge of computer science, while role-playing games may require a background in psychiatry or social psychology. Furthermore, the use and development of gaming for a specific problem requires a thorough understanding of the problem. Good understanding of the problem coupled with good judgement is, in many instances, more important than knowledge of specific gaming techniques.

Although these considerations discouraged us from attempting any kind of generalized handbook, we still saw the need for a specialized monograph. We felt this monograph should fulfill two aims: it should be helpful in introducing systems scientists to operational gaming, *and* it should give some international perspectives on operational gaming, thereby utilizing and building on the unique gaming material available through the IIASA research network.

Looking at the first aim, introducing a systems analyst to gaming, we can group the analyst's probable questions in the following hierarchy:

Assuming that he is interested in analyzing some specific problem his first question should be: Is gaming a method that can be helpful in analyzing problems? To answer this question of "to game or not to game" a systematic overview of the types of gaming available is first required, and this can be found in Parts II and III of the book. The answer to the question of whether gaming is appropriate or not also very much depends on the actual problem at hand. In this respect, much can be learnt from reading case studies on how gaming has been used in a variety of areas (agriculture, construction, industry, transport, etc.) and for different purposes (planning, model tests, improving communications, etc.), and noting how the method varies for different applications. We think that Part VIII should be particularly useful in this respect, but examples of interest are also to be found in Parts IV, VII, and IX of the book.

Once gaming is decided upon as a method for analyzing a particular problem, another question arises: Is it more appropriate to use an existing game or to construct a completely new game? Before constructing a completely new game, it is often worthwhile to investigate the possibility of using an existing game. However, an existing game will often require some modification in order to adapt it to the particular problem at hand. Furthermore, the most suitable game is often unavailable in the country of the new user. In such cases, the international transfer of a suitable game may be contemplated because, worldwide, there exists a large number of games for different purposes but these games are scattered over a great many countries. Both the international transfer process and any special modifications involved, e.g., on moving a game from one computer to another (problems also encountered when transferring games within countries), are discussed in Part V. It is also hoped that many of the other chapters, e.g., those in Part IV, will give some ideas on where to find a suitable game.

In some cases it can be appropriate to use not just one single existing game, but to use parts from two or more different games. The merging of games is discussed in Chapters V:b and VI:b.

If one decides to construct a completely new game it appears that one of the most crucial decisions to be made concerns the size of the game. Both the effort and the money involved, as well as the number of times the game can be played, will depend on its size. Part X is devoted to the tradeoff between the size of the game and its degree of realism.

Once one has decided on the size of the game, one can proceed to develop it step by step. Part IX of this volume is concerned with the methodology of developing games in a systematic manner.

In connection with the development of the game, the constructor may be interested in including various special methods like decision aids, man-computer dialogues for establishing parameters of payoff functions, or robots, i.e., artificial players in the form of computer programs. The first two methods are described in Part XI, and robots are briefly discussed in Part X.

When playing operational games the choice of suitable players is important and this is discussed briefly in Chapter X:a. Finally, when considering the coupling between the gaming activity and the total decision process, i.e., the implementation of the results of the gaming activity, some of the discussions in Part VII may be of interest.

As a monograph with its focus on the international approach, the book contains material of interest for a wide group in the gaming community, including experienced gamers. Thanks to IIASA's special position, this volume contains much material never before published in the English language. First of all there are overviews of gaming in the socialist countries, with a special chapter on gaming in the USSR: there is also a review of gaming in Japan. In addition, there is a unique group of three chapters on the international transfer of games: one on transfer between capitalist countries, one on transfer between socialist countries, and one on gaming transfers between the two systems. There is also a section on East-West trade games, dealing with US-USSR trade and GDR-UK trade.

Several other chapters provide a basis for international, and in particular East-West, comparisons of approaches to different gaming issues. Good examples are Part III, dealing with taxonomy and the theory of operational gaming; Part VII, on the use of gaming for futures research; and Part IX, on methods of development of operational games. Finally, Chapter VIII:b provides a comparison of the playing of the same game in two western countries and two socialist countries.

A BRIEF OVERVIEW

I will now give a personal, and hence perhaps biased, outline of the various chapters, pointing out various features that I feel are of particular interest.

The book starts with a state-of-the-art survey by Shubik (USA). This chapter relates game theory, experimental gaming, and operational gaming to each other, as well as providing a general background which sets the tone of the book, stressing, among other things, the importance of gaming as a complementary method for checking increasingly complex computer models, particularly regarding their assumptions about human behavior.

Section III provides some first steps towards a taxonomy and theory of gaming. Three typological approaches are presented, which, although different, are complementary rather than contradictory.

My own chapter can be seen as an extension of some of the ideas in this introduction: it also relates gaming to game theory and similar concepts. A more fundamental discussion of issues relating to model building is provided by Niemayer (FRG). Marshev and Popov (USSR) also contribute to the taxonomy of gaming, at the same time suggesting some principles for a theory of gaming.

Part IV provides an overview of gaming in some other countries about which very little is to be found in the English-language literature. Assa (Bulgaria), who for several years has been involved in the joint annual meetings on gaming within the CMEA (Council for Mutual Economic Assistance, also known as Comecon), gives an overview of the gaming activities in the socialist countries connected with the CMEA meetings, with a special emphasis on planning games. The Soviet Union has a long tradition in civilian operational gaming going back to the 1930s. Marshev gives an overview of the main schools of gaming in the USSR and also describes some specific details of a game for the construction of management information systems in the largest dairy plant in the USSR. Osawa gives an overview of gaming in Japan, including reports on operational games concerning, for example, the location of nuclear plants.

Part V deals with the international transfer of games. Although it focuses on international transfers, much of the material, e.g., that on transferring from one computer to another, also applies to transfers within a single country. However, it is of course the problems that arise when moving a game from one country to another that are of the greatest interest here, particularly whether the transfer processes are substantially different between different economic systems. We were thus fortunate in being able to assemble three complementary chapters: one on transfer between western countries; one on transfer between socialist countries; and one on the transfer of a western game to a socialist country.

The first of these, by Hutchings and Robertson (UK), contains much useful material for the constructor who wants to create a game that will later be transferable to other computers, other users, and other countries. In particular, the advice on how to structure the computer program of the game in suitable modules appears to be of fundamental importance.

The chapter by Gernert and his colleagues Habedank and Wagner (GDR) in collaboration with Assa (Bulgaria) deals not only with some examples of the transfer of games from one socialist country to another but also with the merger of two games, one on the firm level (from the GDR) and one on the branch of industry planning level (from Bulgaria), to form a new more complex game for the study of the interaction between branch planning and the individual firm.

The chapter describing the transfer of a game from the United States to Hungary is written by Mozes (Hungary), Uretsky (USA), and McWilliams (USA). This chapter not only reports the process of the transfer, including the critical testing phase, but also examines how the game was changed for use as a research tool for testing management reactions to a proposed change in the corporate tax system in Hungary. It also illustrates the thesis that international transfer of games is fundamental to the transfer of gaming methodology. A good starting point for gaming activity in a specific field in a particular country might be to import a game, get acquainted with it by playing it, and then modify it to suit the country's needs. Gradually this process may, as was the case in Hungary, inspire the creation of new games, which in turn might be exported to other countries.

On comparing the three chapters in this section, it appears that many of the transfer problems are the same whether the transfer is made between western countries or between socialist countries. The changes that have to be made due to different currencies, tax laws, and other institutional differences, etc., are of course significant in both cases. A fundamental difference between transferring games between capitalist countries and between socialist countries appears to be the fact that the widespread use of the same family of computers with the same operating systems in the socialist countries made transfer much easier than in the western countries where many different computers and even more operating systems exist. Finally it should be noted that the extra institutional changes required when changing from one type of economic system to another do *not* appear to be insurmountable.

Part VI, on East-West international trade games, is a special case of international gaming transfer. Teams from two countries, with different social systems, submit parts of a game and jointly they merge these into a new game that can then be played in both countries. Besides containing a review of two gaming projects on a subject of great international interest, namely East-West trade, this section raises several gaming methodological issues of importance.

The US-USSR trade game work described by Uretsky combines gaming with case studies of different kinds; in particular, the idea of composite cases should be noted. The use of the diary methodology in a game is also of interest. The GDR-UK trade game described by Gernert (GDR) and his British collaborators Copeland and Pope concerns the modification of an existing game to be used with new game modules from another country to form a new international game. It also deals with merging the computerized gaming approach underlying some modules with the free-form approach of other modules.

Part VII deals with the uses of gaming for futures research and scenario generation. The three chapters contain a common message: gaming not only has potential for forecasting what the future will be like: it could also get people involved in discussing what they consider to be a desirable future.

Klabbers (The Netherlands) deals with the role of gaming within futures research and public policy making. He distinguishes between a macro-cycle of the whole combined analysis and decision process and a micro-cycle of the pure research process. The focus of discussion is on how the gaming activity can be best put to use. Klabbers also discusses which types of gaming are suitable for different levels of policy making and different phases of the policy-making process.

Wasniowski (Poland) provides two examples of games for futures research. One is concerned with long-term regional development and the other deals with the future development of the computer industry. Scenario projects provide, as pointed out by Becker (The Netherlands), an important method for futures studies. In his chapter he shows how various forms of gaming are suitable for different phases of a scenario project.

Part VIII deals with three examples of how gaming can be used in specific areas of decision making.

Rybalskij (USSR) presents games for the construction industry; these have been used not only for training within the industry itself, but also for the development of construction plans, *inter alia*, in connection with the Olympic Games in Moscow in 1980.

My own contribution to this section presents a game depicting a decision situation in Southern Sweden on cost sharing between municipalities regarding jointly built water facilities. The original purpose of the game was to test certain game-theoretical methods of cost allocation. The chapter includes a discussion on the use of gaming for testing theoretical models. The game has been played with water planners, not only from Sweden, but also from Bulgaria, Italy, and Poland. One interesting finding was that water planners from all these countries reached very similar results, more similar than, for example, the results obtained by planners and students from the same country.

Somogyi and Kisimre (Yugoslavia) present a game on cattle breeding. This game is of interest not only for its level of concrete detail, but also because it illustrates that operational gaming does not necessarily involve a conflict between participants. Gaming is sometimes a kind of heuristic programming device to find better solutions. As the authors point out, there is an element of competition, however, in the fact that several players using the same game with the same configuration of initial values can strive to reach better results than the others.

Part IX deals with the *development* of operational games. Duke (USA) describes a systematic ten-step methodology for developing a game, applying it to a specific operational game developed for the Conrail Corporation in the United States. He shows that by involving the top management in the systematic build-up of the game quite unexpected but beneficial results for the corporation were obtained. Yefimov and Komarov (USSR) describe in detail a method for developing games, with particular emphasis on the different documents that aid systematic game construction.

Part X deals with the question of how large and complex a particular game should be. As mentioned at the outset, this is one of the most fundamental questions to be asked when starting the development of a new game. My own chapter focuses on the advantages of small operational games. Willmer (UK) presents a specific method to aid in determining the appropriate level of complexity of a game and discusses this method in relation to one of his own games which uses robots to simulate the roles of certain players.

Part XI introduces some special methods in operational gaming. Schuenemann (FRG) describes the advantages of incorporating a decision aid, in the form of a linear programming package, into a game. My chapter discusses the use of interactive man-computer dialogues for allowing the players themselves to decide on the parameters of the payoff functions. This is illustrated by a game dealing with certain impacts of coal burning, where the player, by using dialogues, can determine the parameters establishing, for example, the costs of coal mining for different countries.

Finally, in Part XII, I summarize the main topics and issues raised, relying partly on the discussions during the various IIASA meetings on gaming, and conclude with an examination of the future prospects for operational gaming.

REFERENCES

Boocock, S.S. and Schildt, E.O. (1968). *Simulation Games in Learning*. Sage, New York.

Cruickshank, D.R. and Telfer, R.A. (1979). *Simulation and Games: An ERIC Bibliography*. Eric Clearinghouse, Washington, D.C.

Duke, R.D. (1969). *Operational Gaming and Simulation in Urban Research: An Annotated Bibliography*. Environmental Simulation Laboratory, Ann Arbor, Michigan.

Elgood, C. (1981). *Handbook of Management Games*. 2nd edition, Gower, Aldershot, UK.

Gibbs, G.E. (Ed.) (1974). *Handbook of Games and Simulation Exercises*. Spon Ltd., London.

Gibbs, G.E. (1978). *Dictionary of Gaming, Modeling and Simulation*. Sage, New York.

Greenblat, C.S. (1972). Gaming and simulation in the social sciences: A guide to the literature. *Simulation and Games*, 3: 477-491. (Contains several bibliographies from 1968-1971 not listed here.)

Greenblat, C.S. and Duke, R.D. (1981). *Principles and Practices of Gaming Simulation*. Sage, Beverly Hills, California. (Bibliography: pp. 255-280.)

Guyer, M. and Perkel, B. (1972). *Experimental Games: A Bibliography (1945-1971)*. Mental Health Research Institute Communication, No. 293. Ann Arbor, Michigan.

Horn, R.E. and Cleaves, A. (1980). *The Guide to Simulations/Games for Education and Training*. Information Resources, Lexington, Massachusetts.

Rohn, W.E. (1980a). *Litteratur-liste über Planspiel-Veröffentlichungen*. (Mimeograph based on a gaming file.)

Rohn, W.E. (1980b). Deutsche Planspiel-Übersicht. Methodik und Didaktik des Planspiels. *Beiträge zur Gesellschafts- und Bildungspolitik Institut der deutschen Wirtschaft*. Deutscher Instituts-Verlag, Köln.

Shubik, M. and Brewer, G.D. (1972). *Reviews of Selected Books of Gaming and Simulation*. R-732-ARPA. RAND Corporation, Santa Monica, California.

Shubik, M., Brewer, G.D., and Savage, E. (1972). *The Literature of Gaming, Simulation, and Model-Building: Index and Critical Abstracts*. R-620-ARPA. RAND Corporation, Santa Monica, California.

Smith, P. (1975). *Bibliographie rond Operationele Spielen*. (Mimeograph based on a gaming file.) Utrecht.

Stadsklev, R. (1975). *Handbook of Simulation Gaming in Social Education - Part 2. Directory*. University of Alabama, Tuscaloosa, Alabama.

Werner, R. and Werner, J.T. (1969). *Bibliography of Simulations: Social Systems and Education*. Western Behavioral Sciences Institute, La Jolla, California.

NOTES

1. For a short history see Shubik, Chapter II of this volume.

2. See Marshev, Chapter IV:b of this volume.

3. A more thorough discussion of purposes is presented in Chapter III:a of this volume.

PART II

GAMING: A STATE-OF-THE-ART SURVEY

Chapter II

GAMING: A STATE-OF-THE-ART SURVEY

Martin Shubik

Yale University, New Haven, Connecticut (USA)

1. INTRODUCTION

There are many different aspects of gaming, but in this survey the stress will be laid on gaming for policy formulation and implementation.

I wish to divide my remarks into:

-- Comments on the general context of gaming and its relationship to other subjects.
-- A note on the history of gaming.
-- A brief discourse on various types of gaming.
-- A review of the uses of gaming.
-- A comment on the prospects of gaming in civilian bureaucracies.

2. THE GENERAL CONTEXT OF GAMING

It is important first to provide a contextual reference. This is particularly relevant because one of the most dangerous gaps that exist between the practitioners and the developers of methodology and theory, in operations research in particular and the behavioral sciences in general, is that in the development of theory many of the simplifying assumptions are implicit, not explicit. The great difficulty in discourse between those with a research paradigm and those with a problem is caused frequently by the fact that some implicit assumptions made by the research worker happen not to be the implicit assumptions made by the person with the problem.

I want to contrast briefly three different topics which are highly interrelated but very different. They are: gaming, simulation, and game theory. All of these topics have undergone major development over the past three decades and they are frequently confused.

Gaming, I believe, has its closest connections to the behavioral sciences. In contrasting it with the others I stress that gaming is people oriented. The individual plays a central role in gaming of virtually any variety. There are two features upon which gaming lays stress. One is sensitivity analysis and the other is model critique. The good gamer is always conscious of the frailties of the model and the model is up for inspection virtually all of the time.

Simulation, especially as it is done today, tends to be more computer oriented than people oriented. The size, complexity, and sophistication of simulations have grown, but just because a program is large and complex really gives us no clue as to whether it is good or bad. The good or bad features have to be determined through an *ad hoc* examination of the particular simulation in question.

The role of simulation has undoubtedly become more intertwined with econometric methods and with general planning methods. If the word simulation had been mentioned to an econometrician 20 years ago it would have been like mentioning the Anti-Christ to one of the faithful. Now, however, styles have changed and econometricians are working hand-in-glove with the simulators. The general idea of the computer as a device for manipulating very large planning models has been accepted in areas where 20 years ago it would not even have been considered.

This is not an unmixed blessing. One of the problems with the growth of computer size and the sophistication of computer technology has been that it is now possible to manipulate easily models in which such a low amount of critical evaluation has been invested that it is dubious whether it was worth building the model in the first place. One of the advantages of the bad old early days of computers was that it was so hard to use a computer that, if you did not specify your problem carefully, you could not get it on the computer. Nowadays computer systems are sufficiently sophisticated that it is much easier to run programs with logical flaws. The system might even patch up your program. But unfortunately, although a computer may be able to patch up your program from the point of view of faulty programming, the feature that may be wrong with large-scale models is not the programming logic, but the inference that went into the selection of certain aspects of the model building. As the computer is, as yet, unable to walk around and look at the world, it is not able to correct modeling errors. Simulation, although not a prime subject, is thus of importance to the extent that gaming can be seen as a debugging device for large-scale simulations.

The third topic is *game theory*, which is oriented towards mathematical methods in the study of decision systems and is clearly related to a study of conflict and cooperation. The people who develop the mathematics of game theory are in general very different from those who work in experimental gaming and the people who do experimental gaming are to a great extent quite different from those who utilize operational gaming. In developing useful applications we have a problem in the difference between the culture or the sociology of the individuals involved in different scientific efforts. The social psychologists frequently have difficulty talking with the game theorists and the experimental psychologists have a great deal of difficulty talking with people whose bent is more managerial. At most business schools in the United States, for example, there are psychologists whose main concern is with managerial psychology and they have considerable difficulties in talking with those who are more interested in experimental psychology or operations research.

3. THE HISTORY OF GAMING

I would like to proceed with a brief comment on the history of gaming. The largest and oldest use of operational gaming has undoubtedly been within the military. The modern origin of operational gaming is usually attributed to the Prussian war staff. However, already in the writings of Sun Tsu, the great Chinese general of the 5th century B.C., one can find both the concepts of operational gaming and some elements of the theory of games, at least in its two-person zero-sum form. This work had to wait for about 25 hundred years before anybody did anything about its game-theory aspects and about 23 hundred years before anybody really took up the gaming aspects of this work.

I note the military background of operational gaming because it is important that we ask ourselves if, for peaceful purposes, we can learn from techniques which have been successfully applied to war. Why should or should not some aspects of operational gaming be transferable to non-military problems? Is there something peculiar about the nature of war that rules out the possibility of using these techniques for peaceful planning? I believe that this is not the case, but it is something that has to be investigated more closely.

4. TYPES OF GAMING

I am well aware of the dangers in trying to present a taxonomy on the uses of gaming, but if utilized with skepticism taxonomies are frequently useful. An immediate use involves comparing one expert's taxonomy with someone else's to examine differences in world view.

The *forms* of gaming are quite different in their uses. The two contrasting forms that we frequently encounter are rigid-rule gaming and free-form gaming.

Rigid-rule gaming comes in at least two packages, noncomputerized and man-machine gaming. There has been a considerable swing, in particular in the United States, towards the machine. In many instances man is being pushed further and further away as an inconvenient appendage to processes that can be simulated more expeditiously with a digital computer. I tend not to support this trend, especially in applications to management problems. As regards human affairs, I believe that large-scale digital computers are excellent for reducing enormous quantities of accounting data, but when you start to generate large numbers of behavioral equations for models, I feel much more comfortable to know that every now and then some human being with experience is required to examine and to challenge these behavioral equations. Once you have a model with many behavioral equations and charts and flow diagrams, it is nice to have some form of device which can ask a few relevant questions before somebody looks at his watch and says, "We don't have enough time to consider that: we have thirty more charts to get through in the next ten minutes".

In order to be able to challenge these behavioral equations they have to be seen. The more that is hidden in bigger and fancier black boxes the less is seen and the more one promotes a division between the users--receiving the oracular pronouncements from the black box--and the priests of the model, i.e., those who feed the black box.

Certain types of gaming may have rigid rules although they are non-computerized, such as, for example, simple production inventory scheduling games. For example, it is possible to train lower management staff in production inventory scheduling games using nothing more than a large board on which there are colored pieces of wood of various lengths representing the length of time to do a job, with different colors indicating the priority of each job. Every aspect of this model is immediately visible. A foreman can look at the configuration of the board and say "This certainly doesn't look like my shop. You must be out of your mind if you think that that's what the machine configuration looks like in our industry." Because of "game transparency", a perfectly ordinary experienced foreman could say whether this game was of some use or not. Although the rules are rigid, they are understood by both the user and the constructor.

In rigid-rule gaming one must contrast noncomputerized games which, in general, can be presented so that the rules can be understood fairly quickly and man-machine games, where the mere fact that an individual sits down in front of a computer console means that somebody has to accept the validity of whatever is in the black box.

The other type of gaming is *free-form gaming*, where the individuals constructing the game and the individuals playing the game accept as a fact of life that neither the constructors nor the players know all of the rules in advance.

The general philosophy of free-form gaming is the very reverse of the philosophy of rigid-rule gaming. The rules are meant to have some validity in rigid-rule gaming. In free-form gaming the understanding, either implicitly or explicitly, is that the game is not completely known and that the playing of the game will in itself serve as a device for generating a better understanding of the rules. Immediately one should be able to see that the emphasis on the participation and quality of the individuals must be much higher when using free-form gaming. The value of a free-form game may be highly related to the expertise and sophistication of both the players and the referees.

One type of serious free-form game may call for a fully organized three-team structure for a two-team game or a two-team structure for a one-team game. In general, most games that are useful for planning purposes involve either one team against an environment or two teams in a situation of conflict. Military gaming is very heavily a two-team game; one usually postulates an opponent. In business gaming, in general, the competitive environment consists of oneself and an aggregate of the others. The others may in some business games actually be two, three, four or more separate teams but frequently the others are lumped together as a reactive environment. In general there are one or two teams of critical interest. There may be an extra team which consists of expert referees. In a free-form game it well may be that the most critical team is the referees. The sociologist Herbert Goldhammer was one of the early instigators of the three-team game. He worked in the context of the political military exercise, but the validity of this type of game goes well beyond the military. The idea is that when you have individuals who themselves are experts studying an area, and where the rules are really not known, an efficient way to organize is to have three teams: the referees and the two opposing teams. After the teams have made a move, the referees take a look at the move. The referees, being a team of experts themselves, could say "That's not really a plausible move". Then the game comes to a halt and the two teams plus the referees discuss whether the rules should permit such a move.

The purpose of such an exercise is to explore the feasibility and the plausibility of the model. To a great extent, good long-term planning is closely related to such a process. It is not too difficult these days to employ people to run regression analyses, to build simple simulations, to make quick statistical checks, etc. The real trick is to have some faith in the model being built; that is to have some faith in the essential assumptions behind the model. The development of free-form gaming came about as an explicit recognition of the fact that frequently the problem is not how the game is played or how the model is manipulated, but rather the validity of the assumptions that went into the model in the first place. The question runs: Is there a methodology which helps investigate the validity of the model? One might say this is the method of sensitivity analysis. It is in fact far more. It is not just a way to check parameter values. It is an approach to the question as to whether you have the right *structure* for the model.

5. USES OF GAMING

I will suggest five major crude subdivisions of gaming as regards its uses. There could be more, but further refinement does not seem worthwhile. The subdivisions that I would like to suggest are: (1) training, (2) teaching, (3) operational gaming, (4) experimentation, and (5) futures studies, i.e., structural brain storming.

Operational gaming can, in turn, be split into: (a) policy formulation, (b) dress rehearsals, i.e., actual testing of plans, and (c) gaming for sensitivity analysis and commentary on plans.

Experimentation can be divided into two rather different, although allied topics, namely theory validation and theory generation. Frequently in the running of a good experiment one finds things that one was not looking for. A reason for running a formal experiment is often not to test the value of some parameter or a particular hypothesis, but to find out what happens to the system when you do not have too many intervening variables interacting at the same time. That is a far cry from the classical sort of experiment that used to be the great love of the experimental psychologists 20 years ago.

I shall first contrast training and teaching.

Frequently when one is *training*, one is not particularly interested in going into conceptual details with the individuals one is training. For example, in the inventory scheduling game mentioned we were not trying to convert lower management staff into heuristic programmers. We only wanted to illustrate some of the aspects of the scheduling problem.

The uses of gaming in training are large. At this moment, there is a large and specialized body of application not only in the West but also in the East. The use of simple games for production or inventory control is fairly well developed. This use is sufficiently specialized and sufficiently well under control that it is not of prime concern to us here.

In *teaching*, as compared to training, one wishes to get across concepts and abstract ideas.

At the university level and at some of our business institutes the uses of gaming have been linked to the teaching of production, control, and accounting. Although one does not use large-scale business games merely to teach accounting forms, one of the great uses of large-scale business games has been to call attention to accounting concepts. It is quite easy to teach people how to fill in forms, how to run production schedules, and how to manage the substance of a bureaucracy. It is another thing to get them to raise pertinent questions as to why a procedure is being followed.

The use of large-scale managerial business games is of concern in this context. In the last 20 years there has been an enormous growth in the use of these games. There is virtually no major business school that does not have some use for a business game.

In the United States, in some of the larger corporations the use of business gaming at the upper managerial levels has peaked and dropped. In IBM more upper management games were played 10 years ago than today. I can speak from experience as a builder of one of the major IBM games, the Financial Allocation and Management Game, built for upper-middle management training within IBM. Several years after its introduction it was decided to use that game for a *lower* level of management. The important question was: Do management games capture enough of the real problems of upper management? There was a clear consensus that the formal management games did capture enough for *middle* management training but there was *not* a consensus that they caught enough for *upper* management training.

This type of question has also come up in military college training. The observation has been that games at middle management level undoubtedly have a valuable role, but as to the value of games at upper management levels there is more doubt.

This distinction is closely tied in with the contrast between free-form and rigid-rule gaming. The games that have been successfully used at business schools have mostly been rigid-rule games, essentially large-scale computerized games which spew out large amounts of data and which represent a fair amount of the bureaucratic work of the middle managerial levels, but do not represent, or do not catch the flavor of the vaguer and less structured sort of conceptualizing work of the upper level of management.

More recently the type of gaming represented by the large-scale management game has spread. There has been a development of urban gaming and of societal-problem gaming. One of the fundamental conceptual difficulties of gaming techniques in this area has been precisely the problem mentioned above regarding middle and upper management in managerial gaming. When you try to construct games to handle societal problems, for example slum clearance, the problem is not in the playing of the game, but in the model itself. Are we capable of conceptualizing adequately at that level to make it worthwhile building rigid-rule games for such problems? I have some serious reservations. Here is the question of free-form versus rigid-rule gaming once again.

I have a brief comment on *research* gaming. This is a growing and important field. The people involved frequently have very little to do with the people working on operational gaming for managerial uses. In the last 20 years there has been an enormous upswing in the performance of simple experiments in social psychology and experimental psychology. There is now a small discipline entitled "experimental economics". There have been several conferences devoted specifically to work in experimental economics, where, for example, experimentation on different price formation mechanisms has taken place. We now have some tentative results in this particular area. Frequently, when we make assumptions about cooperative or competitive behavior, these are assumptions based on casual empiricism. Research gamers are trying to find out if we can get some sort of validation concerning such behavior.

In this context I mention a couple of subjects which concern the interface between operational and experimental gaming. One is panic behavior, related to the general question of stability in social systems. An operational problem that many of us face is the question of how to control hijacking. What is the nature of the steps one can take in the case of aircraft hijacking? Many of our assumptions that go into trying to answer this question at an operational level involve the motivation of those who try to take over the planes and the nature of crowd behavior when a plane is taken over. These odd-ball subjects that we refer to every now and then, and which have considerable operational implications, we know very little about. The experimental gamers, working in highly artificial situations, are at least beginning to ask questions such as: Can you cause a panic in a simple market game? The answer to that question is Yes! In running an experimental business game with a stock market attached to it, we were able to cause a rather spectacular panic, in the middle of the game, which I had not foreseen. This brings back the difference between experimental gaming from the point of view of theory *generation* and experimental gaming from the point of view of theory *validation*. Sometimes when you run an experimental game you find that you can cause behavior that you did not even think was part of the game you were running.

6. GAMING AND BUREAUCRACIES

The last subject I want to touch on briefly concerns the prospects for gaming in civilian bureaucracies, be they government agencies, private corporations, or some other type of organization. The question that I want to raise is: What does the upper bureaucracy learn from gaming exercises when, for example, trying to estimate what will happen in the future and when trying to convey it to someone?

In this connection I would like to make a semantic note. In academic circles one talks about members of upper bureaucracies as "decision makers". I suggest instead we use the phrase "responsibility taker". I am not quite sure what a decision maker is, but I am rather more sure what a responsibility taker is. It is someone who finds that, when something goes wrong in a part of the bureaucracy, he is meant to be responsible for the fact that something went wrong. This is much more congenial to my view of the way institutions work than to attach this vague word "decision maker" to him.

I raise this point because a responsibility taker finds that the only real asset he has is time. He tries to allocate this time as parsimoniously as possible. When for example an operations researcher comes to this responsibility taker with a 35-page questionnaire, he will frequently not fill it in, or if he fills it in, he may fill it in casually.

The questions we have to ask against this background are as follows: How does this study get used? Do responsibility takers like people in their organizations to play games? And if they do, how do they use the output of these games? What are the motivations for having people play games and for using the results of the games? Do games have a value to responsibility takers or are games primarily self-training devices for analysts?

If you are going to keep a stable of analysts and experts in a major bureaucracy they have to at least educate themselves. A perfectly legitimate use of gaming might be to keep these individuals self-trained. The games may be conceptual devices for the analysts. It is not necessary that they be regarded as useless if that is all they do. It is also not necessary that the criterion of usefulness be that you get three corporate presidents to participate in the game you design. It may well be that there is a usefulness to a game in a bureaucracy even if it never gets to the explicit level of top management.

Finally it should be stressed that gaming as an on-going part of a decision process in a large organization is intimately related to the neural network of that organization and to having the planners, the gamers, and the managers communicate in a natural and high-trust mode. Possibly one of the reasons why gaming has been so effective in some military establishments has been historical--the level of trust between the different individuals existed and was long-term in nature. It is important to consider how such levels of trust and communication can be established in the civilian field.

PART III

TOWARDS A TAXONOMY AND
THEORY OF OPERATIONAL GAMING

Chapter III:a

WHAT IS OPERATIONAL GAMING?

Ingolf Stahl
*International Institute for Applied Systems Analysis,
Laxenburg (Austria)*

1. INTRODUCTION

This book deals mainly with operational gaming. Before we proceed to discuss various aspects of operational gaming, we shall try to define more clearly this and some of the related concepts.

The need to establish definitions arises because there appears to be great confusion regarding the concept of gaming. Interpretations of this term in the literature differ greatly. Furthermore, different types of gaming, such as operational gaming, research gaming, etc., have different interpretations. There also appears to be confusion about the difference between gaming and game theory.

It thus appears essential to discuss definitions at an early stage in the book in order to help clarify various points in later chapters. It should be stressed that the attempts at definitions presented here are my own and that there is not necessarily any wider agreement on them. It is, however, my hope that they will stimulate a more general debate on these issues, which may in the future lead to wider agreement on how best to define these terms.

Before proceeding to the definitions themselves, we should say something about the principles of definitions. First we will follow the principle that the definition should as far as possible correspond with what appears to be the common usage of the term. This principle works in two directions. For example, we have to define "gaming" so that it is not too wide, i.e., including many activities that no one would regard as gaming. On the other hand the definition must not be so narrow that it excludes activities that most regard to be gaming. Furthermore, the definition should be precise, reasonably short, and consistent with other definitions in our typology.

Of the two words "operational" and "gaming", it appears that the word "gaming" provides the greatest difficulty due to widespread disagreement and confusion, whilst at the same time being the more fundamental concept. Therefore we start with the definition of the word "gaming" and then towards the end of the chapter discuss the term "operational" more thoroughly. Here we will merely repeat that operational gaming focuses on decision making, planning, and implementation.

We begin by relating the word "gaming" to the more generally used word "game", defining gaming, in the first step, as "the playing of games". The words "playing" and "game" are next defined with reference to operational gaming and we examine how these terms are used in other scientific areas, such as "game theory". As our next step, we define a "game" as an "institutional model of a game situation".

The necessary further definitions of the concepts "institutional model" and "game situation" are developed in Sections 2 and 3 below. In Section 4, we discuss to what extent our definition of gaming, which focuses on game situations with more than one independent decision maker and excludes "games against nature", deviates from others' usage of the term.

To complete the definition of gaming as the "playing of games", we next define the term "playing", in Section 5. Having then completed our definition of "gaming," we move in Section 6 to draw a clear dividing line between "gaming" on the one hand and "game theory" on the other.

We then proceed, in Section 7, to define various types of gaming according to their purpose, focusing on those characteristics that distinguish operational gaming from other types of gaming.

Finally, in Section 8, we draw a distinction between "rigid-rule" gaming and "free-form" gaming as these concepts occur elsewhere in this book.

2. DEFINITION OF THE "INSTITUTIONAL MODEL" CONCEPT

Without going too deeply into the theory of science we shall, for our present needs, define "model" as a "simplified representation".[1] Hence a game is a simplified representation of a game situation. As examples, one can view the games "chess" and "Monopoly" as very crude representations of two "game situations": a battle in Persia in the first millenium BC and real-estate dealings in Atlantic City in the 1930s, respectively.

It should be stressed that a game is *not* a complete model of a "game situation". If we consider a model as a set of assumptions, we can divide a model of any system involving humans into two types of assumptions: institutional and behavioral.[2]

Institutional assumptions concern the physical properties of the game situation, for example, how many players there are, how and when action may be taken, what physical payoffs are paid out, what information is available, what time span is involved, etc. In an experimental replication of the situation the experimenter has control over the factors covered by these institutional assumptions.

The behavioral assumptions concern the properties of the players, their thought processes and patterns of behavior. In an experimental replication of the situation these assumptions *cannot* be controlled by the experimenter.

Here we shall use the term "complete model" for a model that contains both institutional and behavioral assumptions about a game situation. A complete model can therefore describe how the game is played, i.e., assign a solution to the game situation. An "institutional model" of a game contains only institutional assumptions; since the behavioral assumptions are missing, no solution can be assigned to the game situation.

Using these definitions we can regard a game as an "institutional model" of a game situation. In gaming the game constructor provides, at most, this institutional set-up, mainly in the form of rules, scenarios, and possible paraphernalia, such as a board, cards, etc.[3] The behavioral assumptions are not specified because the players are allowed to play in whatever way they choose.

This definition of a "game" as an "institutional model" of a game situation will later help us in two ways: to make a clearer distinction between gaming and game theory (Section 6) and to divide gaming into two main groups as regards rules (Section 8).

3. DEFINITION OF THE "GAME SITUATION" CONCEPT

Before deciding on our own definition of a "game situation" we must recognize that the word "game" is used in the literature (for example on game theory[4]) in connection with two types of decision situations, namely those of "strategic games" and those of "games against nature".

By "strategic game situation" we refer to a situation with the following characteristics. There are *several* decision makers and the decisions made by each will noticeably influence the payoff of some of the others. Hence there is a strategic interdependence between *at least two* decision makers, in the sense that neither can make an optimal decision without first considering what decision the other player is likely to make.

Strategic games can, in turn, be divided into two subgroups: games of conflict and games of coordination. In a game of *conflict*, the payoff of one party will, at least as regards some change in decisions, go down when another party's payoff goes up. In a game of *coordination*, every change in decisions which gives a higher payoff to one party will also lead to *higher* payoffs for the other parties.[5]

In "games against nature" there is no strategic interdependence between the decision makers. Even though there can easily be more than one decision maker in such a situation, no decision maker will, when considering his decisions, take into account how those decisions will affect the other decision makers. He will regard the decisions of the others as exogenous variables. An example of this is the "pure competition" case for agricultural production. A farmer can choose to regard total supply on the world market as completely determined by "nature", without having to distinguish whether any increase in supply and the ensuing fall in price is due to weather conditions or to the decision by many farmers to plant more.

We will restrict ourselves here to strategic games only, and will therefore exclude "games against nature" and other similar games where there is no strategic interdependence between the decision makers.

Within the category "strategic games" it should be stressed that we are just as interested in games of coordination as in games of conflict. Games of coordination are probably in reality more common than can be inferred from the scant treatment they receive in the literature in English, and hence they merit further study.

4. EXCLUDING "GAMES AGAINST NATURE"

The main reason for excluding "games against nature" and similar one-person game situations, is that if we included such situations in our definition of gaming for operational purposes this definition would become far too wide. To further clarify this point we can distinguish the following three types of such game situations, each involving, in principle, only *one* decision maker.[6]

1. Situations in which there is *stochastic variability* of the system. This category covers many common entertainment games, including such "games of chance" as roulette. In the field of research we have different types of stochastic simulation models, concerning, for example, production or inventory policy. While most of these simulations were previously noninteractive, with the simulator supplying all the decisions at once at the beginning of the procedure, they are now increasingly becoming interactive in character. The simulator, working via a terminal, can revise or change the decisions after receiving some preliminary results.

2. Situations where a decision maker has *several objectives*. In this type of situation the decision maker cannot, *a priori*, state his preferred tradeoff between these different objectives. Nature is, in most cases, deterministic, but could also be stochastic. A large number of man-computer interactive methods has emerged for eliciting the implicit multiobjective tradeoff from the decision maker and thus establishing an optimal solution.

3. Situations that have a complicated structure, but where the decision maker has a *one*-dimensional objective, in principle allowing for optimization. The structure of some problems is so complex that no straightforward optimization method, using a reasonably small amount of computer time, can be applied. For solving such problems in a satisfactory manner one often resorts to heuristic programming, relying on "rules of thumb", often generated by human intuition. Many of these heuristic programs are interactive, allowing the "heuristic optimizer" to modify his rules after receiving feedback about how the objective function has changed as a result of earlier decisions.

One can find examples of all three types in which the model of the situation is called a game. This is especially the case with parlor games, but is also true of some educational games.[7] Some of these games can also have an operational purpose.[8]

It appears unreasonable to include in the gaming concept *all* situations in each of the three categories above. For example, taking type 1 situations, gaming would then include all interactive stochastic simulations. Within type 2 situations, gaming would then include all interactive multiobjective methods, and type 3 situations would extend gaming to include all interactive heuristic programming.

The problem is on the other hand that our definition above, which excludes "games against nature" in this wider sense, will be somewhat too narrow with regard to normal usage, since we have noted that some people regard certain simulations of situations of these types as gaming. The question is then whether it is possible to subdivide these three categories so that just these specific cases could be included in the overall definition of gaming.

Unfortunately, this appears to be impossible. It is very difficult to see why certain cases have been referred to as gaming and other very similar cases have been called stochastic simulation, interactive simulation, interactive heuristic programming, etc. The use of the word gaming is perhaps somewhat more frequent when the simulation activity has had an entertainment or educational purpose and where gaming-type paraphernalia such as boards, etc., is used, but there are also procedures called gaming where these factors are not present. We could perhaps change our definition of gaming to include some, but not all one-person simulations that are referred to as gaming, but our definition would then become more complicated and less precise, and would be less in line with our general typology. This does not seem to be a reasonable sacrifice.

Our definition of gaming will thus inevitably be at odds with how *some* other people use the term. However, since we regard our definition as preliminary and as a basis for discussion, we do not intend to be dogmatic! This book includes reports on many gaming activities that fall within the terms of our definition, but also presents accounts of cases where the term gaming is used in a different way (see for example Chapter VIII:c).

5. DEFINITION OF THE "PLAYING" CONCEPT

Having defined a "game" as a certain type of "model", it is appropriate to regard the playing of a game as a kind of "human manipulation" of this model. However, we do not imply just *any* kind of manipulation but rather have in mind the following characteristics:

1. Each role (of importance) in the model is manipulated by a particular player.

2. The manipulation carried out by each player is *not* necessarily aimed at finding an optimal solution.

3. The manipulation carried out by each player is interactive. By "interactive" we mean that *several* decisions are made by the same decision maker and that at least some decisions are made *after* feedback has been received about the effects of other decisions.

We can, in line with a definition accepted by other authors, refer to the manipulation of a model of a social system (not aiming at optimization) as simulation. Since in gaming the model of the game situation does not contain any behavioral assumptions and the players are free to behave as they please, playing obviously involves simulation, and not optimization. It is, however, a special kind of simulation, unlike ordinary simulation in which all manipulation is performed by the one person running the simulation. This is because in a model of a strategic game situation several decision makers are involved and the role of each (important) decision maker is played by a separate player. Hence, we exclude from our definition of gaming those game simulations where *one* person plays the role of every decision maker by, for example, supplying behavioral equations.

Finally, as noted above, we wish to include the interactive element in the definition of gaming. Without this addition the definition of gaming would be too wide, since it would then cover many activities where decisions are made at only *one* single point in time. Furthermore, it appears that most games regard the interactive process as the key element in gaming. The only possible narrowing effect of including the word "interactive" in our definition is that some very simple experimental games (for example, Prisoners' Dilemma games)[9] with only one round of play have to be excluded, but we believe that this omission is reasonable.

Summing up, we have therefore defined gaming as "an interactive simulation, involving more than one player, of a strategic game situation". The discussion thus far is illustrated in Figure 1, which shows the relationship between the various situations. The relationship between gaming and game theory shown in the figure will be discussed more thoroughly in the next section.

6. RELATIONSHIP BETWEEN GAMING AND GAME THEORY

As mentioned in the introduction there is often confusion regarding the difference between gaming and game theory. We will now discuss this problem further.

Game theory, in contrast to gaming, provides a *complete* model of a game situation. While in gaming the game constructor supplies (at most) only the institutional model of the game situation, the game theoretician will also supply the behavioral assumptions. The counterparts of these assumptions in gaming are supplied, consciously or unconsciously, during the play by the participants in the game.

Game theory, however, does not provide the *only* type of complete model of game situations. Game theory is characterized by the fact that the behavioral assumptions are of a special type: namely, they are assumptions of *rational* behavior and expectations. More specifically, the following assumptions (see Stahl, 1972) can be identified:

1.   Rational behavior, implying attempts at maximizing one's payoff (utility) and unlimited computational ability;

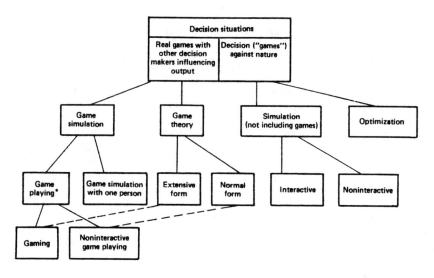

*Game playing here means game simulation with several persons

Figure 1. Relationship between different types of game situations and models.

2. Correct expectations of the behavior of the other parties;
3. Correct expectations concerning the expectations of the other parties.

While assumptions 1 and 2 are fundamental for all equilibrium-point concepts, all three assumptions are implicit in so called "perfect" equilibrium points (Selten, 1974). It is important that we should also allow for other complete models of game situations where the behavioral assumptions do not require "100%" rationality. As mentioned above, we can refer to complete models of social systems (i.e., those including the behavioral assumptions defining the manipulation of the model) that are not of the optimizing type as simulations. By analogy, we can call complete models of games "game simulations".

In cases where one person, such as the model constructor, is the sole manipulator of the model, i.e., the sole supplier of the behavioral assumptions, we have a "game simulation with one person". One problem with such a model lies in the determination of the behavioral assumptions. Unlike in game theory, assumptions of nonrational behavior cannot be determined on purely deductive grounds: empirical study is required. Here gaming can play a constructive role in supplying the behavioral assumptions and can complement game theory by providing steps towards a more general "theory of game playing", including, in addition to game theory (relying on full rationality), a theory of game playing with restricted rationality.

Other ways in which gaming can complement game theory include providing an "acid test" of game-theoretical models. This will be discussed in Chapter VIII:b.

Before leaving the relationship between gaming and game theory we shall briefly examine the two main forms of presenting game theory: the extensive form and the normal form. In the extensive form the game is described as a tree where every possible choice is represented by a branch. All choices which are made at a certain point of time, with given information, are represented by branches from the same node.

In the normal form the game is "collapsed". Each decision maker will at the start of the game choose *one* strategy, where a strategy is defined as a total plan of how to behave in every conceivable situation. In the normal form every decision maker thus makes only one real decision and hence there is *no* interaction. It should be stressed that it is only due to the assumptions of rationality mentioned above that in game theory one can, for most analyses, regard a game in the normal form as equivalent to the same one in the extensive form, even for games involving many decisions by each player.

As soon as one turns to a theory of "nonrational playing", the normal form will, in most cases, no longer be of interest, since there is no intrinsic reason why the parties should commit themselves to such strategies, if they are not following game theory's rationality assumptions. The analysis in the extensive form will still be of interest, since it relies only on the institutional assumptions. Hence, there is a connection between gaming and game theory in the extensive form. The normal form, which does not allow any interaction, is only of interest from a simulation viewpoint for the case of very simple noninteractive games such as the "Prisoners' Dilemma" games mentioned above.

7. TYPOLOGY OF GAMES AND DEFINITION OF "OPERATIONAL"

We will now offer a definition of the word "operational". It seems appropriate to start by defining various types of gaming in a sort of typology based on the purpose of the game, and in particular, on the planned usage of the results of game playing. This typology focuses on what *kind* of benefits can be obtained, what *time* scale the benefits relate to, and *who* obtains the benefit.

We shall deal with five types of games:

1. Entertainment games;
2. Educational games;
3. Experimental games;
4. Research games;
5. Operational games.

The five types are presented in Figure 2, which also gives our view of the connections between the different types of game.

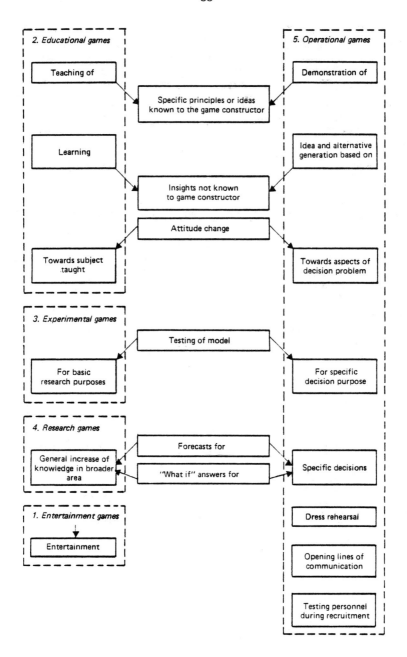

Figure 2. A typology of games.

1. Entertainment Games are games in which all positive results derived from the game are obtained during the playing of the game. After the game is finished there is no remaining value, either to the players or to others (except that some players might have gained or lost some money).

2. Educational Games are games in which all the direct benefits are obtained by the people playing the game, but these benefits to the player are of a long-term and more general character. Any benefits to outsiders are due to the long-term effects of the players being able to carry out certain tasks more efficiently than would otherwise have been the case.

3. Experimental Games are games aimed at testing theories or other general hypotheses, without a specific empirical content, without a specific situational context, and without having any specific type of application in mind. The main planned benefits of the game lie in a report to outsiders on the results of the game playing.

4. Research Games are games with the purpose of obtaining empirical material (e.g., in the form of forecasts) concerning a fairly broad subject area and where the application of this material for decisions is not immediately apparent. The main planned benefits lie in the reporting of the results to an outside audience.

5. Operational Games are games with the purpose of aiding decision making, planning, and policy implementation in specific situations. The main benefits are fairly immediate. No reporting to outsiders is required.

One can, as shown in Figure 2, distinguish between different operational games on the basis of the specific purpose of the game or the specific way in which its benefits can be obtained. In Figure 2 nine such purposes are listed:

1. Demonstrating principles,
2. Generating ideas,
3. Changing attitudes,
4. Testing models,
5. Forecasting,
6. Answering "what if" questions,
7. Providing dress rehearsal,
8. Establishing communication,
9. Testing personnel during recruitment.

As shown in Figure 2, several of these purposes have very similar counterparts in other kinds of game, for example, educational games. The difference lies, as stated above, in the planned ultimate usage of the results of the gaming activity. Self-evidently there are no really clear-cut borderlines between the five types of games in Figure 2. The differences between these types of games are in many cases differences of degree. This is particularly true as regards the difference between operational games and educational games. Many games lie in between these categories and often the same game is used for both purposes. Certain educational games, focused on the teaching of specific tasks, can for example be very close to operational games for demonstrating specific issues to management or for dress rehearsals. The main difference is that the new knowledge obtained, for example by a manager, is more immediately put to use in the case of the operational game than in the case of the educational game.

There are also great similarities between certain research games and operational games. The main differences are usually that the research games deal with a more general subject area and are not decision focused, while the operational games deal with a specific problem and are decision focused. Once again, many games lie between the two categories.

Noting these parallels, it seems appropriate to define a new category of *operational research games* lying between these two types of games. An operational research game, like an operational game, has the ultimate purpose of being an aid for decisions, planning, and policy implementation, but unlike the operational game it is not focused on one single decision situation but rather on several situations involving a specific *type* of problem. The operational research game is thereby directed more towards the development of methods than the pure operational game. Another difference vis-a-vis the pure operational game is that the planned value of the game lies in communicating the results to future decision makers, while in the (pure) operational game no such communication is necessary.

On the other hand, the main difference between a research game and an operational research game concerns how far away one is from applying the knowledge acquired. The operational research game should deal with data from a real decision situation and the players in the game should at least be "real decision maker similar",[10] i.e., persons familiar with the type of decision involved, although not necessarily the actual decision makers themselves.

An operational research game, like an ordinary research game, is more limited in scope than a (pure) operational game. Looking at the nine specific purposes of an operational game identified above, the operational research game would mainly deal with points 4-6: testing of models, forecasting, and answering "what if" questions. To some extent, point 2, generating new ideas, might also be involved: as in many experimental games, the new insights generated when seeing the game played in an unexpected way might be the most valuable outcome. The other purposes listed do *not* have direct counterparts in operational research games, nor in ordinary research games.

In this context, experimental games should also be discussed due to their similarity to research games. While the experimental testing method can also be used in research and operational games, the term "experimental games" is reserved here for games with a basic research purpose, by analogy with the term "experimental economics". Since experimental games are also connected with research, the games referred to here as "research games" should perhaps more rigorously be called "nonexperimental research games" or "other research games". However, for the sake of simplicity, we will retain the shorter term "research games".

To illustrate the differences between experimental, research, operational research, and operational games, we present in Table 1 the main differences between four games that could possibly be applied to the water cost-allocation problem described in Chapter VIII:b.

Table 1. Differences between four types of game[a].

| Dimension | Type of game | | | |
	Experimental	Research	Operational research	Operational
1. Subject	Six-person core game	Cost allocation	Cost allocation in water management	Cost allocation in one specific water project
2. Purpose	Testing cost-allocation methods	Testing cost-allocation methods	Finding cost-allocation methods suitable for water projects	Speeding up agreement in actual project
3. Players	Undergraduate students	Graduate students in economics	Water planners in different countries	The actual decision makers
4. Data	Artificial figures, round numbers, symmetry	Figures artificial but derived from economic theory	Real figures from some water project	Figures from specific project
5. Setting	No administrative setting	Indication of artificial administrative setting	Real administrative setting outlined	Administrative setting exactly known

[a]As applied to the cost-allocation situation described in Chapter VIII:b.

The table deals with the following five dimensions of difference:
1. Subject of the game, i.e., the issue with which the game deals;
2. Purpose of the game;
3. Type of players used;
4. Type of data or figures used;
5. Level of detail as regards the description of the "administrative setting of the game": i.e., information on factors that, in addition to the numerical payoff functions, might influence the decisions of the players, such as who the real actors are, what the time horizon of the problem is, etc.

The information in each element of the matrix in Table 1 is intended only as an example, with the aim of making the differences between the four types of games more apparent. The table shows that roughly the same game could be used for various purposes, but that the types of players, the actual data, and the background information would vary.

8. RIGID-RULE AND FREE-FORM GAMING

In conclusion, utilizing some definitions presented earlier in this chapter, we will now define for use in later chapters two main types of gaming that differ as regards who determines the institutional assumptions of the game.

1. Rigid-Rule Gaming. In "rigid-rule" gaming all the institutional assumptions in the model of the game situation are supplied by the game constructor. Hence, all the rules of the game are exactly defined at the start of the game, often in the form of a computer program. The outcome of every possible combination of players' decisions is thus exactly defined.

2. Free-Form Gaming. In "free-form" gaming at least some of the institutional assumptions are supplied by the game participants. In a free-form game the players will thus, to some extent, invent the rules as the game goes on. The outcome of a particular decision might, for example, be the subject of discussions among the participants. In some cases the game constructor will only supply a small part of the institutional assumptions, in the form of a scenario.

Usually management games, where the players decide on quantities such as price, production, etc., have been of the rigid-rule type, while games involving the exchange of verbal messages, such as international diplomacy games, have been of the free-form variety. In Chapter XI:b we shall see, however, that computerized games can also be of the free-form type.

REFERENCES

Aubin, J.-P. (1979). *Mathematical Methods of Game and Economic Theory.* North-Holland, Amsterdam.

Bacharach, M. (1976). *Economics and Theory of Games.* MacMillan, London.

Bell, D., Keeney, R.L., and Raiffa, H. (Eds.) (1977). *Conflicting Objectives in Decisions.* Wiley, Chichester, UK.

Davis, M.D. (1970). *Game Theory: A Nontechnical Introduction.* Basic Books, New York.

Findler, N.V., and Meltzer, B. (1971). *Artificial Intelligence and Heuristic Programming.* Edinburgh University Press, Edinburgh.

Hawes, D.M. (1973). Operational gaming in the planning of the geologically troubled colliery. In M. Ross (Ed.), *Operational Research '72*. North-Holland, Amsterdam.

Jones, A.J. (1980). *Game Theory: Mathematical Models of Conflict*. Ellis Horwood, Chichester, UK.

Lehman, R.S. (1977). *Computer Simulation and Modeling: An Introduction*. Wiley, New York.

Luce, R.D., and Raiffa, H. (1957). *Games and Decisions*. Wiley, New York.

May, F.B. (1970). *Introduction to Games of Strategy*. Allyn and Bacon, Boston, Massachusetts.

Owen, G. (1968). *Game Theory*. Saunders, Philadelphia, Pennsylvania.

Rapoport, A. (1966). *Two-Person Game Theory: The Essential Ideas*. University of Michigan Press, Ann Arbor, Michigan.

Rapoport, A. (1970). *N-Person Game Theory: Concepts and Applications*. University of Michigan Press, Ann Arbor, Michigan.

Rapoport, R., Guyer, M.J., and Gordon, D.G. (1976). *The Two Times Two Game*. University of Michigan Press, Ann Arbor, Michigan.

Selten, R. (1974). *Reexamination of the Perfectness Concept for Equilibrium Points in Extensive Games*. WP-23. IMW, University of Bielefeld, FRG.

Stahl, I. (1972). *Bargaining Theory*. EFI, Stockholm.

Vorobev, N.N. (1977). *Game Theory: Lectures for Economists and System Scientists*. Springer Verlag, New York.

Zeigler, B.P. (1976). *Theory of Modeling and Simulation*. Wiley, New York.

NOTES

1. For a more extensive discussion on modeling, see Niemeyer (Chapter III:b of this volume) and Zeigler (1976).

2. For a more detailed definition see Stahl (1972).

3. In free-form games (see Section 8 of this chapter), only parts of the institutional assumptions will be provided.

4. The literature on game theory is quite large. For overviews we refer the interested reader to Luce and Raiffa (1957), Owen (1968), Rapoport (1966, 1970), Davis (1970), May (1970), Bacharach (1976), Vorobev (1977), Aubin (1979), and Jones (1980).

5. A common situation involving a game of "coordination" is the case of two people on each side of a door that can open in either direction.

6. For references on type 1, see Lehman (1977); for type 2, Bell et al. (1977); and for type 3, Findler and Meltzer (1971).

7. Among these are several well known games from the socialist countries (see, e.g., Part IV of this volume).

8. For a game of type 1 see, for example, Hawes (1973); for a game of type 3 see Chapter VIII:c of this book.

9. See, for example, Rapoport et al. (1976).

10. This term is discussed further in Chapter X:a.

Chapter III:b

A CONTRIBUTION TO THE TYPOLOGY OF GAMES

Klaus Niemeyer
IABG, Ottobrunn (FRG)

1. INTRODUCTION

Ever since computers and computer models became available, gaming has become an increasingly interesting instrument in many disciplines. At the same time, new approaches within the theory of science have been developed to classify and systematize this methodology. As a stimulus for further work, this paper proposes an approach that describes the gaming method on the basis of Stachowiak's model theory (1973).

An explication of gaming in a formal meta-language based on mathematical logic seems necessary. In this paper, a game is considered as an experimental tool in order to perceive or anticipate the dynamics and the behavior of systems that contain cooperative and/or antagonistic intelligent subsystems. In contrast, classical game theory is considered as a rather specific, mathematical approach to optimize strategies and tactics in well defined game situations.

It is proposed to interpret the game setup as a model. The operation of the game is a time-dependent process or a simulation. On the other hand, a game is a supersystem composed of intelligent subsystems (referred to as K-systems)[1] and of models that serve as communication entities between the K-systems. Therefore the key elements in the explanation of gaming should be models and K-systems.

2. MODEL THEORY

The model theory of Stachowiak (1973) includes a systematic approach for the explication of a model. Attributes are used to describe and classify the most important characteristics of models:

- purpose;
- relationship between model and original;
- contraction.

2.1. Purpose

The pragmatic attribute of a purpose for models is also valid for games. The pragmatic way of thinking is considered to be in better correlation with experience than, for example, the critical rationalism by Popper (1973). With respect to the application of models to support decision makers, we do not consider verification or falsification of models, based on the criteria postulated by Popper, to be as important as the acceptance of the models by the decision maker. There are many models in use that have been proven false or that cannot be falsified/verified in principle. Stachowiak (1973, p.132) states: "Models are not *per se* related to their originals. Models are substitutes for the original:

- for defined, cognising or perceiving and acting, model-using subjects (K-systems);
- within defined time frames;
- by restrictions on given mental or real actions."

Models are developed and applied in order to fulfil given goals or motivations.

2.2. Relationship Between Model and Original

Normally the model is seen as a representation of its original, but a model can also be seen to be a prototype for a future construction. Thus there is a certain relationship between a model and its original in reality, or between the future construction and its model in reality (Figure 1). Therefore, the representational character of models alone does not reflect the prototype-construction relationship, which seems to be the reason for many misunderstandings.

While the model credibility discussion (Crosbie, 1976; Schruben, 1980; Bretzke, 1980) is often restricted to the representational character, the intention of the application of the model is based on the character of the prototype. In this paper, models of the representational character are classified as perception models, and models of the prototype character as anticipation models.

In correspondence to Figure 1 the model-original relationship can be formulated in the following notation based on set theory:

Perception model h

$$h = h_a \cup h_g$$
$$O = I \cup g_o$$
$$R : g_o \to h_g$$

Anticipation model f

$$f = f_g \cup f_a$$
$$C = J \cup g_c$$
$$A : f_g \to g_c$$

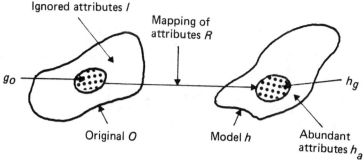

Perception

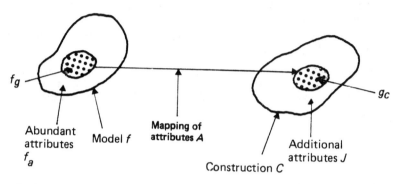

Anticipation

Figure 1. Relationship between model and original.

with

h, f	= sets of model attributes;
O	= set of attributes of the original environmental object;
C	= set of attributes of the desired future construction;
h_a, f_a	= sets of abundant attributes, which are only necessary to realize and operate the model (e.g., as regards computer models, the computer hardware, or input-output routines);
g_o	= set of attributes of the original that are relevant for the purpose of the model;
g_c	= set of attributes of the construction that are relevant for the purpose of the model;
h_g, f_g	= sets of attributes of the model that correspond to the sets of relevant attributes of the original and construction;
I	= set of ignored attributes of the original, which are not relevant for the purpose of the model;
J	= set of additional attributes of the construction, which are not relevant for the purpose of the model;
R	= mapping relation for the perception;
A	= mapping relation for the anticipation.

The model theory of Stachowiak (1973) does not explicitly distinguish between perception and anticipation models. In the formal explication of the model, both characters are closely linked in the sense that a repertoire of perception models is the prerequisite for the anticipation model and the anticipation model is the automatic consequence of a perception model as the purpose of the model-generating process. Since model generation can be seen as a process within a hierarchical structure of K-systems, the more explicit distinction between the two model types is proposed.

For models we state:[2] The generation of models is a process in time following the law of causation. Hence the model-original relationship can be separated into two aspects:

- the model is the representation or mapping of the original (perception model);
- the model is the prototype or standard for a future construction (anticipation model).

A model is *either* a model of an existing object, entity, or system, which could also be a model, *or* a model for a desired object, entity, or system, which has been changed or manipulated or the behavior of which has been forecast.

2.3. Contraction

The contraction denotes that models simplify the original or the future construction in order to reduce the complexity of the reality, to systematize facts, or to transmit knowledge and information, etc. Normally only a few attributes, elements, or parameters are taken into consideration, namely those important or relevant for the desired purpose. The many attributes, elements, or parameters that have a noise effect, reduce the clarity of results, or have little relevance are not taken into consideration. A model is easier and less expensive to manipulate than the original or a construction. For models it is stated: "A model does not represent all attributes of the original. A model represents only those attributes that are relevant or suitable for the generator or user of the model" (Stachowiak, 1973, p.132).

3. K-SYSTEMS

3.1. The Single K-System

The K-system is seen as the general representation (model) of an intelligent cybernetic system.[3] The K-system forms a feedback system together with an external object in the environment that is of interest to the K-system (Figure 2). This acting K-system or subject can be a human or any capable biological structure, a computer, or a composite of these elements, e.g., groups, organizations, etc. (aggregation of K-systems).

The K-system is, in a simplified manner, a repertoire of perception models, anticipation models, and a motivator for an acting subject. The perception models are representations of the external existing object; the anticipation models are prototypes for the desired object and produce guidance for the manipulation of the existing object or the construction of a new object.

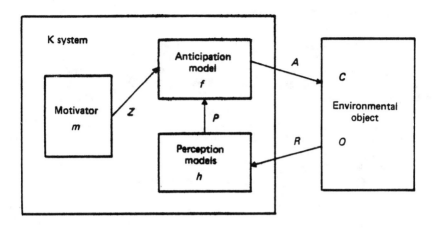

Figure 2. The K-system.

In addition to the notation illustrated in Figure 1 we may formulate:[4]

$$Z : m \rightarrow f_m$$
$$P : h \rightarrow f_p$$
$$f = f_m \cup f_p$$

with

m	=	set of motivational attributes or objectives of the K-system;
h	=	perception model or set of relevant perception attributes;
f_m, f_p	=	sets of attributes of the anticipation model;
Z	=	mapping relation for the motivational attributes;
P	=	mapping relation for the perception attributes.

The anticipation model f is controlled by the motivator and is based upon the set of relevant perception models. The set of relevant perception models h of the existing original object O in the environment can be seen as a repertoire of models out of which are selected those models and attributes suitable for fulfilling the set of objectives and motives m. The mapping of the motivational attributes m and perception attributes h results in the set of anticipation attributes f, which are relevant for the desired new construction or manipulation of the existing object.

The basic motivation is assumed to be a change of the external object so that the stability of the feedback cycle will be increased or the chance of survival of the K-system will be maximized in the sense of the theory of evolution. The perception and anticipation models within the K-systems are called endogenous models. A K-system has the ability to increase the quality of the endogenous models with the tendency of an increasing adaptation and approximation of the external environment (learning).

3.2. Aggregation of K-Systems

The external object of a K-system can also be a model. At the same time, this exogenous model may also be the external object or exogenous model of a second or third K-system. Simultaneously it is the object of the manipulations of all participating K-systems or their endogenous anticipation models, respectively, or the original for the endogenous perception models. The exogenous models are the essentially intellectual connections between the K-systems. The jointly formulated and manipulated exogenous models are representations or prototypes of the jointly perceived or anticipated external environment. In Figure 3 the exogenous models are denoted by h, f, and m.

The models h, f, and m should be inter-subjective entities that are as precise as possible. These models are the elements of communication between the K-systems. They perform the linkage in order to organize a K-system on a higher level. A model is an exogenous model in relation to a K-system, or a model-using subject, if the same model can be realized and accepted by another K-system (process of communication). An exogenous model becomes an endogenous model of the K-system on the next higher level.

If the K-systems organize a specialization of work, the overall system can be seen as a K-system K_n on the next higher level. The K_n system would contain the subsystems responsible for perception. K_{n-1}^p, anticipation, K_{n-1}^a, and motivation, K_{n-1}^m. The level is indicated by the index n. The elements of this system are the participating K-systems and their exogenous models h, f, and m, which now become endogenous models for the superimposed K_n system.

A very high-level K_n system is, for example, a national organization. Let the water resource O be the external object. In this example the sub-K-systems and models can be interpreted as follows:

K_{n-1}^p = research institutes that only do research in relation to the water economy of the country;

K_{n-1}^a = planning organization or administration;

K_{n-1}^m = political domain, which collects and integrates the motivations and goals of all participating K-systems;

h = repertoire of exogenous perception models of the water resources held by the research institutes (e.g., data, theories);

m = set of motivational or objective attributes (e.g., laws, regulations, etc.);

f = exogenous anticipation models, held by the administration, that determine the directives and specifications of a new or changed water supply system as well as its expected effectiveness.

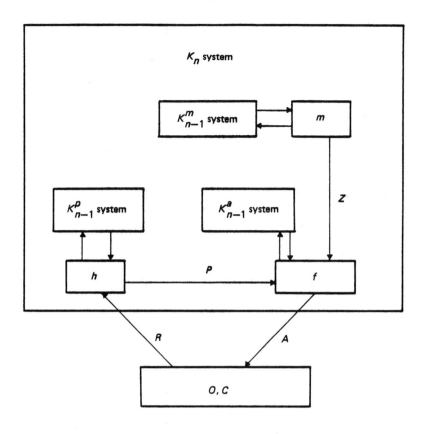

Figure 3. Aggregation of K-systems.

4. SIMULATION

A game constitutes a subset of a simulation, which is a dynamic process in time. A theory of simulation as defined by Zeigler (1976) could also serve as a basis for a formal explication of a theory of gaming. As in any simulation, several characteristics are valid for the gaming process (Koller, 1969).

4.1. Experimentation

A simulation is the application of an experiment on the basis of a suitable model or experimental construction. The methods and principles of scientific experimentation in the implementation, application, and evaluation phases are fully applied. The credibility and/or acceptability of the results is determined by the experimental frame (Zeigler, 1976, p.294), the purpose of the investigation, the model used, and the reproducibility of results.

4.2. Dynamics

Time is the independent parameter in a simulation. From an initial state or situation, the time and state of the model are changed and advanced either continuously or in time steps or at events until a final state has been reached (time-step simulation versus event simulation, time-step gaming versus event gaming). The problem of time synchronization (game time versus real time) has to be taken into consideration in several gaming applications, e.g., in simulators for training.

4.3. Determination of Final States

A simulation is a stochastic simulation if relevant processes are based on random events in the simulation. Based on identical initial states, the random events produce significant different final states within the reproduced simulations. A sample of simulation runs results in a probability distribution of the final states.

A simulation is deterministic if no relevant random events influence the processes. In this case, reproduced simulation runs should result in identical final states.

5. GAMING

A game (Figure 4) is characterized by the interaction between a K-system L (control) and a setup S, which can be considered as the representative (perception model) or prototype (anticipation model) of the environmental situation W (in relation to L). By analogy to W, S consists of one, two, or more K-systems (gaming parties) and a model g_L, which represents the external object g relative to the participating K-systems. If only one K-system participates in the setup S, the setup may be defined as a simulator. The game is a conflict (or competition) game if at least two K-systems with antagonistic goals participate. The K-systems with identical goals can be seen as being in coalition and can be organized as a K-system on the next higher level.

In Figure 4 some relations in a game are identified. The mapping relations Z, P, R, and A, as well as the set of attributes m, f, and h, have the same meanings as in Figures 1, 2, and 3. The participating K-systems in the game setup S have the notations x and y. They represent the K-systems x' and y' in the environmental situation W. The mapping relation and the sets of attributes are indexed by K-system notation (e.g., R_x is the mapping relation for the perception of K-system x).

In the environmental situation W the K-systems x' and y' are in competition with respect to the external object g. For each K-system the external object g and the opposite K-system are the elements for perception and manipulation. This is, for example, indicated by the mapping relation $A_{x'y'}$ which means that the K-system x' manipulates the K-system y' by way of $f_{x'}$. The same relation exists in the game setup S.

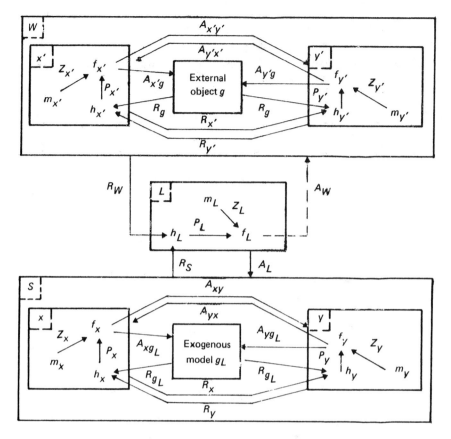

Figure 4. Relations in a game.

The following relations can be identified for the gaming situation S and for the environmental situation W (indicated by ').

A_{xy} = manipulation relation of K-system x on y;
A_{yx} = manipulation relation of K-system y on x;
A_{xg_L} = manipulation relation of K-system x on g_L;
A_{yg_L} = manipulation relation of K-system y on g_L;
R_x = perception relation of x by K-system y;
R_y = perception relation of y by K-system x;
R_{g_L} = perception relation of g_L by K-systems x and y.

The K-system L, which is the control-system (e.g., the game director or designer), describes the external object g using g_L or develops an exogenous model g_L based on the original g.

The relations for the K-system L are as follows:

R_W = perception relation of the environmental situation W by L;
R_S = perception relation of the gaming setup S by L;
A_L = manipulation relation on the gaming setup S by L;
A_W = manipulation relation on the environmental situation W by L.

Specific characteristics of the game can be defined based upon the expression of the sets within the game. For example:

- The degree of influence on the opposing K-system is defined by the relations A_{xy} and A_{yx}. There is no influence if $A_{xy} : f_x \rightarrow \phi$ and $A_{yx} : f_y \rightarrow \phi$.

- The degree of influence of the K-system L on the participating K-systems x and y is defined by the relations A_{Lx} and A_{Ly}. A *free-form* game is conducted if $A_{Lx} : f_L \rightarrow \phi$ and $A_{Ly} : f_L \rightarrow \phi$.

- The degree of reconnaissance is defined by the relations R_x and R_y. A *covered* game is conducted if R_x and R_y filter the information similarly to what must be expected in the real situation.

- The degree of effectiveness of a game for the K-system L is defined by the relation R_S. The effectiveness is a prerequisite for the acceptance of the game.

If the terminology of Shubik (1975) is used, several types and classes of games follow directly out of the relations and sets in Figure 4. Basically the motivator m_L and the relation Z_L determine the setup and the purposes of S. The games can be classified as follows:

Research Gaming

Development of a repertoire of perception models h_L within L to examine the phenomena of a potential conflict scenario W through application of gaming experiments and simulations S.

Operational Gaming

Development, test, and validation/verification of anticipation models f_L; design and realization of models to test concepts and plans in order to control the potential conflict scenario W.

Educational Gaming

Development of the repertoire of perception models h_x and/or h_y of the participating K-systems x and/or y; transmission of knowledge and experience to the gaming parties.

Staff Exercise

Development, test, and validation/verification of anticipation models f_x and/or f_y of the participating K-systems x and/or y (also x' and/or y'); the learning and training of action and goal-oriented planning.

Litigation

Influence and change of the motivation m_x and/or m_y of the participating K-systems x and/or y controlled by the K-system L in order to control the conflict scenario W.

Dialogues for Improved Communication

Joint formulation and adaptation of the external model g_L by the parties x and y in the sense of a dialectic method.

The elements of the game determine several well known forms of application of gaming. A few examples are collected in Table 1 (see also Bowen, 1978; Huber and Wobith, 1979; Stahl, 1979, 1980; Marshev, 1983).

Table 1. Some forms of the game.

	K-system L	Exogenous model g_L	K-system x	K-system y
Staff exercise	human	plan, map, concept	human $x = x'$	-
Tests of command/control systems	human	computer	human, computer $x = x'$	computer
Test of management information systems	human	computer	human, computer $x = x'$	-
Manual games	human	plan, map, board	human	human
Computer-assisted games	human	plan, map, computer	human	human
Interactive games	human, computer	computer	human	human
Interactive simulations	human, computer	computer	human	-
Closed simulations	computer	computer	computer	(computer)

REFERENCES

Albus, J.S. (1981). *Brains, Behavior and Robotics.* McGraw-Hill, Peterborough, New Hampshire.

Bowen, K.C. (1978). *Research Games: An Approach to the Study of Decision Processes.* Taylor and Francis, London.

Bretzke, W.F. (1980). *Der Problembezug von Entscheidungsmodellen.* Mohr, Tuebingen.

Crosbie, R.E. (1976). The Credibility of Computerized Models. *Simulation Councils Proceedings Series,* 6 (2), December.

Huber, R.K. and Wobith, B. (1979). Spiele der Militaerischen Systemanalyse. In R.K. Huber, K. Niemeyer, and H.W. Hofmann (Eds.), *Operationsanalytische Spiele fuer die Verteidigung.* Oldenbourg, Munich.

Koller, H. (1969). *Simulation und Planspieltechnik.* Gabler, Wiesbaden.

Marshev, V. (1983). Gaming in the USSR. In I. Stahl (Ed.), *Operational Gaming: An International Approach.* This volume, Chapter IV:b.

Popper, K.R. (1973). *Logik der Forschung.* Mohr, Tuebingen.

Schruben, L.W. (1980). Establishing the credibility of simulations. *Simulations,* 34 (3): 101-105.

Shubik, M. (1975). *Games for Society, Business and War.* American Elsevier, New York.

Siebecke, R. (Ed.) (1979). *Die experimentelle Methode in der Sozialistischen Betriebswirtschaftslehre.* 3/1. Friedrich-Schiller-Universitaet, Jena.

Stachowiak, H. (1973). *Allgemeine Modelltheorie.* Springer, Vienna.

Stahl, I. (1979). *A Proposal for IIASA Research on Gaming.* WP-79-30. International Institute for Applied Systems Analysis, Laxenburg, Austria.

Stahl, I. (Ed.) (1980). *The Use of Operational Gaming as an Aid in Policy Formulation and Implementation.* CP-80-6. International Institute for Applied Systems Analysis, Laxenburg, Austria.

Zeigler, B.P. (1976). *Theory of Modelling and Simulation.* Wiley, New York.

NOTES

1. In accordance with Stachowiak the intelligent subsystems (cybernetic systems) are designated as K-systems (K=Kybiak).

2. This statement is a variation of the corresponding statement by Stachowiak (1973, p.131): "Models are always models, namely mappings or representations of natural or artificial originals, which could also be models".

3. Although the K-system has been structured in a different, more detailed manner by Stachowiak (1973, p.67ff), the specific character is considered to be identical to the simplified structure of the K-system as defined in this paper. As a feedback system it also corresponds to the structures seen by Albus (1981) and others.

4. The abundant and ignored attributes are not noted further.

Chapter III:c

ELEMENTS OF A THEORY OF GAMING

Vadim Marshev
Moscow State University, Moscow (USSR)

A.K. Popov
Inform-Electro, Scientific Research Institute, Moscow (USSR)

1. INTRODUCTION

From a phenomenological point of view, management games are models which reflect to some extent the different sides of socioeconomic systems of different complexity and on different levels. Such models also represent systems of symbolic actions and interactions of the participants according to the given status of the rules, the goals of the game, and a set of behavioral norms (which are familiar to the participants from their own experience or from the literature).

The main idea in the theory of the management game is to consider the game from a *semiotic* point of view, i.e., from the point of view of:

1. Mathematical structure (syntax of the game);
2. Interpretation (semantics); and
3. Design and use (pragmatics of the game).

An overview of the elements of these three parts of the theory, as well as an indication of the relationships between them, is given in Table 1, and further details are given in the next three sections.

2. SYNTAX

Practically every game is defined by regulations, i.e., by a list of rules. In this list one must distinguish between the syntax rules (internal regulations describing the game independently of interpretations) and the design and use of the game in special cases. The list of rules consists of seven sublists according to the elements from which the game is constructed:

1. A set of pieces (a set of things to play with). We will call "pieces" those things that the players manipulate, such as production facilities, material and financial resources, etc.

2. A game space. In the course of the game, we must somehow allocate the pieces in space. Usually, this allocation is well defined by the rules, and the exact places and order of the allocation is described in the rules for the initial step and for the process of playing. Thus, not only is the set of places for pieces set, but so too is the relation between them. Let us name the set of places "the game space" and the set of places, together with the structure of this space, the "scheme of the game space".

3. A set of game positions. When a set of pieces is put in a certain way, we say that it has a certain position in the game. Let us call a "position" the placement of pieces according to the scheme of the game space. In every game there are rules to describe two special subsets of positions: a set of initial and a set of final positions. Rules for finishing the game are also included, so that the sublist of rules defines the positions of the game (initial, intermediate, final) and also the end of the game.

4. A manipulation set of the game. This sublist of rules defines the possible moves or manipulations as transformations of the positions.

5. Functions for evaluating the final position (as well as other positions) for each player and team.

6. The number of places for players in the game.

7. The role of the player in the game. Here we are defining the *right* to have a certain amount of pieces of different types with the positions taken by these pieces, the *duty* of the player to make a sequence of moves, the *obligation* to fight in order to reach personal goals in the game, and the *right* to have various sorts of information about the game. As usual, the access to information is implicitly defined for each player within the context of the game.

3. SEMANTICS

Within the interpretation of the game as a formal system, we can conceptualize the multiple or simple "mapping" or correspondence between the elements of the game and the "elements" of some conceptual class of substantive areas.

The totality of the interpretation of the game as a formal system is called the semantics of the game, and these are set by a part of the rules in the external regulations. A key term in the analysis of the semantics of simulation games as models of social systems is the term "role".

A simulation game is basically a symbolic representation of the role structure of the social system being analyzed. The essence of the modeling is the analysis of the empirical and theoretical structure of the social system, which is the totality of the interrelated roles of the participants, and the standardized relationships between these roles. This structure is reflected in the structure of the formal system of the game, which includes the roles of the participating teams and the relationships between roles.

Table 1. The elements of the semiotic theory of gaming.

Syntax	Semantics	Pragmatics
Management game	Social system	
Player	Player--a participant in the social system	Team of players
Set of pieces	Resources of participants	Team of game conductors
Game space	Set of places for resource allocation	Format of the game
Set of game positions	Socioeconomic situations	Materials for the game
Game manipulation set	Relationships between participants in social situations	
Evaluating functions	Evaluation of social situations	
Final game positions		
The number of game places and roles of players	Roles of participants	

The interpretation of the simulation game is called *correct* if each correct position of the game corresponds to a time description of the social system. The interpretation is called *adequate* if every position which corresponds to a true description of the social system can be reached from the initial position. These two properties of the interpretation of simulation games are evident analogues of noncontradiction and completeness in a formal system.

4. PRAGMATICS

The methodology and methods for the preparation, conduct, and analysis of simulation games comprise the pragmatics of the game. Using the pragmatics, we can divide management games into free-form and rigid-rule games.

A rigid-rule simulation game has a very formal set of regulations with which we can make an algorithm for the right moves. There is a distinction between manual and computer-based rigid-rule management games.

A nonformal, nonrigid simulation game is called a free-form game. One must distinguish between pragmatic and syntactic elements in the construction of the management game. In rigid-rule games, we have both elements, while in free-form games the syntactic elements are largely not made explicit.

The following are the main pragmatic elements in the construction of the game:

1. A team of players, to represent the corresponding participants in the socioeconomic system;

2. A team of conductors, to represent the environment or other vital participants in the socioeconomic system which are not directly represented in the game;

3. The format of the game, which includes rules for the conduct of the game and methods for presenting information, together with the procedure for conducting both rigid-rule and free-form games;

4. The materials for the game include office equipment, e.g., terminals, telephones, calculators, etc.

There are three stages in the design and use of the management game: (i) preparation, (ii) conduct, and (iii) analysis.

(i) Preparation includes the construction of the pragmatic elements and the formal system of the game (if it is a rigid-rule game); the choice of a suitable game among those available and its adaptation to the required goals; the planning of the game; and the instructions to the teams before they begin to play.

The real cases for the construction of the game are usually taken from managerial practice. The construction of a game presupposes that the following actions and requirements have been fulfilled:

1. The concrete practical aim of the game has been defined.

2. The object(s) for the game setting has been chosen (it can be a department, production unit, enterprise, division, machine, brigade, etc; here we must also define the client of the game and the level of administration to be simulated).

3. A group of people has been assembled for the design of the game.[1]

4. This group is fully acquainted with the materials to be used as the basis of the game. For the construction of the game it is vital to study the accumulated experience from the construction of similar games. Moreover, the material must be theoretically re-examined from the point of view of management science, taking into consideration facts and activities which preceded the modeled event or phenomenon.

5.   The time interval, i.e., the time for decision making and imple-
     mentation of the solution, has been defined. In the description
     of the game we specify several things: the resources of the par-
     ticipants, the boundaries of their activity, the rules for moves
     and for evaluation of positions.

6.   Those facts which are independent of the positions of the game
     have been specified.

7.   Instructions for the players and conductors have been com-
     posed.

8.   Initial information for the starting scenario which is necessary
     to begin the game has been designed (books of facts, figures,
     schemes of information flows).

(ii) Conduct of the game has the following general pattern. After the
instructions have been given out and the players are acquainted with the
initial information, play begins, and the start of the first round is
declared. The play continues according to a previously specified scheme
and can be generally presented as a process of receiving, analyzing, generating, and transmitting information both within and between teams.

(iii) Analysis of the game includes analysis of the process simulated,
analysis of the play and of the work of the conductors, analysis of the
pragmatics, and exposure, analysis, and improvement of the elements in
the construction of the game.

It should be mentioned once more that the degree of adequacy of
gaming as a scientific research method is determined by the degree of
completeness of the semantics. As a result, such problems as validity
and verification of the solutions of the game have not yet been solved.

5. CLASSIFICATION OF MANAGEMENT GAMES

The above elements of the theory of management games permit us to
outline a classification of such games. Games developed so far can be distinguished according to the following characteristics:

1.   The structural elements of the game: one- or several-person
     games; with opposing or similar interests; with numerical or
     ordinal functions for evaluations of the players' positions.

2.   The procedures and means of conducting the game: free-form
     and rigid-rule games (manual and computer-based).

3.   The subject of simulation: structure of the economy; level of
     production; stages in a production process, etc.

4.   Purpose: educational, research, operational/practical.

It is extremely important from the viewpoint of both theory and practice
to determine the place of a game in the classification.

Let us elucidate the third, and from our point of view, most important indicator in the classification, the *subject* of simulation. The common
indicators for all games from this viewpoint are:

1. The place of the simulated subject in the structure of the economy (industry, agriculture, transport, etc.);
2. The level of the subject (economy, branch, production unit, enterprise, division, etc.);
3. The stages of the "public production process" (including actual production, supply, sale, financing);
4. The structure of the elements and parameters of the production process (staffing, technology, products, labor productivity, capacity, quality, etc.);
5. The stages in production management (goal setting, forecasting, planning, organization, administration, analysis, evaluation, control);
6. The level and functions of the managerial stage (line and functional managers at top, middle, and lower levels);
7. The methods of management (economic, social, organizational, etc.).

6. FIELDS OF APPLICATION OF THE MANAGEMENT GAME

We shall finally turn to a typology of applications. In order to improve management, the gaming method is used in three areas--educational, research, and operational/practical--with corresponding functions in each.

(i) *The educational area--management training*
1. Demonstration function: games are used as a means of demonstrating the concepts, principles, methods, and procedures used in management.
2. Training function: games are used as a means of training, developing managerial skills, and teaching methods of problem solving.
3. Motivation function: games are used as a means to involve a person in the educational process and to provide natural motivation.
4. The function of improving activity: games are used as a method for active and intensive education.

(ii) *The research area--the formulation of management theory*
1. Heuristic function;
2. Verification function;
3. Formalization function;
4. Organizational function.

Among these research functions we carry out at present only the organizational function, which is performed during the process of designing and using the management game. In this process, it is possible to divide and coordinate the labor of scientists, specialists, and managers. As a result of their participation in games, theoretical research is carried out. This research requires much effort but is also very important. However, the effort required exceeds the psychological and physiological limitations not only of the individual researcher, but also of the total number of researchers at present involved in the design and use of management games.

(iii) The operational area--the rationalization of management

1. Analytical function: analysis of elements of the actual management system (organizational structure, staffing, decision making and decision implementation, process methods of management, managerial techniques, etc.).

2. Planning function: the design of various elements in the management system.

3. Experimental function: experiments using developed elements of the management system under game conditions.

From experience we can conclude that the gaming method can be successfully used in studies of the following applied problems:

- Studies of the management process;
- Methods of influencing various management objectives;
- The problem of short-term planning;
- The problem of forming the organizational structure of the objectives of management;
- The problem of division of functions and agencies within the management system;
- The decision-making process and the implementation of decisions on both the macro and the micro levels;
- Problems of global modeling;
- Problems of modeling in international relations, etc.

NOTE

1. For the construction of the game it is reasonable to bring in specialists in management, economics, mathematics (programming), psychology, education, etc., as well as from the field being modeled.

PART IV

OVERVIEW OF GAMING IN VARIOUS COUNTRIES

Chapter IV:a

MANAGEMENT SIMULATION GAMES: A COMPARATIVE STUDY OF GAMING IN THE SOCIALIST COUNTRIES

Isak Assa
*International Institute for Applied Systems Analysis,
Laxenburg (Austria)*

1. INTRODUCTION

The "Management Simulation Games" project reported on here began in 1974 as an essential part of the CMEA's[1] research plan. Scientists from six socialist countries gathered to work on the idea of developing a new tool for systems analysis in large socioeconomic systems. The material reviewed here covers a major part of the research to date on gaming in Bulgaria, Czechoslovakia, the GDR, Hungary, Poland, and the USSR. The basic information for the analysis and comparisons is drawn from the proceedings of eight successive seminars on management simulation games, held in Prague (1974/1975), East Berlin (1975), Budapest (1976), Warsaw (1977), Sofia (1978), Tbilisi (1979), Prague (1980), and Jena (1981).

Many results concerning problems of the taxonomy, design, application, transfer, and implementation of the management simulation games for educational and research purposes have been reported at these annual seminars. The research work carried out in each particular country has had its own specific features: an overview is given in Table 1.

The scientists from the GDR have directed their efforts towards the construction of educational games. Participants in the seminars from Humboldt University in Berlin, Friedrich Schiller University in Jena, Wilhelm Pieck University in Rostock, the Bergakademie in Freiberg, etc., have gained considerable experience in the application of gaming in their educational programs.

Scientists from Czechoslovakia have distinguished themselves in the methodological field by developing procedures for the design and computer programming of games. The Institute for Management Studies in Prague has reported on a multilevel management game for planning purposes at the level of corporations.

Methodological problems in the field of gaming are also of interest for participating scientists from Poland. The Institute for Scientific Organization and Management in Gdansk has achieved a great deal in the field of didactics and psychology in gaming. Games in accounting are being developed at Lodz University, and production planning games at the enterprise level are under preparation at Warsaw University and the Institute for Organizational Studies and Training of Managerial Staff (also in Warsaw).

Table 1. The use of management simulation games in institutions represented at the CMEA gaming seminars.

Country and institution	Field of application	Participants in gaming activities
Bulgaria		
Institute for Social Management, Sofia	Inventory planning Industry planning Distribution of resources	Students Top managerial staff
Karl Marx University of Economics, Sofia	Site location Transportation Economic mechanism	
The Bulgarian Academy of Science	Global modeling Management information systems	
Czechoslovakia		
Institute for Management Studies, Prague	Production planning at the enterprise level	Students Managers
The CSSR Academy of Science		
Institute of Philosophy and Sociology, Prague		
GDR		
Humboldt University, Berlin	Production planning in industrial enterprises Regional problems International Trade	Students Postgraduates Managers
Bergakademie, Freiberg		
Friedrich Schiller University, Jena		
Technical Institute, Leuna-Merseburg		
Wilhelm Pieck University, Rostock		
Institute of Engineering, Zittau		

Table 1. *Continued.*

Country and institution	Field of application	Participants in gaming activities
Hungary		
Research Institute of the Ministry of Labor, Budapest	Industrial planning Inventory problems Transportation	Students Managers
Karl Marx University, Budapest		
Poland		
Warsaw University	Accounting Planning at the national	Students Managers
Lodz University	and enterprise levels Human relations	
Institute for Organizational Studies and Training of Managerial Staff, Warsaw		
Institute for Scientific Organization and Management, Gdansk		
USSR		
Institute for Control Sciences, Moscow	Planning Simulation of different	Students Postgraduates
The USSR Academy of Sciences, Novosibirsk Branch	economic mechanisms Inventory problems Transportation Allocation of resources Global modeling	Managers
International Research Institute for Management Sciences, Moscow	Management information systems Trade Regional studies	
Moscow University		
Financial and Economic Institute, Leningrad		

Bulgarian scientists set themselves the task of combining, through gaming, the search for more efficient decision-making methods and the development of active techniques such as games, to facilitate the training of top managerial staff. In the Institute for Social Management in Sofia several games are being used for educational and research purposes.

The most notable feature of the research work being carried out by Hungarian scientists is the construction of a large number of computer games in the Research Institute of the Ministry of Labor in Budapest. The papers from this group discuss in great detail the methodological and implementation problems encountered in the design of games using computers.

Practically all areas of gaming are covered by publications of scientists from the USSR. Special mention should be made here of the achievements in the mathematical theory of gaming made by scientists engaged in research at the Institute for Management Sciences in Moscow, the Novosibirsk Branch of the USSR Academy of Sciences, and elsewhere. Considerable work in operational gaming is taking place in Moscow University and in the Leningrad Financial and Economic Institute.

The games discussed in the seminars were developed mainly for the field of economics. Some theoretical and practical work is also going on in gaming for other areas, such as military affairs, foreign trade, organizational behavior, human relations, politics, ecology, etc., but these applications were not covered in the seminars.

It should be pointed out here that there were many differences, mainly concerning methodological problems, between the scientists at the beginning of the project. Some of these still exist, but, in our opinion, these differing viewpoints actually contribute to a better understanding of how gaming should best be used in the systems analysis of complex socioeconomic systems. A number of questions were frequent topics of discussion:

- What are the advantages and benefits of using gaming in systems analysis?
- Can we solve the problems examined by methods other than gaming?
- What is man's role in gaming?
- Does the game used converge to an optimum solution?
- What kind of practical problems can be tackled successfully through gaming?

The reader will find some answers to these questions in the following sections.

2. REASONS FOR THE DEVELOPMENT OF MANAGEMENT SIMULATION GAMES

The fact that management simulation games are able to combine the heuristic capabilities of man and the computing capabilities of the machine can be considered the *first* reason for the use of gaming in economics and the social sciences.

The *second* reason is that a large gap still exists between management theory and managerial practice. Scientists and model builders have noted the lack of interest shown by managers in making decisions with the help of models. On the other hand, scientists often decline experimental opportunities if these require time-consuming data collection or if the statistical and empirical information available is considered inaccurate or insufficient. At present, there is a serious lack of communication between the decision makers and the model builders; this situation has arisen for a number of reasons:

- Practical management requires the construction of simple and realistic models which are easy to cope with and to understand, but modelers often supply complex or unrealistic models with incomprehensible results.

- Model building, data collection, and model verification and implementation are interdependent activities, but modelers often treat them separately.

- Social and economic reality is far too complex for one person to comprehend, regardless of his profession, training, or knowledge. Management problems require a team of specialists that can provide a framework for interdisciplinary communication and a better background for the study of complex phenomena.

Therefore, the growing need for closer cooperation between scientists and decision makers has led to the widespread application of management simulation games. Gaming can convey information to the manager about scientific planning methods, forecasting, etc., in a simple and understandable way.

The *third* reason stems from the following. Previously, there was a generally held opinion that problems in management could be solved by the use of large optimization models. However, it is now widely recognized that the decision-making process involves more than just making a choice. It comprises a set of interconnected activities, such as goal setting, gathering and processing the required information, definition of the problem, generation of alternatives for the different courses of action, estimation of their possible outcomes, and finally the actual commitment to some course of action and its realization. These phases in the decision-making process are shaped by different people, at different times and locations, and under different circumstances.

The most efficient way to solve a complex management problem that comprises a system of decisions is to divide it into decision stages. This approach introduces the concept of hierarchy and subdivides the decisions into a number of subdecisions sequentially in time. The combination of the quantitative approach and the introduction of the concept of hierarchy into decision-making has resulted in a new method: *situation analysis.* The idea is to identify those situations that are the key points in the decision-making process and to facilitate their resolution by appropriate methods and techniques. The interaction of the various "resolved situations" can be handled successfully by the management game structure through efficient use of a sophisticated computer system.

The *fourth* reason for the development of management simulation games concerns educational and training applications. The gap between management theory and managerial practice is very often explained by the lack of interest shown by managers in the preparation and analysis of decisions with the help of mathematical models. The reasons given for this lack of interest are many and varied, ranging from insufficient knowledge about the capabilities of models, computers, and new management approaches to organizational deficiencies and psychological barriers. However, the rapid development of technology and the growth of computer applications in management have persuaded decision makers that it is necessary to periodically update their knowledge about developments in planning methods, forecasting, computer science, management technology, etc. The use of gaming as an essentially new educational technique has been found very suitable for imparting this advanced and sophisticated information.

3. METHODOLOGICAL PROBLEMS IN THE DESIGN AND IMPLEMENTATION OF GAMES

Serious attempts to develop gaming theory have been made by the Soviet scientists V. Burkov of the Institute for Control Sciences and Y.B. Germayer of the Computer Center of the USSR Academy of Sciences. The two books written by these scientists (Germayer, 1976; Burkov, 1977) have been widely used by scientists from the socialist countries as methodological guides in the construction of the model systems used to simulate the object of the gaming exercise. They deal mostly with the mathematical background of gaming theory and with the problems of interaction between the different models used by the participants in the game.

We shall give here a brief summary of the basic principles and concepts of Burkov and Germayer's interactive system theory.

Each participant in the game is considered as an interactive element with certain behavioral features. The interactive elements can be situated in different management levels, which also differ from each other with regard to the type of information processed in order to make a decision. Thus, the theory deals with multilevel management simulation games and applies the basic concepts of hierarchical system theory.

In the case of a two-level management simulation game, the single interactive element on the first level is called the "control unit", while those on the second level are called "users". The "control unit" governs the behavior of the interactive elements on the second level: it plays a coordinating role in order to achieve a higher payoff for the system as a whole.

The game is designed on the basis of the existing relationships between the decisions made by the interacting elements. No decision maker (user or control unit) can make a decision without considering what decisions the other decision makers may make. This interdependence is considered by Germayer as nonconflicting because it can be controlled and directed towards a situation in which the system as a whole benefits, through several interactions between the participants in the game.

The basic concepts of interactive system theory are as follows:

- The control unit works with insufficient information about the characteristics of the second-level interactive elements (users).
- Each interactive element has its own objective function. This function may or may not be known by the control unit.
- Each interactive element knows the strategy of the control unit and also the abilities of the control unit to influence its behavior.
- Each interactive element can use this information in order to fulfill its goals.
- Each interactive element has the opportunity to optimize its actions according to its desired development perspective and interests.
- Each interactive element may or may not know the objective functions of the other elements.

Management games with similar structures are very appropriate for simulating the planning process in socialist economies. "Nonconflicting" situations are involved and the hierarchical structure of the games corresponds to the structure of the system where planning decisions are made (Panov, 1978). The planning procedure is interactive and based on the dialogue between the elements in a multilevel management system. The most straightforward way to simulate dialogues between the corporations, the individual plants, and the planning body is, in our opinion, the management game approach.

Some scientists working on gaming believe that management simulation games can be usefully applied to the strategic planning and testing of economic and social mechanisms (Assa, 1978). Another viewpoint is that games should be used to study the problems which arise in the functioning of large organizations (Yefimov and Komarov, 1980).

The serious lack of methodology on gaming for operational purposes leads to different views about the structure, application, design, and interpretation of games. One commonly held opinion, for example, is that the following procedure should be used when building a game for operational purposes. First, the object for research (enterprise, plant, organization, etc.) is chosen and a model for its behavior developed. Second, the model is tested using real data, and third, a game situation is constructed in which the model is used for decision making.

In other words, emphasis is laid on the construction of the simulation system of models and often very little attention is paid to the design of the game situation (roles, scenarios, and rules). However, a considerable amount of work has been done on the latter problem by Yefimov and Komarov. Using the example of a game built at the enterprise level, they developed a procedure for the design of a gaming situation (Yefimov and Komarov, 1980).[2]

In this paper we shall describe three approaches that can produce tentative structures for gaming situations and illustrate each one with appropriate examples. The three approaches differ in terms of the ways in which they stratify the management process.

The *first approach* is based on the stratification suggested by Mesarovic and Pestel (1974) and adapted by Klabbers (1975). Under this approach, large organizations are viewed as socioeconomic systems which are goal-directed and self-organized. They respond to the changing environment by consciously varying their structure in order to attain their goals. They are characterized by a large degree of uncertainty, which is a consequence of a lack of knowledge about the system's elements and their interrelationships. In order to study the interrelationships between the system elements through gaming, the management process is disaggregated into three strata--the norm stratum, the decision-making stratum, and the causal stratum.[3] The causal stratum is related to the activities through which the system's input/output processes are accomplished. The decision-making stratum is related to the formation and implementation of goals, policies, and strategies. The norm stratum is related to norms and values which govern the decision-making process.

As an illustration of this approach for structuring the management process in a large organization the management game IM-1 ("Economic Mechanism") (see Assa et al., 1976) can be used. It was developed in the Institute for Social Management in Sofia for educational and research purposes. This game is described in greater detail in Chapter V:b of this volume. Here we shall only present a few salient features to illustrate the approach.

The goals of the game are:

- To impart knowledge about different economic instruments and to study their functioning in a given enterprise; and

- To test different economic mechanisms at the enterprise level.

The enterprise in the game is represented by a simulation model (see Figure 1) based on a system of simultaneous equations. The equations are regressions estimated from statistical information gathered for the enterprise over a certain period. Sixteen economic instruments through which the decision maker (director, planner, chief of the production sector, etc.) can influence the functioning of the enterprise serve as input to the simulation model. The outputs from the model are seven economic factors that describe the state of the enterprise during each period.

The participants in the game must achieve a planned set of target figures for these factors by varying the economic instruments available according to the defined economic mechanism. By economic mechanism we mean here the assumed rules, norms, and laws for the interrelations between the different participants in economic and social life.

The decision maker in the game acts according to the information that he receives from:

- The simulation model of the enterprise;
- The economic mechanism;
- The other decision makers; and
- The decision support system.

The decision support system contains additional models which, if the decision maker so requires, can be run to obtain forecasts, trends, general data, etc.

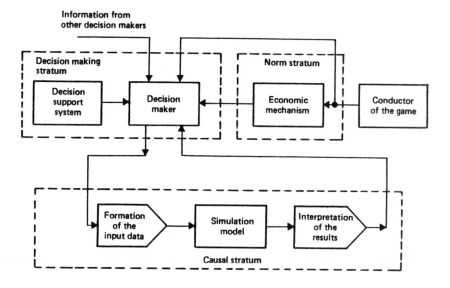

Figure 1. The management game IM-1 ("Economic Mechanism").

The conductor of the game can change the economic mechanism and study the corresponding changes in behavior and decisions. The advantage of being able to study the psychological interrelations between the different decision makers and the considerable knowledge which the participants obtain by using the computer should not be underestimated.

The *second approach* to developing structures for gaming situations involves attempts to describe the management process as an information process decomposed into several interconnected phases forming the so-called management cycle (Nikolov, 1971).

The management cycle illustrated in Figure 2 is constructed by applying the "management by objectives" concept. The process of management is decomposed into several different phases expressing the main management functions. It is an aggregated cycle and can be adapted to management at various levels of the economic system, including individual enterprises, larger organizations, and the economy as a whole.

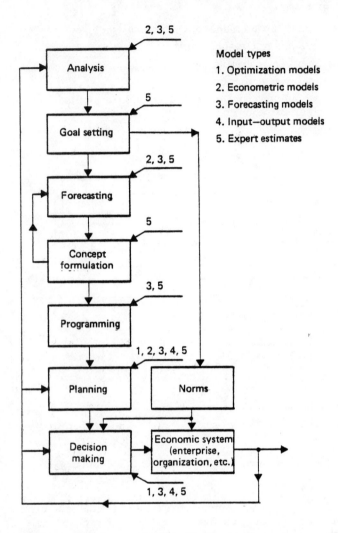

Figure 2. The management cycle and types of models used in each phase.

Several types of model are also mentioned in Figure 2 in order to illustrate their relationship to each particular phase (Assa and Petrov, 1978). The list is not complete but shows the stage reached in the development and application of each model type. Combinations of statistical, optimization, and numerical methods, and also expert estimates, are used to facilitate the decision-making process in each phase of the cycle. The role of the management cycle here is to provide a general framework for interdisciplinary research and to help link the models into one interactive procedure. It also introduces the important concept of hierarchy.

A similar structure for the gaming situation has been used in the construction of the multilevel game "Management of an Industrial Production Organization" in the Institute for Social Management in Prague (see Fotr et al., 1980). This game uses a complex dialogue procedure to represent the entire mangement process of a large organization. The organization consists of a central management level and three production enterprises. The goal of the game is to construct an appropriate five-year plan for the organization. Three different roles exist in the game: those of a central managerial board of the organization, managerial boards for each production enterprise, and a game conductor playing the role of an industrial ministry. Each of these is responsible for different management functions. The participants in the game can make use of a sophisticated decision support system, i.e., a system of models which is designed to solve problems that can arise during the operation of the organization. An information system covering numerous economic parameters and instruments has been adapted to aid decision making in building the plan. This management game is run on a computer system using a large number of terminals in the Training Center of the Ministry of Industry in Prague.

The *third approach* which is used for the structuring of the game situation is closely related to the concepts of game theory and interactive system theory (see Germayer, 1976: Burkov, 1977). As an illustrative example we shall discuss the game "Mono-Resource Allocation Planning", a result of collaborative work between the Institute for Social Management and the Institute of Engineering Cybernetics, both in Sofia (Assa and Tzvetanov, 1979). A diagram of the game is given in Figure 3.

The problem of planning resource allocation is structured as a two-level hierarchical system in which the first level is represented by the central unit (CU) and the second level by a number of users. The CU can influence the planning process, i.e., the actual behavior of the users, through the implementation of various economic instruments such as prices, penalty functions for unused resources or surpluses, premium functions, etc.

The conductor of the game is able to introduce different laws or rules for the distribution of the resources and can study the behavior of both the CU and the users. Each user has specific demand and production functions. It can optimize its resource-ordering policy in the desired direction by using the modules especially designed for that purpose. Each user may or may not know the demand and production functions of the others, depending on the rules introduced by the conductor of the game. In this way, different scenarios can be generated in order to study various distribution mechanisms.

The game is designed on the basis of four algorithms, which solve the following problems:

- Choice and estimation of the distribution rules used by the CU;
- Estimation of the value of the resource requirements;
- Estimation of the planned distribution of the resource by the CU; and
- Estimation of the user's strategies in the game.

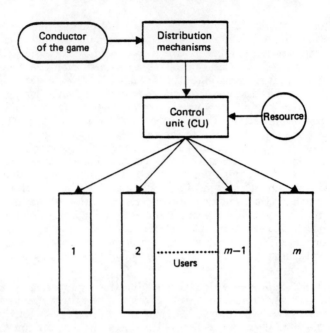

Figure 3. A management game for resource allocation planning.

The algorithms are designed to solve the problems with monotonous and stepwise decreasing demand and production functions. The game is implemented in FORTRAN on an ICL 1904A computer. The programs are structured in a modular fashion. By running the game it is possible to test the concept of rational behavior and to arrive at an equilibrium point in the resource allocation exercise.

The three illustrative examples given above are only a small part of the large number of games reported in the seminars. On analyzing their structure and fields of application, we find that most of the games consist of two main elements, a simulation system of models and a game situation, and that one or other of the approaches discussed above are used in their construction. Most games are interactive.

Two main directions can be distinguished in the recent development of management games:

The *first* is connected with the study of various mechanisms in large corporations based on simple interactive models. There is a widely held opinion that, with the help of small and simple models, new theoretical ideas and hypotheses can be tested. Examples include the study of different economic mechanisms and their impact on the economy, and investigations of the influence of different organizational structures on the functioning and management of large organizations.

The *second* direction is closely related to the actual functioning of various social and economic mechanisms in the economy. Here complex systems of models are required in order to provide a framework for scientific and practical results, and relatively sophisticated models, programming techniques, and computer operating systems are needed.

4. DESIGN OF THE SIMULATION SYSTEM OF MODELS IN GAMES

Many scientists feel that a model must have an interactive mode of communication before it can be classified as a game. However, a large number of the educational games reported in the seminars were simply models designed to solve problems in different fields. The "game situation" in these games was simply routine work with the model involving changing its input and interpreting the results.

Nevertheless this type of work in gaming has contributed to the fast development of models, programs, and techniques which have been successfully applied in the building of new games.

Some authors think that it is more convenient to start building a game by using existing models. However, one should bear in mind that these models have to be connected by a game-situation framework.

Two major problems can be distinguished in the building of a simulation system of models--the computer programming involved and the informational basis of the game. Leading contributions in this field have come from scientists from Czechoslovakia, the GDR, and Bulgaria (see Fotr and Hajek, 1978; Vieviger, 1978; Assa and Petrov, 1977). These efforts have been directed towards the building of a standard type of program with a modular structure which would make it usable for a number of different games. The unified inputs and outputs of these standard programs enable researchers to use them as modules in the game structure and to generate different scenario algorithms for the solution of various game situations.

A bank of programs has been collected in the Institute for Social Management in Sofia (see Assa and Petrov, 1977), consisting of programs in FORTRAN IV for the following tasks:

- The solution of large systems of linear equations with embedded topological and sparsity techniques for different types of matrices.
- The solution of continuous linear optimization problems with embedded reinversion subroutine, sparsity, and topological techniques.
- The solution of large transportation problems using graph theory.
- Statistical analysis (regression, correlation, and factoral).
- The solution of nonlinear systems of equations.

- The solution of integer 0-1 variable linear optimization problems.

- Random number generation and filters for different probability distributions of the time series.

This bank of computer programs was assembled to overcome the difficulties which often arise in connecting the models in an iterative procedure when standard computer programs with complex inputs and outputs are used.

There are two main viewpoints concerning the generation of the game's informational basis. The *first* one emphasizes the model side. First of all an adequate model should be built for the description of the game situation and then appropriate information should be sought for its solution. The *second* one takes into account the fact that the information is often scarce and inaccurate. Therefore, this second group suggests that an appropriate model should be built on the basis of the information available.

The optimum approach probably lies somewhere in between. If efficient methods and programs are developed for the processing of the available statistical information, practically any kind of data can be generated for the game. Several games reported use Monte Carlo techniques, random number generators, and filters for different probability distributions in order to enrich the existing data.

Summarizing the previous discussion, the following common characteristics can be derived:

- All reported management simulation games are realized on computers.

- The most widely used computer language is FORTRAN IV; a very small number of games use PL/I and ASSEMBLER.

- The programming of games is generally performed without the use of standard computer programs which facilitates their transfer.

- The modular structure of the games facilitates modification.

- Games use realistic statistical information.

5. MULTILEVEL MANAGEMENT SIMULATION GAMES

Multilevel management simulation games have also been developed: these reflect the structure of the planning system in the socialist countries. Within the hierarchical management structure, dialogues take place both horizontally and vertically, and the multilevel MSGs mirror this feature.

Vertical lines of communication exist on a sectoral level between the planning authorities, ministries, enterprises, and plants, and on a regional level between the planning authorities, the region, and the subregions. Horizontal communication channels exist between the ministries, between the enterprises, and between the regions and the sectoral ministries, enterprises, and plants.

This structure and intercommunication is illustrated by the multilevel game KOMBINAT. This game is designed on the basis of two other games, IM-1 ("Economic Mechanism") and the management game BES-1. The latter was developed by scientists at the Humboldt University in Berlin (see Gernert and Habedank, 1980). The KOMBINAT game covers the dialogue taking place between the ministry, the enterprises, and the plants in the process of constructing the plan. The game situation is structured by applying the management cycle approach. IM-1 has been described above. BES-1 is a game on a plant level. It simulates the functioning of the plant in each three-month period during the whole planning horizon. The simulation model uses statistical data which reflect its "economic past". The game is mainly intended for educational purposes.

The connection of BES-1 with IM-1 will, when complete, open possibilities for research and operational use: the multilevel IM-BES game is still under development. The decision-making process in the game is implemented by means of discussions and consultations with the conductor of the game. This is a collaborative venture between Bulgarian and German scientists.[4] In the same way as the Czechoslovakian game "Enterprise", it is also intended to build a system of models for decision-making in conjunction with this game.

There are also plans to construct a game with a structure similar to that of a system of models developed for the Silistra region of Bulgaria at the International Institute for Applied Systems Analysis in Laxenburg, Austria. This game is intended to facilitate the dialogue between the national and regional authorities in the strategic regional development process.

6. APPLICATIONS OF MANAGEMENT GAMES

It is probably fair to say that the main area of applications of the management simulation games developed in the socialist countries has been in economics. For example, participants from almost every country reported games concerned with inventory problems (see Assa et al., 1978; Dimitrova and Marchev, 1978). The management of the inventory process is a relatively developed part of operations research. The gaming situation in these games is usually constructed by using a random number generator and filters with specified probability distributions in order to simulate the processes of supply and demand in the warehouse. These games have been used mainly for educational purposes.

Another fairly common topic for research in gaming during the past five years has been the development of games based on the production process at the plant level. The management game DOENTS ("Decide") designed by scientists in the Research Institute of the Ministry of Labor in Budapest simulates the production process in a toy factory (see Doman, 1976).

The decision-making process in a chemical production plant is modeled by the game IU-IV, developed by Fotr and Hajek (1976) from the Institute for Social Management in Prague. The BES-1 game developed by H. Gernert from Humboldt University in Berlin and discussed above also describes the production process and the relationship between the managers in a general factory.

A number of games described by scientists from the Institute of Control Sciences in Moscow deal with the management process at the plant level: these are the games "Project", "Plan", "Competition", "Maintenance", "Assignment", and "Stimuli of Production" (see Burkov et al., 1978).

The management game "Quality" analyzes the factors which can influence the quality of production in the shipbuilding industry and was developed by A. Stoer, from Rostock.

"Red Weaver" is a game developed by Djakubova and Yefimov (1978), which studies the management and production processes in a plant in the textile industry.

Several games were constructed and run in the USSR in order to analyze the characteristics of a management information system (MIS) in large organizations (see Yefimov and Komarov, 1978). This idea was first suggested by Davis and Taylor (1975) and it is now widely used for assessing the efficiency of management information systems.

Management simulation games are considered by gaming specialists in the socialist countries as a powerful and effective tool for educational purposes. According to answers to a questionnaire, ninety percent of them are convinced that in the future gaming should be directed at educating students and managers (see Dobrinski and Janeva, 1978). Eighty percent of the games reported in the seminars are educational. They are used in Humboldt University in Berlin to teach students from the Department of Economics and Statistics, in the Institute for Social Management in Bulgaria to train top managerial staff in the application of quantitative methods and computers in social management, in the Institute for Organization Studies and Training of Managerial Staff in Warsaw in the field of economics, and so on. (see Table 1).

From the many applications reported, several major conclusions can be drawn:

- The development of management games for educational purposes is done on the basis of simulation models and management information systems.

- The construction of a game requires first, the specification of those elements which could be useful in fulfilling the educational goals and second, the preparation of a scenario for a quasi-gaming situation with appropriate illustrative data.

- The participants in the game get acquainted with the actual application of models in various sectors of the economy, and study how to act in different situations generated by realistic social and economic mechanisms.

The researcher who designs an educational game must bear in mind two very important rules. First, the educational game should reflect a real-life situation and second, the didactic goals must be precisely and clearly formulated. The didactic and psychological problems in the field of gaming are a major research topic in the Novosibirsk Branch of the

USSR Academy of Sciences and the Institute for Scientific Organization and Management in Gdansk. The studies are directed towards describing the specific influence of the manager's personality in the decision-making process. The particular manager is characterized by his knowledge, experience, intuitive skills, attitude to the social and economic environment, habits, etc. The researchers in this particular field have made successful progress by analyzing the "history" of each game. Every management simulation game is considered to generate its own history through its being played by various participants differing in education, profession, age, and so on (see Mironosezki, 1978).

Valuable results have been obtained by scientists in Gdansk and Smolensk, based on a sociological and statistical analysis of the history of a game that was run with more than 1500 participants, including students, managers, scientists, etc. (see Repinski, 1978; Wach, 1978).

7. TRANSFER OF MANAGEMENT GAMES

The research reported earlier has led to collaborative work between groups of scientists. The Hungarian game DOENTS ("Decide") has been transferred and introduced into the educational program in Freiberg University (GDR) and in the Institute for Social Management in Sofia (Bulgaria). The game BES-1 designed at Humboldt University (GDR) has been connected with the Bulgarian game IM-1 ("Economic Mechanism") designed by scientists from the Institute for Social Management. This transfer is discussed in greater detail by Gernert et al. in Chapter V:b of this volume.

Scientists from the Universities of Budapest and Warsaw have a great deal of experience in the transfer of games. In these two universities, the New York University Management Game, designed by Myron Uretsky, has been successfully transferred and implemented for the education of students and managers. The game is treated as an "economic laboratory". Details are given by Uretsky et al. in Chapter V:c of this volume.

Scientists from the GDR (M. Gernert) and Poland (A. Metera) are working on the problem of building a computerized bank of management games. Existing games in the socialist countries are classified and stored in a computer in Warsaw. Considerable efforts were devoted to the game identification problem. Each game is now uniquely defined by a set of parameters which has been approved and accepted by all the socialist countries. The existence of such a bank will hopefully stimulate further transfers of games and gaming ideas (see Siebecke, 1979).

The seminar in Prague in 1980 discussed the problems of gaming in a new and different way. Two large multilevel games were analyzed from the standpoint of using such types of games for planning purposes in the socialist economies. The completion of this task will require an interdisciplinary team of specialists and international collaboration between scientists from various CMEA countries.

REFERENCES

Assa, I. (1978). *Management Games in the Decision-Making Process.* Informatika 78, Bled, Yugoslavia.

Assa, I. and Petrov, S. (1977). *Programming and Information Problems in the Design of Management Games.* Proceedings of the International Seminar on Management Games, 4th, Warsaw. (In Polish.)

Assa, I. and Petrov. I. (1978). *Cybernetics Approach to the Management of Economic Systems.* Amsterdam VIII. Proceedings of the International Congress on Systems Research and Cybernetics (World Organization of General Systems Research and Cybernetics).

Assa, I. and Tzvetanov, I. (1979). *The Management Game "Mono-resource Allocation Planning".* Institute for Social Management, Sofia, page 130. (In Bulgarian.)

Assa, I. Gevrenov, S., Kolarov, N., and Petrov, S. (1976). *The Management Game "Production Enterprises Economic Mechanism".* Proceedings of the International Seminar on Management Games, 3rd, Budapest. (In Russian.)

Assa, I., Kechayov, A., Ivanov, M., and Gateva, N. (1978). *Inventory Process Management.* Proceedings of the International Seminar on Management Games, 5th, Sofia. (In Russian.)

Burkov, V. (1977). *Foundations of the Mathematical Theory of Active Systems.* Nauka, Moscow. (In Russian.)

Burkov, V., Ivanovski, A., Nemzeva, A., and Shepkin, A. (1978). Proceedings of the International Seminar on Management Games, 5th, Sofia. (In Russian.)

Davis, R. and Taylor, B. (1975). Systems design through gaming. *Journal of System Management,* 26:36-42.

Dimitrova, I. and Marchev, A. (1978). *Inventory.* Proceedings of the International Seminar on Management Games, 5th, Sofia. (In Russian.)

Dobrinski, R. and Janeva, I. (1978). *Management Games--Today and Tomorrow.* Proceedings of the International Seminar on Management Games, 5th, Sofia. (In Russian.)

Doman, A. (1976). *Decide!* Proceedings of the International Seminar on Management Games, 3rd, Budapest. (In Russian.)

Djakubova, T. and Yefimov, V. (1978). *The Management Game "Red Weaver".* Proceedings of the International Seminar on Management Games, 5th, Sofia. (In Russian.)

Fotr, I. and Hajek, S. (1976). *The Management Game "IU-IV".* Institute for Social Management, Sofia. (In Russian.)

Fotr, I. and Hajek, S. (1978). *Tentative Programming Structure of a General-Type Management Simulation Game.* Proceedings of the International Seminar on Management Games, 5th, Sofia. (In Russian.)

Fotr, I. and Hajek, S. (1980). *Management of an Industrial Production Organization.* Proceedings of the International Seminar on Management Games, 7th, Prague. (In Russian.)

Germayer, Y.B. (1976). *Games with Nonconflicting Interests.* Nauka, Moscow. (In Russian.)

Gernert, H. and Habedank, M. (1980). *The Multilevel Planning Game "KOMBINAT"*. Proceedings of the International Seminar on Management Games, 7th, Prague. (In Russian.)

Klabbers, J.H.G. (1975). *Interactive Simulation: On-Line Interaction between Man and Machine for the Study and Management of Social Systems*. Annual Conference of ISAGA (International Simulation and Gaming Association), 6th, Milan.

Mesarovic, M.D. and Pestel, E. (1974). *Multilevel Computer Model of World Development Systems*. Proceedings of the IIASA Symposium on Global Modelling, 1st, Laxenburg, Austria.

Mironosezki, N.B. (1978). *Active Educational Methods in the Training of Managerial Staff*. Proceedings of the International Seminar on Management Games, 5th, Sofia. (In Russian.)

Nikolov, I. (1971). *Cybernetics and Economics*. Nauka i Izkustvo, Sofia. (In Bulgarian.)

Panov, O. (1978). *Choice of the Type and the Characteristics of Management Games for Research and Training Purposes*. Proceedings of the International Seminar on Management Games, 5th, Sofia. (In Russian.)

Repinski, J. (1978). *Use of Management Games in Educational Courses and Seminars*. Proceedings of the International Seminar on Management Games, 5th, Sofia. (In Russian.)

Siebecke, R. (Editor) (1979). *Die Experimentelle Methode in der Sozialistischen Betriebswirtschaftslehre*. P. 143, No. 3/1, Oekonomisches Labor, Friedrich Schiller University, Jena.

Vieviger, B. (1978). *A Methodology for Development Simulation Models*. Proceedings of the International Seminar on Management Games, 5th, Sofia. (In Russian.)

Wach, T. (1978). *Participants' Behavior in the Decision-Making Process in Games*. Proceedings of the International Seminar on Management Games, 5th, Sofia. (In Russian.)

Yefimov, V. and Komarov, V. (1978). *Management Games Used in the Development of MIS*. Control Systems and Machines, No. 1. (In Russian.)

Yefimov, V. and Komarov, V. (1980). *Introduction to Management Simulation Games*. Nauka, Moscow. (In Russian.)

NOTES

1. CMEA (also known as COMECON) stands for the Council for Mutual Economic Assistance.

2. This is explained in more detail in the paper by Yefimov and Komarov in Chapter IX:b of this volume.

3. See also Chapter VII:a of this volume, by Klabbers.

4. This is discussed further by Gernert et al. in Chapter V:b of this volume.

GAMING IN THE USSR

Vadim Marshev
Moscow State University, Moscow (USSR)

1. INTRODUCTION

Man has devised many useful techniques for dealing with behavioral problems connected with the management of socioeconomic processes. Most of these methods are based on formal logic, and their formal structures have become progressively more complicated in an attempt to model real-life situations more closely. However, throughout this period of increasing complexity, decision-making specialists were aware that many *human* factors are also involved which normally end up in the Procrustean bed of formal models because they are very difficult (and often impossible) to incorporate in the framework of models.

Model designers gradually became aware that it would be sensible to incorporate people within the models, and so, in a new type of combined model, people were invited to act out their real-life roles and to re-create their behavioral patterns under experimental conditions. The term "games"[1] (e.g., business or production games) soon came into use to describe these combined "formal logic and people" models.

Gaming techniques are now rapidly gaining in popularity. Hundreds of business and management games[2] have already been designed, scientific investigations of gaming are taking place throughout the world, including the USSR, and the number of articles on the subject continues to grow. The following sections present a brief history of gaming in the USSR and discuss the current state of Soviet studies.

2. A BRIEF HISTORY OF GAMING IN THE USSR

The first publications on business and educational games appeared in the USSR in the 1930s (Ostrovsky, 1933; Birstein, 1938). The first Soviet business game, an "organization of production" experiment, was carried out at the Leningrad Engineering and Economic Institute in 1932 by M. Birstein. The purpose of the game was the rapid preparation of a program to introduce new technology in the Leningrad Textile Factory (LTF). The managers of some subdivisions of LTF were included as players of this game. At the same time, discussions were held among senior factory officials about the best methods of implementing the new system. It was found that the game produced a program four times more quickly than high-level discussions, and that it required only half as much labor (Birstein, 1976). An additional advantage of the gaming approach was that the players were able to assimilate some of the skills associated with the new technological system while the game was in progress.

There were no large-scale computers or other means of rapid calculation available in the early days of gaming. The gaming approach generally requires a considerable amount of routine calculation, and in the absence of computational aids it was necessary to carry out these calculations manually. This quickly acted as a strong disincentive to the use of gaming and for the next 20 years the subject all but disappeared. Interest in gaming eventually reawakened in the USSR during the 1960s, coinciding with the increasing availability of large computers which removed some of the constraints on calculation.

Since then interest in gaming has been growing rapidly in the USSR. More than 200 articles and monographs on the subject have already been published, and a number of professorships and laboratories for gaming studies have been created in universities and technical institutes. The number of organizations and specialists involved in the design and use of games continues to increase. There has been some success in using gaming both as a method of teaching and as a means of designing and implementing management information systems (MIS) and new organizational structures for various scientific and production industries, although a number of research problems still remain.

All gaming activities in the USSR are centralized and coordinated by the Coordinating Council on Gaming, based at the Ministry of Higher Education,[3] and by the Scientific Council on Cybernetics of the Academy of Sciences. An annual conference, the All-Union Conference on Gaming, is held in the USSR under the leadership of the two councils mentioned above.[4] Soviet experts also take part in other international conferences held in the socialist countries.

There are two distinct types of conferences on gaming in the USSR. One type considers the design of software, while the other deals with the problems of gaming as a method of decision making and teaching.

The most recent All-Union conference was held in September 1981 in Novosibirsk and was attended by about 200 researchers and users. Four of the five sessions were devoted to the playing of 15 new computer-based games, followed by discussions. The participants came to the conclusion that at the present stage in the elaboration of this relatively new kind of simulation, gaming conferences should give priority to demonstration, that is the playing of new games, rather than to talking about games, their advantages and disadvantages, without preliminary demonstrations. The necessity of accumulating experimental game statistics was stressed. It was also emphasized that discussions of methodological problems of gaming, on the potential of this type of simulation, and the representation of the behavior of socioeconomic systems should be held on a more fundamental theoretical level.

Gaming is also one of the topics of other conferences. For example, at the All-Union conference on management training problems held in Moscow in April 1981, which attracted more then 200 participants--senior administrators and managers from the major sectors of the Soviet economy--there was a special section on gaming.

3. THE FOUR MAIN APPROACHES TO GAMING IN THE USSR

There is no general agreement among Soviet scientists on all aspects of gaming (definitions, evaluation of efficiency, effectiveness, etc.) but at present four main methodological approaches may be distinguished. The similarities and differences between these four approaches are described below.

3.1. The Syroezhin Approach

The group of scientists led by I. Syroezhin at the Leningrad Financial and Economic Institute (LFEI) considers that there are three different and sometimes "noncoincident" economic interests[5] in socialist economic systems, i.e., private, collective, and social interests. The Syroezhin group sees management games as a unique tool for revealing and reconciling noncoincident economic interests of the parties concerned. The basis of any game is seen to be the relationship between different kinds of resources and information about these resources.

According to this group the structural elements of any game are:

1. *Players*, to represent various economic interests;
2. *Rules*, to regulate and direct the relative prominence and interaction of economic interests according to the ideas of the designer about the object of the game; and
3. *Information*, to provide details about the changing status of resources during the game.

Syroezhin believes that replacing this information by data from real sources will turn any game into a natural experiment. The LFEI group classifies games into four groups:

1. Educational games;
2. Games for testing managers;
3. Games for operational decision making; and
4. Research games.

Syroezhin considers that the results of operational games are especially valuable if the players are those people who will actually be applying the results of the game in the future. Each of the four classes of games has specific distinguishing features. The rules of the game and the algorithms for handling both the database and information are of great importance in educational games, while the choice of members of the control and game teams is more important in games designed to test managers.

Similarly, the structure and rules of the game are of great significance for operational decision making, whereas research games place more emphasis on the structure of the database.

The conceptual basis (a theory of socioeconomic organizations) underlying all the games designed by the LFEI group is described in Syroezhin (1970). The group has designed many games, including IMPULS, ASTRA, EPOS, and LOTOS, which involve variations in the organizational structure of different scientific and production industries (Gidrovich and Syroezhin, 1976). An example of a game with a strong operational focus is *Marketing Council* (Katkov, 1981), designed as a part of a real process of management planning in the largest shoe factory in Estonia. The most recent big game developed by the group is *Nautilus*, designed according to instructions from the Russian Ministry of Higher Education,[6] in which players are asked to allocate research projects, money, and other resources to different scientific institutes and universities for the planning period under consideration.

3.2. The Yefimov and Komarov Approach

V. Yefimov of Moscow University and V. Komarov of the Novosibirsk Institute of Management Systems define a management simulation game in stages, by defining a "game", then a "simulation model", and finally a "management simulation game".

A *game* is defined as a type of human activity in which other types of human activity are reconstructed. The game is played under artificial, experimental conditions.

A *simulation model* is a model of a system that can be used to conduct investigations into that system and which can simulate the functioning of the system over an extended period of time.

A *management simulation game* is one containing a simulation model describing an organization active in the production sector of the economy.

The structure of a management simulation game of this type is shown in Figure 1 (see Yefimov and Komarov, 1980). The Yefimov group classifies games into four categories:

1. Educational games;
2. Decision-making games;
3. Projection games; and
4. Research games.

These games are characterized by the facts that they operate in real time and that they involve real managers, i.e., future users of MIS. The researchers realize that under the conditions described above it will become almost as difficult to design games to model an MIS as to design the MIS itself. With this in mind, the Yefimov group proposes to design simple invariant or frame games on the basis of the "software package for production management" and other standard MIS subsystems. The group would like to explore new aspects of MIS design in their choice of players and in the rules of the game.

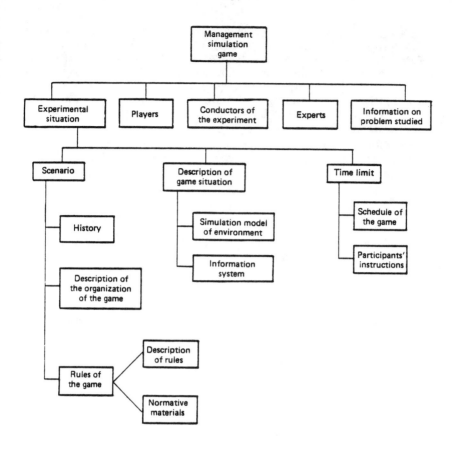

Figure 1. The structure of the management simulation game according to Yefimov and Komarov.

The Yefimov group has constructed many games, including *Production Subsection* and *Red Weaver II* (see Yefimov and Komarov, 1980), although their best known and most successful product is the *Management Project* game (see Komarov, 1979). This game was intended to provide an MIS for a research institute, and was especially interesting because the potential users took part as players. The game involved the participants in the design of the MIS and took them through the procedure for approving operational control systems (all in accordance with the rules of the game). The result was the procedure necessary to develop a real MIS.

In a sense, this game is an invariant or frame game, and has been used to design many other new games for MIS development. In particular, Komarov based the new game *MIS R&D* for the Research Institute of the Ministry of Forest Industry on the *Management Project* game (see Komarov, 1979). V. Shtytman and others from the Cheljabinsk Project Bureau for MIS have used the game to approve and implement a new MIS project for the Cheljabinsk building organization (see Business Games and their Computer Program Supplies, 1980).

The Yefimov-Komarov approach is also illustrated by the article on a method for developing management simulation games in Chapter IX:b of this volume.

3.3. The Burkov Approach

The group led by V. Burkov at the Institute of Management Problems of the USSR Academy of Sciences defines a management game as a model of human interactions culminating in the achievement of certain economic or political goals. The game has the following structure:

1. Purpose;
2. A method for estimating the extent to which the game has achieved its purpose;
3. Formal rules; and
4. Informal rules.

Points (1)-(3) correspond to the definition of an ordinary formal model, although the last item is one of the basic characteristics of a management game in that it reflects the human element. Point (4) represents active competition between people attempting to reach elevated goals. The methodology of the games is described in Burkov (1977), Burkov et al. (1977) and Assa (Chapter IV:a of this volume).

The Burkov classification of games includes the usual categories of educational, operational, and research games, but also defines two other classes, one of which has complete information, and one which has not. The Burkov group has constructed many games which are basically designed to verify the results of the active system theory, as described in Burkov (1977).

3.4. The Marshev Approach

The group led by Marshev at Moscow University defines a management game as a representation of management processes composed of the following elements:

1. A *model* of interrelated dynamic sequences of economic (or business) events;

2. A set of participants (the *players*);

3. A set of *goals* and *rules*;

4. A set of symbolic *actions* made by participants according to the goals and rules of the game, i.e., experimenting with the players and the model according to the rules.

Gaming here includes the design and use of management games for the education and training of managerial staff, for operational decision making, and for research into management problems. Figure 2 illustrates the group's view of the general structure of a management game.[7]

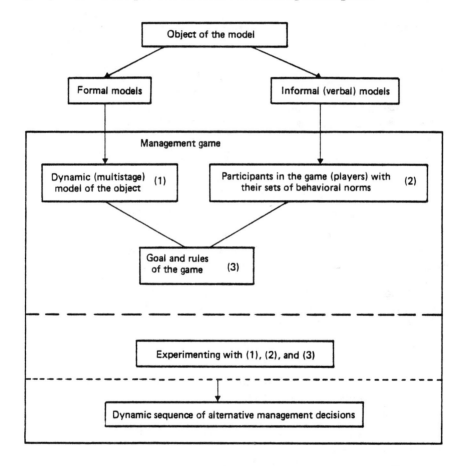

Figure 2. The structure of the management game according to the Marshev group.

All of the Marshev group games are designed on the basis of the semiotic theory of gaming (Marshev and Popov, 1974; Marshev, 1980), which considers the management game from three points of view:

1. Syntax (the mathematical structure of the game);
2. Semantics (the interpretation of the game); and
3. Pragmatics (the design and use of the game).

The foundations of the semiotic theory of gaming and the multi-dimensional classification of games used by the Marshev group is described in detail in Chapter III:c of this volume.

The Marshev group started designing educational games in 1972 and then later, with increasing experience, turned to the design of operational games. Various parts of the educational games were included as formal models of subsystems in the later operational games when appropriate. In particular, the educational game *Milk* representing the planning and production processes at the Moscow Milk Factory (see Smolkin, 1978) was used in designing the subsystems for the factory's MIS. On completion, the subsystems were included in the MIS of the milk factory. More information about this game is given in Appendix A, which also contains information about other operational games, including those for the automobile industry and postal services.

4. OTHER GAMING ACTIVITIES IN THE USSR

Only the more interesting aspects of other work on gaming carried out in the USSR will be considered here.

A group of scientists from the Central Economic-Mathematical Institute of the Academy of Sciences of the USSR (Oleinik, Krukova, and others) has been very active in this field, and has designed a system of games called PAUTINA intended to investigate the problems involved in road haulage of furniture in Moscow (see Krukova and Oleinik, 1980). The game represents management activities in a motor transport enterprise, in furniture factories, and in furniture shops. The PAUTINA system consists of three big games:

1. An annual planning game;
2. A game dealing with operative planning and management of the road haulage processes; and
3. An accounting game.

The first experiment with PAUTINA was carried out in the spring of 1979 and work on the project continues.

V. Rybalskij from the Kiev Building Institute has designed an operational game system called KROSS, consisting of four big games, which was used to train managers in the new building management system introduced for the construction of the Moscow and Kiev Olympic facilities (see Rybalskij, 1980 and Chapter VIII:a of this volume). In this game the players design a network representing the construction of the Olympic buildings and choose paths to optimize certain criteria (critical path analysis). The game lasts for three days and is played for six hours each day.

A gaming group from Novosibirsk University (Syskina, Anochin, and others) has developed a game called *Sajans* (see Malov and Syskina, 1976; Ionova et al., 1976), concerned with the optimal siting and building of industrial plants in the large Siberian region of Sajans. The group is now designing a system of games, based on the world global model, to simulate trade between the four regions of the world (see Business Games and their Computer Program Supplies, 1980). The Academy of Foreign Trade is continuing to work on the USA-USSR trade game (see Chapter VI:a in this volume).

REFERENCES

Assa, I. (1983). Management simulation games: a comparative study of gaming in the socialist countries. In I. Stahl (Ed.), *Operational Gaming: An International Approach*. This volume, Chapter IV:a.

Birstein, M. (1938). The experience of the organization-production tests. *Light Industry*, 3. (In Russian.)

Birstein, M. (1976). Soviet business games in the 1930s and problems of contemporary business game development. In *Business Games and their Computer Program Supplies*. CEMI, Academy of Sciences of the USSR, Moscow. (In Russian.)

Birstein, M. and Timofievsky, A. (1980). *Catalog of Soviet Games*. Leningrad. (In Russian.)

Burkov, V. (1977). *The Basis of the Mathematical Theory of Active Systems*. Nauka, Moscow. (In Russian.)

Burkov, V., Emeljanov, S., Ivanovsky, A., Nemtzeva, A., Sitnikov, V., Sokolov, V., and Shepkin, A. (1977). *Method of Business Games*. International Centre for Scientific and Technical Information, Moscow. (In Russian.)

Business Games and their Computer Program Supplies (1976). CEMI, Academy of Sciences of the USSR, Moscow. (In Russian.)

Business Games and their Computer Program Supplies (1980). *Economic Mathematical Methods*, XVI(2). (In Russian.)

Davis, R. and Taylor, B. (1975). Systems design through gaming. *Journal of Systems Management*, September: 36-42.

General Branch Methods MIS Design (1972). Minsk. (In Russian.)

Gidrovich, S. and Syroezhin, J. (1976). *The Game Modeling of Economic Processes*. Ekonomika, Moscow. (In Russian.)

Ionova, V., Malov, V., and Syskina, N. (1976). Possible uses of the business game technique in planning territorial production complexes. In M.K. Bandman (Ed.), *Applied Questions of Using Optimization Models for Territorial Production Complexes*. Institute of Economics and Organization of Industrial Production, Siberian Branch of the Academy of Sciences of the USSR, Novosibirsk.

Katkov, A.L. (1981). Gaming simulation as a tool of management planning: a social experience. *Simulation and Games*, 12(2): 153-166.

Komarov, V. (1979). *Management Simulation Games and MIS*. Nauka, Moscow. (In Russian.)

Krukova, L. and Oleinik, J. (1980). On directions of use of business games. *Economic-Mathematical Methods*, 16: 848-863. (In Russian.)

Krukova, L., Alamazian, A., and Asmov, A. (1979). On the question of psychological research in gaming. In *Business Games and their Computer Program Supplies*. CEMI, Academy of Sciences of the USSR, Moscow. (In Russian.)

Malov, V. and Syskina, N. (1976). *The Business Game "Sajans"*. Novosibirsk University, Novosibirsk. (In Russian.)

Markin, I. (1979). *MIS in the Milk Industry*. Ekonomika, Moscow. (In Russian.)

Marshev, V. (1980). *Gaming: Problems of Theory and Practice*. CP-80-6. International Institute for Applied Systems Analysis, Laxenburg, Austria.

Marshev, V. and Popov, A. (1974). Management education and research into management problems. *Proceedings of the Scientific Method Conference*. Riga. (In Russian.)

Ostrovsky, J. (1980). *The Emergency Procedure: Games on the Shatura*. Techprog, Moscow. (In Russian.)

Rybalskij, V. (1980). Net planning and building management. *Economics and Industry Product Organization*, N9. Novosibirsk University, Novosibirsk. (In Russian.)

Simulation Games for Training and Mastering Management Innovation (1976). Moscow University, Moscow. (In Russian.)

Smolkin, A. (Ed.) (1978). *Collected Business Games*. Moscow Worker Publishing House, Moscow. (In Russian.)

Syroezhin, I. (1970). *Essays on the Theory of Production Organizations*. Ekonomika, Moscow. (In Russian.)

APPENDIX A: THE GAME *Milk*

The game *Milk* was designed at Moscow University by Marshev and Markin (see Smolkin, 1978). It represents the planning procedures and processes used for the manufacture of dairy products (milk, cheese, yogurt, ice cream, etc.) at the Moscow Milk Factory (MMF).[8] The MMF comprises two large enterprises, each of which has two sections (production lines) producing various kinds of dairy products. The players of *Milk* assume the following roles:

- Director of the game. At different points in the game the director will play the role of a minister, a consumer, and a supplier.
- Director of the MMF (DMMF).
- Chief engineer of the MMF (CE).
- Chief of the planning department of the MMF (CP).
- Chief of the mathematical and technical supply department of the MMF (CMTS).

- Two deputy directors of the MMF (DD).
- Four chiefs of sections (CS).
- Eight shop stewards (SS).

The game is played in three stages:

(1) A five-year plan is drawn up, showing the total amount of each product required for each of the five years, with no disaggregation into size or type of product (e.g., only the total amount of ice cream is specified, not whether it should be chocolate or strawberry flavored, or whether it should be sold in large or small cartons).

(2) The factory's operational plans *Techpromfinplan* (technical-production-financial plans) are designed. These deal with the disaggregation of the totals given in the five-year plan into the specific types and sizes of product, and cover various periods of time. Operational plans are designed for periods of one year, one quarter, one month, ten-day periods, and for single days.

(3) The operational plans are implemented and evaluated.

In the first stage the Ministry of the Meat and Milk Industry provides the DMMF with the aggregate totals proposed in the five-year plan. The MMF then designs a "counter plan", prepared by the CP, together with the CE, the CMTS, and the DDs. Taking into account the *real* production capacity of the MMF, the CP calculates the additional requirements (raw materials, etc.) needed to fulfill the five-year plan and sends them to the ministry. If the minister satisfies these requirements the five-year plan is ratified and the first stage of the game is completed. However, if the minister does not meet the requirements, the MMF must find other ways of fulfilling the five-year plan. This may involve a few iterations within this first stage.

In the second stage the CP, the CMTS, and the CSs prepare the detailed (disaggregated) plan *Techpromfinplan* for various periods up to and including one year. The operational plans for the enterprises and the sections are then finalized.

In the third stage the operational plans for various periods are implemented and evaluated. This means that the real production processes are represented by a system of models which is then solved using standard software packages.

Milk was initially played at Moscow University with students taking the roles described above. After several experiments with the "educational" game, the designers decided to invite real managers from the MMF to participate as experts, and to evaluate the decision-making processes and decisions involved in the game.

Together with the managers of the MMF computer center the researchers then decided to use the gaming approach and this particular game to design an MIS for the MMF, roughly as described in Yefimov and Komarov (1980), Komarov (1979), and Davis and Taylor (1975). This decision was made primarily because no one was happy with the usual procedure for designing and implementing an MIS.

The procedure takes place in a number of stages (see General Branch Methods MIS Design, 1972):

(1) Before the project starts, there is an investigation of the existing management and production systems used by the organization being modeled (in this case the MMF).

(2) The technical aims of the MIS are decided upon.

(3) Drafts of the MIS are drawn up.

(4) MIS technical project design (resource requirements, cost assessment, etc., for various drafts) is carried out.

(5) MIS working project design (construction of the final draft) is carried out.

(6) MIS is put into experimental operation.

(7) MIS is implemented.

Practical experience has shown that in many cases the future users of the MIS do not take part in the design process. Furthermore, the MIS is usually tested only in the final "implementation" stage, which means that users' suggestions for improving the MIS or eliminating any faults noticed during testing can be incorporated only at the final stage, i.e., long after the design phase has been completed. These problems increase the time taken to put the MIS into operation and reduce the overall efficiency of the system because designers are not usually interested in making changes once the MIS has been implemented. A new procedure for MIS design was therefore developed, as follows:

(1) Before the project starts there is an investigation of the management and production systems in use at the MMF.

(2) The game *Milk* is played with the managers of the MMF.

(3) The technical aims of the MIS are worked out by comparing the real system with the game management system.

(4) Variants of the game management system are generated using the software package for the production and accounting processes. These variants must be compatible with the technical requirements outlined in (3) above.

(5) Decisions are projected and adjusted according to the conditions laid down by the game management system.

(6) The game *Milk* is played with the future users in order to train them.

(7) The MIS is put into operation at the MMF.

During the game the players introduced many changes, particularly in the production models and the procedures used to collect and utilize information. The players also informed the designers of the game about the problems which could arise when introducing the MIS in the MMF. This was very helpful in the design of both the game and the MIS. Playing the game *Milk* as one of the first stages in the MIS design procedure has also benefited users. The first benefit was that the MMF workers were able to obtain a better idea of the changes in management that would result from the use of the MIS. During the game they experimented with new planning and accounting methods so that afterwards they could suggest constructive improvements in MIS design. The second benefit was that many new types of MIS planning and accounting procedures were adopted by users after playing the game. Further information about the use of MIS in the milk industry is given in Markin (1979).

The game *Milk* has served as a frame game in developing a series of branch-oriented games because it represents the process of drawing up plans ranging from five-year to daily plans. This process is common for practically all Soviet industrial enterprises. Besides, the game has roles for almost all management levels in branch organizational structures (from a minister to a shop steward). These levels and roles are typical of Soviet production associations and enterprises. Based upon *Milk*, the Marshev group is currently developing similar branch operational games for the textile and clothing industries (the *Textile* game), and for meat and fish processing industries (the *Fish* game).

The Marshev group is currently also under contract to design parts of an MIS for two Moscow motor plants (ZIL and AZLK), in particular to prepare subsystems for production, quality control, accounting, and analysis. With this in mind, the group is concentrating on the technical aspects of the game, designing models of car production and the working environment, as well as deciding on the main roles to be played and the rules of the game. It is hoped that the *ZIL* and *AZLK* games will be played in Moscow by the managers of the car plants concerned.

In addition, the group has now begun the design of an operational game called *Post* under contract from the Ministry of Communications. Some drivers, postal workers, and managers actually working at Moscow post offices will be invited to take part in the game, whereby it is hoped to obtain a simulation model of the optimal distribution of postal vehicles between the various post offices in Moscow, and to ensure efficient transport of parcels between Moscow rail stations, bus stations, and the post offices themselves.

It goes without saying that in each of the games the production and control parameter blocks had to be modified. For instance, in *Textile* we had to introduce a specific control parameter "thread breakage in the loom"; in *Post* we introduced two extra parameters (transport shortages and seasonal variations in the amount of parcels handled by the Post Office); and in the *ZIL* game we introduced the parameter "low quality of semi-finished goods detected after prolonged service", etc.

NOTES

1. More complete and correct definitions of the terms "game" and "gaming" will be presented later.

2. War games, card games, board games, children's games, etc., are not included in this analysis.

3. The author is the head of the Foreign Experience in Gaming subdivision of the Council.

4. The most important reports from these conferences are given in *Collected Business Games*(1978), *Simulation Games for Training and Mastering Management Innovation*(1976), *Business Games and their Computer Program Supplies*(1980), and in Birstein and Timofievsky (1980), which contains short descriptions of 136 Soviet games.

5. "Noncoincident" here implies interests which are slightly different but not diametrically opposed.

6. Russian here refers only to the RSFSR (Russian Soviet Federated Socialist Republic) and not to the complete Soviet Union.

7. In the USSR, management games are used for research in the field of management; design and implementation of new scientific results in management practice; and training of managerial staff.

8. The game takes around 15 hours to play. The computer models are written in PASCAL and are hence transferable.

Chapter IV:c

A REVIEW OF GAMING ACTIVITIES IN JAPAN

Yutaka Osawa
Osaka University, Osaka (Japan)

1. INTRODUCTION

Shortly after the publication of the important work of Ricciardi et al. (1957) and Andlinger (1958), various kinds of business games developed in the United States were transformed into Japanese versions and subsequently used among Japanese managers and students. During the same period, in collaboration with Professor Totaro Miyashita of the University of Tokyo, the present author also utilized this new educational tool and developed several types of games (see, for example, Osawa and Miyashita 1961; Osawa, 1962); the last of this group to be developed (the *Top Management Decision Game--Model 625-B*) has been played under our supervision on about 100 occasions over a 15-year period.

One new development of gaming in the United States in the 1970s, namely, dealing with social phenomena, was noted by engineering researchers in Japan. Professor Tomitaro Sueishi of the Faculty of Engineering, Osaka University and his group have made continuing efforts in the development of gaming for analyzing problems of garbage treatment in urban areas (Sueishi, 1977, 1978). Professor Yoshinobu Kumata of the Faculty of Engineering, Tokyo Institute of Technology and his group have studied the construction of highways and nuclear plants (Kumata and Morita, 1975; Kumata et al., 1976) using experimental gaming techniques.

In this review article, the gaming activities of these two groups are first briefly summarized. Then some findings from our own experience on the educational use of business games are presented. This is not, however, a comprehensive survey of gaming activities in Japan. For example, some commercial institutions are offering businessmen opportunities of participating in business games in order to refresh and extend their managerial abilities. As regards the use of gaming as an aid to policy formulation, research work in Japan has effectively only just begun.

2. GAMING ON ENVIRONMENTAL PROBLEMS

Professor Sueishi and his group, under the sponsorship of the Institute for Systems Science, have been concerned with problems of urban garbage collection and treatment (including wastes emitted by factories) since 1976 (Sueishi, 1977, 1978). First, they investigated the actual mechanism of garbage collection and treatment in various cities, surveyed the development of gaming methodology and practice in the United States for background information, and then tried several gaming experiments using a preliminary version of their simulated garbage system. Later, a revised version of the gaming model was applied to the actual situation in Hiroshima and two experiments were carried out in which various municipal personnel took part.

This latter gaming exercise involved the following roles: (1) the mayor of the city, (2) local leaders of the neighboring rural areas, (3) inhabitants of the city, (4) inhabitants of the rural areas, (5) inhabitants of the area around the garbage-treatment plant, (6) representatives of manufacturers located in the city, (7) garbage collectors, and (8) employees of the garbage-treatment plant. Six hours of gaming allowed for ten rounds of play.

To begin with, a set of rules and a short description of the initial situation as regards the city's garbage treatment arrangements were presented to the players by the gaming operator. Alternative courses of action from which each player could choose were specified to the players. These alternatives were based on the study of various publications and on interviews. The operator generated some events, both spontaneous and planned, in each round. He also assigned the priorities with which each player could respond to a given event. The player with the highest priority then chose some action from his list of actions, and stated the reasons for his choice. Other players could respond to him in turn. The flow of money and amounts of garbage moved and treated were presented on a chart. At the end of the round, each player was asked to report to the operator on how he evaluated the actions taken by the other players and on his own depth of understanding of the garbage problems of the city.

After ten rounds of play, the records of communication flow between the interest groups, and the conflicts that had occurred and had been resolved, etc., were analyzed in detail. Throughout the gaming exercise, there was a tendency for discrepancies of perception of the garbage problem in each group to become wider whenever a concrete plan was proposed.

Sueishi and his group concluded that gaming methodology might be helpful for building a new social system based on mutual understanding. More specifically, the participants in the gaming experiment were able to learn what kinds of issues were involved in the problem, how different the value judgments and behavioral patterns of each group were, why such wide discrepancies in perception of the issues involved arose, etc. It was concluded that, if more people had the opportunity of joining the gaming experiment, it might be helpful in setting up a new social system in which mutual understanding would be reached through information disclosure, hearings, participation of inhabitants in policy formulation, etc.

The approach to environmental problems using gaming followed by Professor Kumata and his group (Kumata and Morita, 1975) was entirely different. They thought that the development plan for a new *power system* and the development program for a proposed *nuclear power plant* should be regarded as separate functions, or at most with the latter as a fairly independent subsystem of the former. In their framework of analysis, the power company set a goal for the amount of power to be supplied and specified the development plan of the nuclear power system based upon this goal. Then, in accordance with the company's plan, a development program for individual plants could be formulated and come into operation. This program might be expected to give rise to various actions and responses by the parties concerned. Intercommunication and interaction between these parties, including the power company, could be viewed as constituting a decision-making process relating to the construction of the nuclear power plant. The company would have alternative development programs. The company's programs and the actions taken by the various other parties concerned could be regarded as the input into the decision-making process, making it possible to compare output with input in order to choose the optimum program for the overall development plan of the company. Whenever the output was judged to be unsatisfactory, a new development program could be generated or, when necessary, the development plan itself modified.

Kumata designed a gaming model simulating the decision-making process of the parties concerned in order to evaluate the alternative development programs. A preliminary survey was conducted of recent cases of power plant construction at three different locations. The following roles were specified: (1) the minister in charge, (2) the governor of the local region (prefecture), (3) the leader of the city concerned, (4) the leader of the opposition, (5) the representative of the power company, (6) three types of representatives of the inhabitants, (7) landowners, (8) fishermen, (9) the press, and (10) public opinion. It was assumed that each actor had his own objectives, and each was asked to optimize specific functional forms representing these objectives. Actions to be taken by the actors, constituting influence and information, were determined by field survey results and by published records from newspapers and magazines.

Sixteen participants joined the gaming experiment and five of them played the role of public opinion. Each period of the experiment was divided into five steps, and in the first three steps communications were exchanged among the actors. In the fourth step actions were taken, and in the fifth and final step the present situations were explained to all the actors by the gaming operator. About 20 minutes were needed to play one period, which corresponded to three months in the real world. Four alternative programs proposed by the power company were operated in turn, with some repetitions.

The performance of each program was evaluated and compared multidimensionally using the following parameters: number of periods required to start on-site plant construction; cost to the power company (including opportunity cost due to delays of schedule); incremental utility of the local inhabitants; stability of the political power bases of central and local government; costs paid as a result of disputes with residents;

etc. It was found that the program that disclosed details of the development plan to the public in earlier periods brought about a more desirable outcome in general.

The group's second paper (Kumata et al., 1976) dealt with a highway construction problem. Roughly the same framework was adopted as in the case of the nuclear power plant problem. Nineteen actors were specified, and five alternative programs were experimentally investigated. These programs differed with regard to whether or not an assessment of environmental changes was introduced, the stage during which local inhabitants took part in the process, and the pattern of communication between inhabitants of the area and local government.

As regards this last problem, Kumata formulated the hypothesis that the decision-making process would produce a more desirable output when an efficient and open system of communication was available. It was found from the gaming experiments that assessments of environmental changes and their release to the public could remove uneasy feelings among the inhabitants about pollution; the overall outcome of the gaming was scarcely affected by the stage at which local inhabitants started to take part in the development process; and finally, a large amount of information could be communicated at the hearing, which appeared as a useful means of achieving mutual understanding. Kumata noted that it was very difficult to identify the precise cause of variations of output in the different cases, since these variations might be due to differences in the development programs, personality traits of the participants in the experiment, or other random factors.

3. SOME EMPIRICAL FINDINGS FROM TOP MANAGEMENT DECISION SIMULATIONS

The *Top Management Decision Game--Model 625-B* was developed by Osawa and Miyashita in 1962 and has since been played, under our supervision, by top executives, middle managers, and candidates for management positions in the leading companies in Japan. Over 3,000 businessmen have had experience with the game.

The essential points of the game can be summarized as follows:

- One product is produced;
- One market exists;
- Four or five companies compete;
- Cartels are not permitted;
- Between four and ten participants represent each company;
- Each company has a different market share and balance sheet at the beginning of the game; and
- There is no random element.

The items to be decided in each period are selling price, marketing expenditure, R&D expenditure, rate of production, investment for expanding productive capacity for the next period, short- and long-term financing, dividend, capital increase, etc. One game period corresponds to three months in the real world. At the end of every year, the profit and loss account and the balance sheet of each company are announced by the game operator, while only the selling prices and stock prices are disclosed in every period.

One of the main features of this gaming procedure is that each company is asked to respond to questionnaires delivered by the game director in the first period of every year. In the first questionnaire the participants are asked about their top management organization, their long-range policy and planning, their management objectives and the quantitative measures expressing them, etc. The second questionnaire asks about the goals for market share, total unit cost, return on investment, size of plant, and amount of inventory. There are also questions regarding break-even points, optimal amount of inventory, pricing policy, and optimum ratio of current assets to current liabilities. The third questionnaire concentrates on how each company analyzes the behavior of its competitors based on their published financial statements. Market shares, marketing expenditures, R&D expenditures, and dividends of the competing companies must be projected here.

These questionnaires are designed in order to force the participants to use various kinds of management tools and ideas applicable to decision making in the gaming situation. This device is most important in order to avoid rash and irresponsible decision making and also to preserve records of the original intentions of each company for later discussion. Neither good performance in the game nor full benefit from its educational effects can be achieved by simply filling out figures on decision items.

Usually, in the opening session, which starts in the evening in the common classroom, the gaming rules are explained using a player's manual for one hour, followed by a one-hour trial period in order to avoid misunderstandings of the rules. After this session, the participants representing each company are put into separate conference rooms where they are required to establish a top management organization. The company's long-range policies and plans for the next day's gaming are also discussed. Next morning the initial conditions are presented and the game commences. It continues for about eight hours. After dinner, the participants assemble in the common classroom again. More than twenty charts, showing the performances of the individual companies as well as the responses to the questionnaires, are then displayed. Following a briefing by the game director on the information in these charts, the "general meeting of stockholders" starts. The president or chairman of each company describes the company's management policy, strategy, and performance. Discussion continues for about two hours and concludes with comments by the game director.

Through this gaming exercise, the participants are expected to obtain the following personal experience:

1. It is generally very difficult to achieve both profit increase and market-share position improvement at the same time. This can only be achieved when the balance between the timing of dynamic and multiple decisions is very well judged.

2. One of the important factors affecting the company's perfor-
    mance is the coordinating function of its decision-making pro-
    cess. Leadership from the chairman is especially required when
    difficulties occur. Usually, a variety of good alternatives to over-
    come such situations are proposed by some participants but
    subsequently phased out in the process of discussion. It is not
    an easy job to incorporate analytical findings based on quantita-
    tive data into the final decisions.

3. When a company tries to determine the cause of its losing
    money, it is most frequent that outside reasons, such as com-
    petitors' aggressiveness or economic depression in the industry,
    are blamed. On the other hand, there is a tendency to conclude
    that a good performance results from the company's own
    efforts. Very often, these conclusions are simply not true.
    Failures by competitors may improve a company's market posi-
    tion, and even in a bad economic climate an individual company
    may improve its position.

In conclusion, we feel that by developing management games and
operating them in practice valuable experience has been gained by all
concerned. Firstly, without the active involvement of the participants,
the educational purposes of the game could never be achieved at all. The
game director should behave like the director of a drama. In the gaming
described above, we believe that none of the participants had a dull time
throughout the long two-day session!

Secondly, when a specific industry was simulated, and the employees
of a company in this industry played the game, some difficulties arose.
Players had comprehensive knowledge about circumstances in the industry, while not all the elements concerning the industry were necessarily
involved in the simulation model. Sometimes the players wasted their
time in discussing items not included in the player's manual. For
instance, in the above-mentioned management game, the type of product
was deliberately not specified in order to minimize these problems.

Finally, it should be noted that the competent manager in the real
world generally displayed his abilities in the gaming situation. It was also
true that the players who were in higher positions in a company would
almost always get a high rating in the game, and vice versa. Although it is
frequently asserted that one of the factors in the success of Japanese
business is the so-called bottom-up style of management, this hypothesis
is, we believe, true only in cases when able junior employees are super-
vised by a capable senior manager.

REFERENCES

Andlinger, G.R. (1958). Business Game--Play One! *Harvard Business
Review*, 36(2): 115-125.

Kumata, Y. and Morita, T. (1975). *An Approach to the Evaluation of Alternative Programs for Nuclear Power Plant Construction Using Gaming Simulation.* Paper presented at the meeting of the Association of City Planning, Tokyo, pp. 73-78. (In Japanese.)

Kumata, Y., Nemoto, T., and Matsuda, K. (1976). *Comparative Evaluation of Alternative Programs for Highway Construction in Urban Areas by Means of Gaming Simulation.* Paper presented at the meeting of the Association of City Planning, Tokyo, pp. 349-354. (In Japanese.)

Osawa, Y. (1962). A model and an operating procedure for a management game. *Sophia Economic Review,* 9: 1-18. (In Japanese.)

Osawa, Y. and Miyashita, T. (1961). A Japanese business management game. In J.M. Kibbee, C.J. Craft, and B. Nanus (Eds.), *Management Games.* Reinhold, New York, pp. 296-312.

Ricciardi, F.M., Craft, C.J., Malcolm, D.G., Bellman, R., Clark, C., Kibbee, J.M., and Rawdon, R.H. (1957). E. Marting (Ed.), *Top Management Decision Simulation.* American Management Association, New York.

Sueishi, T. (Ed.) (1977). *Research Report on the Application of Gaming Simulation to the Problems of Garbage Treatment.* Institute for Systems Science, Kyoto. (In Japanese.)

Sueishi, T. (Ed.) (1978). *Research Report on Area Development Planning Using Gaming Techniques.* Institute for Systems Science, Kyoto. (In Japanese.)

PART V

INTERNATIONAL TRANSFER OF GAMES

Chapter V:a

TRANSFERRING A COMPUTER-BASED
MANAGEMENT GAME BETWEEN CAPITALIST COUNTRIES

D.J. Hutchings and W.C. Robertson
Edit 515 Ltd, Glasgow (UK)

1. INTRODUCTION

This chapter describes the experience of transferring a computer-based management game from the UK to a number of other capitalist countries. The game is the *Edit 515 Management Game*, a complex, computer-based business training game. It was first devised in 1968 and has been run regularly and often since then. To date, at least 20,000 people have taken part in it.

The game is used in the normal way as a training tool to foster an understanding of how a manufacturing company operates as the sum of several parts that must work in harmony to achieve optimum results from the whole, and as a means of improving the communication skills of those taking part. It is used in universities, at seminars, and for in-house training in business organizations, but it is best known in the UK as the basis of a national competition, played annually, in which the winning team receives a substantial prize. In recent years it has been successfully transferred from the UK to France, Portugal, Pakistan, Israel, and Brazil where it is used in a similar fashion. Other transfers are contemplated. This chapter discusses the problems that were encountered and overcome in making these international transfers.

2. DESCRIPTION OF THE GAME

The game is interactive, with up to eight teams of six players each competing at one time. It simulates the activities of companies competing to sell three different products in four market areas, in the face of competition from up to seven rival companies. At each pass of the game, teams are required to make 63 decisions covering marketing, production, personnel, procurement, research and development, etc. Being such a comprehensive simulation, it is complex and for this reason was designed from the start to be computer-based. The game is played in the usual way, with discrete decision cycles, each simulating one-quarter of the calendar year. Criteria for "winning" are usually based on maximizing profit or some management ratio that involves profitability in some form.

As a national competition, the game is played on a very large scale, with over 2,000 people grouped into some 400 teams taking part at any one time in more than 50 games. In practice this means that, typically, 50 passes of the Game System, including data checks, computation, and printing of reports, have to be accomplished in approximately two hours.

To achieve this feat of logistics, the Game System had to be designed to meet certain basic, overall criteria, and it was important that these criteria were maintained during transfers between countries.

1. The game had to operate with as little mediation as possible from the controller. It was necessary to minimize the number of queries from participants who might be having difficulty understanding what was happening. It was also necessary to *avoid* any need for the controller to intervene, in order to make the game unfold in a meaningful way. Ideally the game had to run smoothly and interestingly without action from the controller.

2. The game had to be self-checking and self-correcting. With so much data passing into the system in a short space of time it was not possible to check every decision variable over the range of possible types of error. The Game System had, as far as possible, to identify errors in the input, analyze them, and make a reasonable correction, automatically.

3. The game functions had to be sufficiently robust to protect serious players from the mistakes of those who did not entirely understand what they were trying to do, and from the intervention of "kamikaze" players wanting to introduce chaos into the game.

4. To cover any errors that might slip through the checking system, or catastrophic loss of historic data on which the Game System depends, the state of the game at any time had to be capable of identical reconstitution from the previous, or even earlier, states.

To carry these basic criteria successfully from one country to another required the consideration of three actions: the transfer of the Game System; the briefing of the new organizer/controller; and the transfer of the computer programs themselves.

3. TRANSFER OF THE GAME SYSTEM

To understand the transfer of the Game System it is first necessary to understand the structure of the game under normal running conditions as reflected in the various documents and computer programs:

1. The Playing Manual defines the game, not only for the players, but also for the programmers.

2. The Decision Sheet sets out the decisions required from the players at each cycle of the game, and controls the format in which they are presented.

3.   The Management Report shows the outcome of each cycle. This is interpreted by the players (with the aid of the Playing Manual if necessary) before they make the next set of decisions, thus inaugurating the next cycle of play.

4.   The INPUT program checks the validity of decisions and performs important scaling and editing functions.

5.   The RUN program incorporates the basic model on which the game depends.

6.   The OUTPUT program, through its editing and rescaling functions, creates the Management Report.

The policy in making a transfer of the game between countries is to alter all of these elements, with the important exception of the RUN program, in which every effort is made to avoid change. This forms the constant element to which changes in the other elements are related, and which is known to be correct and functioning.

We first hold discussions with the local organizers to agree upon the appropriate units of currency and other measures appearing in the documentary parts of the Game System--the Playing Manual, the Decision Sheet, and the Management Report. Similarly, any structural or commercial changes (i.e., different methods of taxation, or treatment of depreciation) are agreed upon, as well as any changes to the layout of the Decision Sheet or Management Report. Once agreed, at least two copies of the English version of the Playing Manual are rewritten to include these changes. The first becomes the definitive version for making changes to the program element of the Game System. The second copy is used for translation to the local language.

3.1. The Playing Manual

The Playing Manual, which is an integral part of the Game System, performs three basic functions.

Firstly, it describes in nonfunctional terms the *structure* of the enterprise that will be managed by the teams taking part--the way different parts of each company, such as Marketing, Personnel, Production, etc., fit together to create the whole; the relationships between the competing companies; and how these companies fit into the total economic scenario of the game. The Playing Manual thus creates a relevant "mental image" of the company so that the teams can gain some idea of the company that they are going to manage--it helps to make the company "real". It would be perfectly possible to rewrite the Manual to set the scene differently and change the image of the game without requiring changes in the RUN program, which forms the core of the game. For instance, the companies are currently presented as making three products that are not specified in any way, giving a somewhat neutral image to players but allowing them to fill in the image of what they are making with any products with which they may be familiar. However, the whole game could be presented more specifically, as part of the clothing industry, for example, if the Manual were written in such a way.

To transfer the Playing Manual therefore requires not only that it be translated from English, but that the style in which it is written should be true to the country in which the game is used. The mental image presented by the transferred Manual should relate comfortably to the cultural and commercial practices of the country. The commercial "jargon" must be right, as well as the structure.

Secondly, the Playing Manual describes the *quantitative aspects* of the company. Costs and revenues must be in a relevant currency and the use of resources must be in units that are suited to the country in question. The figures given must relate to the economics of the country. Where, for instance, the cost of fuel is cheap in reality it may be necessary to reduce transport costs relative to those used in the UK version of the game.

Finally, the Playing Manual describes the *mechanics of playing* the game: the playing cycle, the use of the Decision Sheet, and the significance of the Management Report. These details are worked out with the local organizers of the game.

The Playing Manual should be translated by a native of the country, preferably one who has played and understood the English version of the game. When a draft version of the translated Manual and the programs are ready they should be used by local teams to play a series of trials, in which queries, misunderstandings, and inconsistencies are noted as points requiring revision in the Manual. In this way the Manual can be brought up to a suitable standard before it is printed.

The preparation of the Manual is never really complete, however, and only its use in serious game situations over a period of time will show all of its weak points. The UK Playing Manual is constantly being revised to clarify points that appear to be inadequately explained. The English version has been through major revisions in which the layout and handling of the contents have been entirely restructured, and it is now considered to set out the facts of the game in a fairly clear and understandable way. It was a hard-won lesson and the present general structure is thoroughly recommended to those who wish to transfer it to other languages.

The role of the Playing Manual is of special importance in the *Edit 515 Management Game* because of the basic criterion that the game must run with the minimum of intervention from the controller. The Manual therefore becomes central to the Game System, and must be comprehensive and accurate. Participants must be able to turn to it and have confidence in its ability to answer their problems clearly and accurately. However, one advantage of this approach is that the Manual becomes the definitive document to which all other elements of the Game System must conform.

3.2. The Decision Sheet

Input to the system comes from the Decision Sheet, which should be translated using methods similar to those for the Manual. There are certain technical constraints, however. The Decision Sheet is designed so that decisions are represented by a maximum of 160 digits, which can be transferred to two 80-column punch cards for each team. Though the recent introduction of key-to-disc systems renders this discipline somewhat unnecessary, it is still considered to be good practice to limit the space allocated for decisions, as this prevents the game from becoming inefficient. The design and layout of the Decision Sheet are, we believe, responsible for the high degree of accuracy achieved from data preparation. In 12 years of running the game the number of punching errors has been less than ten (in some 50,000 cards), and most of these have been due to poor writing. In order to fit the decisions into the available digits, it is necessary to scale the units in which the decisions are presented. The wording of the Decision Sheet should always specify how the units are scaled and what limits are placed on the decisions that can be made, e.g., the maximum and minimum values that can be used.

The Decision Sheet should be checked against the Playing Manual to ensure that the contents of both are in agreement.

3.3. The Management Report

The final part of the documentation to be translated is the Management Report. There are three matters to consider in transferring this to another country, all of which are constrained by the overall need to retain the present format of two pages of 63 lines, each with a maximum of 132 characters. To achieve this it would be best to follow the general layout of the UK version of the printout.

Firstly, it may be necessary to alter the layout of the financial accounts to follow local practice. The main constraint here is usually the number of lines available. Once the layout has been settled, the maximum physical size of each number appearing in variable form should be considered, and the units scaled so that the length of each number can fit into the space available. The headings should then be translated into local terms, using whatever abbreviations are acceptable and necessary for them to fit into the space available. Finally, the Playing Manual should be checked to ensure that its description of the contents of the Management Report agrees with what will appear in the Report.

The latest development in the transfer of the Management Report stems from Portugal where, instead of the computer being used to print the headings for each item, the Report is printed on to preprinted stationery, so that only the variables need to be printed at run time. This has several advantages--the run time is reduced, and the amount of wording in the headings can be considerably increased because it is not limited to the character set and size available on the computer.

3.4. The INPUT Program

After the transfer of the Game System documents, it remains to bring the computer programs into line with the game as defined in the Playing Manual. The usual procedure is to amend a version of the UK suite of programs in the UK and to test their accuracy before transferring the programs physically to the local computer.

The INPUT program acts as a buffer and interpreter between the external parts of the system and the computer model. The model is a complex system of functions, many of which are exponential or logarithmic and some of which will only work within a limited range of values. The INPUT program ensures that data arriving for use in these functions are properly presented within the correct range. Each decision value is checked to ensure that it lies within the preset range, and that it is consistent with the historical activities of the company concerned. For instance, if the company employs 12 salesmen (as a consequence of earlier decisions), then only a maximum of 12 can be deployed to sell the company's products in the various sales areas. If errors are found, reasonable corrections are made automatically. These are fully described in the Playing Manual. The data are then transformed by linear and matrix scaling processes, which take into account the units in which the decisions are made and any further transformations necessary to convert for currency differences. To transfer the program it is necessary to amend the scaling factors not only for the decision variables themselves but also in the check parameters. Because the INPUT program was designed with this task in mind it is relatively easy to make such changes to the scaling parameters.

3.5. The RUN Program

The decisions are now in a form suitable for presentation to the RUN program. As stated earlier, the policy when transferring the game is to make every effort to leave this element of the Game System unchanged. However, many of the functions and identities have constant elements that will have been changed in the Playing Manual; for instance, the cost of vehicles in the Transport function is fixed and should have been scaled in the Manual, if only because of currency differences. Such fixed parameters need to be changed for the RUN program and are stored in a parameter file.

The more extensive the structural changes specified in the Playing Manual the more difficult it will be to avoid making changes to the RUN program. We try to retain the RUN program in its basic version because, after many years of use and many hundreds of runs, it is known to be free of error in the UK version. Because of its complexity, extensive changes to the program will increase the risk of error, and the difficulty of tracing that error through all three programs will increase enormously.

3.6. The OUTPUT Program

Finally, the OUTPUT program creates the Management Report by carrying out three tasks, each of which requires modification in a transfer.

1. It scales the quantified outcomes from the RUN program to a state compatible with the units and currencies specified for the Management Report in the Playing Manual. In effect this carries out the function of the INPUT program in reverse and, once again, because scaling factors in the program are parameterized the change is relatively easy.

2. It restructures any local commercial practices that may differ from UK practice and that manifest themselves in the Management Report, for example the calculation of the unemployment statistic, or the gross national product. This change may require slightly more elaborate program changes.

3. The headings on the two-page Management Report will require corresponding format statements within the OUTPUT program, and these will require to be changed extensively from the UK version. At this stage it is probably the most onerous programming task in the whole transfer process. Clearly it is not necessary if the Management Report is output onto preprinted stationery.

Thus the transfer is complete. In making the transfer, much of the work can be done by the local organizer under our supervision.

4. BRIEFING OF THE CONTROLLER

4.1. The Role of the Controller

The Game System is designed to run in a control-free state. It runs deterministically without reference to Game Control. Even parameters such as interest rates and market growth rates are varied deterministically by the activities of the participants themselves as the game proceeds. Deliberately introduced random effects are kept to a minimum. Predictability (or lack of it) depends on the ability of the participants to predict what other teams are doing, with only limited information available to them. This is not to say that there is no controller, but in our system his role lies in the creation of the game before the teams take over. The controller has three main tasks to perform: to make each game ready for play; to receive the Decision Sheets, present them to the computer, run the programs, and dispatch the Management Reports; and to intervene and make corrections in the event of errors passing through the screening and checking procedures.

The design is such that every game can start from a different opening position. Both the simulated economic environment and the company that the participant teams take over can be in any one of an infinite number of states that depend on decisions taken by the controller in the setting-up phase. The controller, working through a fourth computer program, the SERVICE program, makes a series of opening decisions that set up the companies in identical "zero states", i.e., as if they had been newly set up with only shareholders' capital and (as yet) no operation. The controller then runs through the game cycle as many times as he thinks necessary, making identical decisions for all companies, to achieve a state that he thinks suitable for starting the game, at which time the teams take over completely.

The SERVICE program has to be taken into account in the transfer process. As the decisions made by the controller in setting up the zero state involve similar units to those used elsewhere in the game, these will have to be scaled to allow for currency and other factors. As with earlier programs, changing the SERVICE program to do this is made relatively easy by the use of scaling parameters.

4.2. The Controller's Manual

The controller requires a comprehensive briefing on the economic concepts that enable him to create a particular opening position for the teams. This is done through the Controller's Manual, which is written in English. So far it has not been found necessary to translate it, mainly because the local game organizers and controllers have had a good command of English, but partly because they use a large amount of computer jargon, which tends to have international use.

One chapter of the Controller's Manual is devoted to the variable decisions that the controller can make to set up the opening position of the game. These variables are: opening capital available, market growth factor, opening skilled-labor wage, and availability of labor. These factors interact according to the normal economic laws in a free economy to create the general economic environment and are sufficiently general in their effect to apply in most capitalist countries.

In setting up a game, the controller must decide the kind of game he wants the teams to play, and the state of each company and the simulated economy when they are taken over by the teams. He must consider such factors as: rate of market growth, product qualities, capital and plant available, availability of labor, interest rates, and wage and salary levels. Clearly some degree of experience is needed to do this, and in the opening stages of any transfer we often create states of the game at which local users can take over.

The mechanics of running the game are explained in detail in the Controller's Manual. This gives comprehensive and detailed information on the structure of the programs, data files, and the sequence of events, as well as examples of the computer commands used. It also explains how large, multi-group competitions can be set up and controlled, sets out the duties of the controller, and gives examples of the administrative documents used for the game in the UK.

One of the basic criteria laid down for the game in the beginning was that it should be able to re-create identical results from the previous, or even earlier, states of play in the event of erroneous data being entered. This is done either directly through the programs in the case of a rerun, using the previous cycle as the starting point, or by reverting to copies of the historical files kept from earlier stages. Procedures for using both of these techniques to re-create the game are explained in the Controller's Manual.

5. TRANSFER BETWEEN COMPUTERS

The transfer of the game from one country to another usually means a transfer from one type of computer to another. In many ways this represents the area of greatest difficulty in the whole process. The programs for the *Edit 515 Management Game* are written in FORTRAN IV and were developed originally on General Electric computers, but now the UK master version is held on a Honeywell 6000 Series machine.

Difficulties arise because different computers use different operating systems, with the principal difficulty arising from the variety of word sizes to be found. For instance, of the computers on which the game runs in full time-sharing mode, the Honeywell 6000 uses a 35/36-bit word, the IBM 370 a 32-bit word, and the DEC 10 a 35-bit word. The consequences of these differences manifest themselves in two ways:

1. Where character variables are used, then in the programs the definitions of these variables in Data Statements, and their corresponding Format Statements, must be amended.

2. Different word sizes lead to differences in the accuracy of numbers, particularly in the decimal portion of real numbers. With double-precision and quadruple-precision numbers, which are used in the programs, this is particularly noticeable. To some extent this difference in accuracy is not relevant because within any one computer and operating system results will always be consistent. It is only when comparisons are made between the results from different machines, such as might be needed for checking purposes, that problems arise.

Apart from the differences in word size, other problems can arise from transfer to a different machine and operating system. One basic feature of the design of the *Edit 515 Management Game* is dynamic file handling. In the UK version, data files are created, or enlarged if necessary from within the programs themselves. Some operating systems (particularly IBM) cannot do this and require all files to be predefined externally to the programs. To overcome this shortcoming, procedures had to be set up using the IBM job control language.

FORTRAN IV can bring problems as well, depending on the type of FORTRAN compiler used. Different versions exist and originally the game programs were written in an enhanced version of the language. Experience has forced us to rewrite parts of the programs so that the language used is drawn only from the most common subset of FORTRAN.

In this connection it should be mentioned that the transfer of the computer program has been aided by adhering to the following "rules" of "defensive programming":

1. Use subsets of FORTRAN IV, adhering closely to ANSI standards;

2. Avoid overlays;

3. Do not use "clever" programming tricks;

4. Do not use machine-dependent routines, e.g., for random-number generators;

5. Use standard compilers and compiler options;

6. Use simple file structures;

7. Use standard input-output devices;

8. Use well tested and "robust" subroutines and functions of modular design that are used in other programs.

The programs now contain their own machine-independent random-number generator, which is seeded from historical data at each cycle of the game and which can be reconstructed to produce an identical number should a rerun of the programs be necessary. Subroutines and functions of this kind are of modular design and can be used in any suitable program.

Problems, however, will arise, even in transfers between identical computers with identical operating systems and with identical computer versions of FORTRAN. This happened to us once. All programs were compiled without error on the new machine but gave unexpected results. It took us two days of searching to discover that the compiler on the new computer had a part missing. (Murphy's law at work: If anything can happen, it will--*Editor's comment.*)

The final problem is the choice of a medium for making the actual transfer of programs. Originally 80-column punch cards were used, but these have now been generally superseded by magnetic tape. This gives rise to problems because different computers use different tape systems. We now use IBM standard (8-track, 1200 bpi, no headers). Most machines now have conversion routines for this.

6. CONCLUDING COMMENTS

Since several transfers have been made from the UK to other countries, it becomes apparent that the conceptual and documentary transfer of the game is not particularly difficult, especially when the local organizers have already played the UK version of the game. The principal area of difficulty lies in the computer technology. This is not likely to improve with time. Having developed a popular and successful game, we must keep up with the technology if the game is to remain so. New problems are appearing as new generations of computers appear, particularly microcomputers. While giving additional flexibility to where and how the game might be used, they bring many new technical problems.

The ease with which the concept and scenario of the game have been accepted in other countries can be explained by the fact that we have always made the transfer to countries with the same economic system, and that the game is concerned with a microeconomic problem that can be replicated all over the western world. Players identify readily with the problems that the game poses, and gain real benefits by taking part. We would like, however, to hypothesize that the basic structure of the model used (as appearing in the RUN program) is sufficiently robust that, with major rewrites of the Playing Manual, Decision Sheet, Management Report, and INPUT and OUTPUT programs, the game could be used also in socialist countries.

Chapter V:b

THE TRANSFER OF GAMES BETWEEN SOCIALIST COUNTRIES

Hans R. Gernert
Humboldt University, Berlin (GDR)

Isak Assa
*International Institute for Applied Systems Analysis,
Laxenburg (Austria)*

Manfred Habedank
Humboldt University, Berlin (GDR)

Wolfgang Wagner
Bergakademie Freiberg, Freiberg (GDR)

1. INTRODUCTION

Since 1975, the year of the first international seminar on simulation games within the CMEA,[1] cooperation between the socialist countries has been developing steadily. Various institutions such as academies of science, special institutions for the further training of experienced managers, and universities are involved in research on gaming models.

It is now widely accepted that economic games always reflect the socioeconomic environment of the country for which they have been developed. One basic condition underlying the rapid progress in this area within the CMEA countries has been the existence of the same social system in all the countries involved. The computer hardware and software available in the different countries is fairly uniform, thus meeting another requirement for the easy transfer of games between the respective institutions. The computer family RYAD jointly developed by the CMEA countries and the corresponding operating systems provide good conditions for running computer-based simulation games in different locations.

From several years' experience of international cooperation we can identify the following main objectives of this difficult but promising task:

- Research on theoretical aspects of game-playing;
- General exchange of experience in the development and use of Management Simulation Games (MSGs);

- Transfer of existing games and their adaptation for use in the new country; and
- Development of new games for educational, research, or operational purposes.

These activities will all be continued in the future. The research on hierarchical multilevel management simulations is regarded as particularly important: it is expected to lead to economic experiments in order to gain insight into the different economic strategies used in the various socialist countries.

The international transfer of games and gaming methodology provides a very important opportunity to disseminate gaming experience. Therefore, this chapter will concentrate on generalizing the results of several attempts to transfer games between socialist countries.

2. OBJECTIVES IN THE TRANSFER OF GAMES

One of the essential conditions for playing games in different countries is obviously that the game should be felt to be reasonably relevant and interesting by players in these countries. Furthermore, the games have to have at least some relevance to actual research, managerial, or educational problems. The specific objectives in transferring a game derive therefore from the specific interests of the institution adopting the model. As regards the main objectives for international cooperation in the field of game playing two main points can be identified: the examination of underlying economic mechanisms in different countries and the transfer of games and gaming methodology to stimulate the development of new games.

2.1. Demonstration of Economic Mechanisms

When using a management simulation game (MSG) it is possible to depict the vertical or horizontal structure of the economy either as a whole or broken down into smaller entities. The comparatively simple games for production and inventory control, already fairly well developed in most countries, are not of immediate interest here. Complex MSGs are far better able to analyze and demonstrate the behavior of the management responsible for developing the part of the real world mirrored in the game.

The reasons for the development of MSGs are described elsewhere (see Chapter IV:a of this volume, by Assa). They include attempts to

- Combine the heuristic capabilities of man and the computing capabilities of the machine;
- Narrow the gap between management theory and managerial practice;

- Introduce situation analysis into management; and
- Improve the level of management education.

Therefore, running MSGs from several countries allows us to study and compare the approaches to economic problem solving in the respective countries. When used to demonstrate given economic circumstances in the various countries the game models should not be altered but should be used in their original versions. This aim in transferring games leads to something approaching experimental economics.

2.2. Transfer of Games and Gaming Methodology to Aid Development of New Games

The exchange of games for this purpose utilizes the experience gained by the game constructor to reduce the otherwise great efforts required to develop the game model alone. The fact that the same socio-economic system is in operation in all the socialist countries is one of the main reasons behind their successful transfer of economic games. In spite of this, however, considerable effort has still been necessary in adaptational research work. The transfer of gaming methodology is therefore equally as important as the transfer of complete games.

Some of the difficulties encountered in the transfer of games have been summarized earlier by Assa (1981) as follows:

- Language difficulties;
- Existing differences in the social and economic mechanisms;
- Choice of appropriate institutional conditions (plant, enterprise, organization, etc.) in each particular country where the game is transferred and adapted;
- Gathering the necessary information; and
- Transfer of the models and the computer programs from one machine to another.

Later in the chapter some of these difficulties will be discussed further.

3. GDR-HUNGARIAN EXCHANGE OF GAMES

During the Second International Seminar of the Socialist Countries on Simulation Games, organized in 1975 by the Humboldt University, Berlin, the management game BES-1 was demonstrated (see Apelt et al., 1975). The philosophy of these seminars has always been to provide opportunities to *play* games of interest and not only to talk about them. Therefore all participants in the 1975 seminar played several periods of BES-1 and could then decide to what extent it was of interest to them.

At the same seminar a paper was presented on the business simulation game DOENTS (Decide), developed at the Computing Institute of the Ministry of Labor, Budapest (Doman, 1975). This game was then played during the Third International Seminar, held in 1976 in Budapest.

Both models simulate the behavior of industrial enterprises. While BES-1 sees the company in a more generalized way and aims at developing different strategic concepts in managing the firm, the model DOENTS is more concerned with simulating the production process of the enterprise in detail.[2] These two games have since been exchanged, i.e., the GDR BES-1 game has been transferred to Hungary and the Hungarian game DOENTS transferred to the GDR. The main incentive for the exchange of these games was the understanding that these models complement one another and that therefore the transfer experiment would be of mutual advantage.

There were three main groups of activities during the implementation of DOENTS and other Hungarian games (see Csaki et al., 1975) on GDR computers and the introduction of these games into educational programs. These involved general preparation, implementation of the computer program, and testing, interpretation, and adaptation.

3.1. General Preparations

On the basis of the translated documentation (briefing papers, user's manual, program description, etc.), an outline of the proposed usage of the game was prepared. Experience gained from those who had previously played the game in its original version was very useful in this respect. The outline included recommendations of the most appropriate game variants to use.

The outline was discussed with the relevant authoritative party (e.g., head of department, scientific council of faculty, etc.) and after mutual agreement had been reached a contract was signed between the original author and the proposed user. This contract contained specific details of all activities such as time schedules, divisions of responsibilities, etc., and included agreements on an intensive exchange of experience over a period of several years. Furthermore, all items to be exchanged within the terms of this cooperation (documentation, computer programs, data, etc.) were fully defined in the contract.

These contractual stipulations may at first sight appear excessive, and there have certainly been examples of games being given away to other institutions without any of the formalities described above. But often these latter transfers have been more or less friendly gestures or only of interest for special game constructors. Without a clear-cut concept of the proposed use of the game in education or research, the transfer of a simulation model can involve a significant risk of failure with all the associated wastes of time and material resources.

3.2. Implementation of the Computer Program

MSGs are characterized by their complexity and rely heavily on computer assistance. The difficulties of transferring computer games are therefore similar to those encountered in the dissemination of other program packages.

It was found advantageous to write the source programs in widely used problem-oriented languages. Specialists in data processing studied the respective job control languages of both computer systems concerned to ensure perfect simulation runs on the new hardware system.

As part of the general documentation mentioned above, a comprehensive program description has proved very helpful. It took about 3 hours to implement the BES-1 game on the computer of the Computing Institute of the Ministry of Labor in Budapest. Both computer systems involved were identical machines of the RYAD family. To prevent difficulties regarding the correctness of the transferred software package, it proved very useful for the first simulation runs to be performed under the guidance and supervision of the original program developer.

3.3. Testing, Interpretation, and Adaptation

The first step in transferring the computer-based games involved several test runs with the original version of the game but on the new computer. The results were then discussed with the author and the validity of the translation of the printed data was checked. Problems sometimes arose here due to slightly different concepts used in business administration and accountancy in the various countries concerned (e.g., valuation methods, taxes, layout of the balance sheet, etc.). Therefore, reprogramming was often needed for the computer output.

The adaptation efforts also extended to other parts of the model. For instance, to use the Hungarian game DOENTS in the GDR it was necessary to change several parameters and data. It is not sufficient just to substitute the word Mark for Forint in the output! All values in the model involving currencies had to be recalculated and program parameters such as wages per hour, price per unit, etc., had to be changed. The results of this adaptation work also found expression in revised briefing papers and in the user's manual.

The agreed long-term cooperation between the original author and the new user proved very helpful, especially during this period of adaptation. In spite of the considerable work involved, there is general agreement that the cost of adaptation is far lower than that required for an institution to develop its own complex MSG "from scratch". It almost goes without saying that the game must be relevant to, and wanted by the receiving institution.

The DOENTS game has been adapted for use in higher education in the GDR by scientists of the Bergakademie Freiberg (see Gallenmueller and Wagner, 1979). The software problems were solved by K. Messerschmidt of Humboldt University, Berlin, and the variant used is entitled BES-3.

3.4. Recent Work: GDR-USSR Transfer

The conclusions drawn from the transfer of the DOENTS and BES-1 games between Hungary and the GDR were recently confirmed and strengthened by the successful transfer of BES-1 to the Kazakh Polytechnic Institute "V.I. Lenin" in Alma-Ata during the autumn of 1982.

It took only a few hours to implement the program package on the mainframe computer of the KPI. The game's authors then played several periods to instruct the KPI scientists on the content and teaching aims of the game in more detail. The Russian-language version of BES-1 is now available to other universities and polytechnics in the USSR.

4. GDR-BULGARIAN COOPERATION IN GAMING

4.1. Introduction

The need to develop multilevel management simulation games arises from the procedure used for constructing plans in the socialist countries. Dialogues take place in the hierarchical structure of the management system, both horizontally and vertically.

Vertical communications exist at the sectoral level between the planning authorities, ministries, enterprises, and plants, and at the regional level between the planning authorities, the region, and the subregions. *Horizontal* communications exist between the ministries, between the enterprises, and between the regions and the sectoral ministries, enterprises, and plants.

One example of a multilevel MSG covering the dialogue between the ministry, the enterprises, and the plants in the process of building and realizing the plan is KOMBINAT (see Gernert and Habedank, 1980). This is designed on the basis of two separate games. The first game, *Economic Mechanism* (IM-1), was developed in the Institute for Social Management in Sofia for educational and research purposes (see Assa et al., 1976). It simulates the development of a complete industrial branch. The second game, BES-1, was developed at the Humboldt University in Berlin and is able to simulate the development of individual industrial enterprises.

By combining these two models, hierarchical structures in management can be simulated. To provide some insight into the difficulties of transferring and combining two models of such different origins, the two basic game models will be described briefly in the next two sections,[3] before we review the new combined game in Section 4.4 and discuss the methodological problems involved in Section 4.5.

4.2. The IM-1 Game

The management simulation game IM-1 is designed to analyze the behavior of a production firm under various changes in the perceived economic mechanism. The latter should be understood as a set of rules and laws, determined in advance, regarding the interrelations between the various economic agents (firms, institutions, individuals, etc.).

The production firm in the game is represented by an econometric model, which is a system of linear simultaneous equations.[4] The variables in the model are divided into two groups: endogenous and exogenous. The endogenous variables together form a state vector which plays the role of a performance indicator for the firm.[5] Its elements are seven variables, which correspond to the seven planned targets to be achieved by the firm at the end of each period: namely, specified values for volume of production, sales, costs, profits, wages, capital, and labor.

The exogenous variables are the "decision variables", with values specified by the players (= the decision makers) at the beginning of each simulation period. By varying the values of the 16 exogenous variables, different state vectors, corresponding to different levels of performance, are obtained. The procedure for evaluating the exogenous variables is not random but is strictly a function of the existing economic norms and rules and of the value of the state vector in the previous period.

The same sort of procedure is also used to determine various schemes for interactive simulation with the model. In the first scheme, each period can be simulated several times until one achieves values of the elements in the state vector that are acceptable, i.e., near to the planned values. This scheme is used mostly when the simulated periods are one year long, thus giving players an opportunity to reconsider some of their decisions, especially about investments, staff recruitment, etc.

In the second scheme, each period is simulated only once. The decision maker must correct some of his earlier decisions at the same time as he simulates subsequent periods. The second scheme is the most usual mode for playing the game when the simulated period is three months long.

The IM-1 game was developed on the basis of a broad econometric analysis of a textile production firm. Factor analyses have shown that the 23 selected economic factors (7 endogenous + 16 exogenous) are sufficient to describe the performance of the firm. An adequate econometric model of the firm was obtained by constructing a system of simultaneous regression equations describing the dependence of the endogenous variables on the state vector of the remaining variables.

The structural form of the equations was chosen through the generation and estimation of 60 different types of regression functions. According to statistical criteria, the most accurate formulation of the production process in the firm is achieved when logarithmic functions are used. To ensure that a fast and simple solution would be possible, the econometric model of the firm was built on the basis of linear regression equations. The statistical data for the econometric model were from a textile production firm, gathered over a period of five years. The use of real data considerably facilitated the estimation and adjustment of the coefficients in the model. The computer program for finding the solution is written in FORTRAN IV. The model is solved very quickly (in less than a second), which is a great advantage, particularly for the interactive mode of operation.

IM-1 is used for educational purposes in the Institute for Social Management, Sofia, and in various management training centers throughout Bulgaria.

4.3. The BES-1 Game

This management game was developed at the Department of Statistics of Humboldt University, Berlin (see Gernert and Koelzow, 1973). It aims at simulating a manufacturing process in order to aid studies in the fields of business administration, finance, and economic theory.

The BES-1 model has been designed and implemented in cooperation with members of several scientific disciplines at Humboldt University, and the managements of a number of industrial enterprises and banks. There has also been cooperation with Czechoslovakian scientists (see Machon, 1970). The industrial enterprise simulated by this model is described in terms of its product line, marketing conditions, fixed and current assets, manpower, and the necessary financial framework. In any simulation period, decisions are taken about purchases of raw materials, manpower, working conditions, investment, research and development, production, turnover, and distribution of profits.

BES-1 is a general simulation model. The number of periods played is variable and depends on the aims of the teaching staff. Each simulated period equals three months of real time. Usually 4-6 periods are played within 3-4 days (about 6 hours a day). The number of teams (3-4 persons each) is variable as well.

The great flexibility of this game is due to the computer software package. The program was first written in assembler (on the ROBOTRON R 300), and then rewritten in PL-1 and FORTRAN. It comprises about 2,500 PL-1 statements.

The development of BES-1 was completed at the end of 1973. Since 1974 it has been applied in training full-time students and high level executives of enterprises in several branches of industry. A recent version of this game is now used in about 15 universities and polytechnics in the GDR and in other socialist countries. It is now the most widely used large-scale rigid-rule simulation game in the GDR. Moreover, it has been increasingly successful very recently in policy-formulation exercises in special training courses for middle and higher industrial management.

4.4. The Multilevel MSG KOMBINAT-1

The structure of this game corresponds to the three levels of management shown in Figure 1.

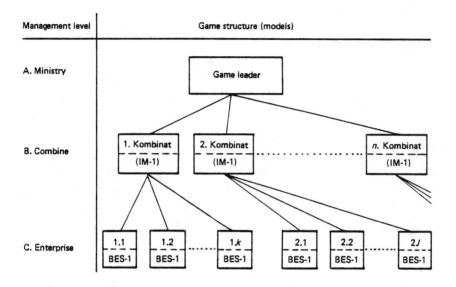

Figure 1. Structure of KOMBINAT-1.

(a) Level of the Ministry of Industry. At this highest level of management the team of umpires represents the centralized planning authority. All influences from the national economy (planned targets, general directions for future development, resource constraints, etc.) are elaborated and fixed by the team of umpires that acts in the role of a minister of industry. In this way the educational aims of the gaming exercise are formulated.

(b) Level of the Kombinat. The industrial structure known as a Kombinat has been developed in the GDR over the last few years. A Kombinat results from the merger of several industrial enterprises producing similar kinds of products. Recently the Kombinat has attained a very important position in the country's economy.

Because the area of responsibility of the Kombinat management is very similar to the decision-making process within a branch of industry, the IM-1 model can be useful in developing economic strategies at this level.

Several interactive runs with IM-1 in the dialogue mode enables the Kombinat team to find a favorable economic strategy for the Kombinat as a whole. There are several Kombinat teams under the management of the ministry, all of them receiving their planned targets from the game leader.

After finding a satisfactory solution, the Kombinat team is responsible for elaborating qualitative and quantitative targets for all the industrial plants subordinate to it. Therefore the general plan figures for the Kombinat have to be broken down to the level of individual industrial enterprises.

(c) Level of Individual Industrial Enterprises. The next lower level of management is represented by the industrial enterprises playing the business simulation model BES-1. These plants differ in size and level of productivity. Their decisions (concerning production volume, manpower, capital investment, research and development, turnover, etc.) are made along the general lines laid down by the Kombinat team responsible, but they will search for better solutions in order to improve efficiency still further. The computerized simulation process of BES-1 takes the decisions and provides feedback on the results to all three levels of management.

4.5. Methodological Problems of Combining IM-1 and BES-1

This successful attempt to combine two independent models into one game nevertheless caused many more problems than did the transfer of the DOENTS game described in Section 3. In addition to the problems associated with translating all the documentation and transferring the computer program, it was also necessary to:

- Create a joint data base for both the models;
- Generate different starting situations for the BES-1 enterprise; and
- Adapt the econometric model of IM-1 to the economic interrelations underlying the BES-1 simulation, in accordance with the economic mechanism in the GDR.

The amount of work invested in transferring IM-1 and merging it with BES-1 into the large multilevel simulation game KOMBINAT was determined by a number of factors: the mathematical formulation of the model; the existing institutional conditions; the differences in economic mechanism; and the organizational structure of the economies.

The new multilevel simulation game contains only the structure, the simulation procedure, and the software of IM-1. From the point of view of the data, a practically new IM-1 game was developed based on GDR data. By playing the BES-1 game for several enterprises over 16 periods, an appropriate amount of statistical data was generated. These data were then used to estimate the econometric model. Due to some differences in organizational structures between the two countries and in the economic mechanisms operating in the GDR Kombinat and the Bulgarian production firm (DSO), some economic factors were replaced by others.

The institutional conditions have also been changed. For the Bulgarian IM-1 a real production firm was used to produce the data. In the case of the GDR IM-1, the required data were obtained by simulation. This caused certain difficulties in the adjustment of the model. This adjustment is required because the model is a system of simultaneous linear equations. In order to assure that the simulated solutions of the model are members of the set of *feasible* solutions, the lower and upper bounds of the exogenous variables have to be determined. By using real institutional conditions this procedure is made considerably easier.

The merger of the two games into a larger one was greatly helped by the fact that IM-1 was programmed in FORTRAN and tailor-made programs were used in the solution procedure. The latter saved a considerable amount of work and time in moving the software from one type of computer to another (from an ICL 1904A to a RYAD ES 1022).

The multilevel KOMBINAT game thus appears to be a good example of the advantages for the development of *new* games of transferring gaming methodology.

5. SOME CONCLUSIONS

Summarizing our experience of transferring games and game-playing methodology, the following conditions are very important for smooth and effective transfer:

- The program should be written in an internationally used, problem-oriented computer language.
- The computers involved should be similar, e.g., with regard to operating systems, compilers, etc.
- The model needs to be extensively described and documented, to enable the user to change some parts of the model on his own.
- The game's authors ought to be very involved and available, because they have to help the new user to adapt and then to run the game.
- It is essential that precise objectives for using the game in education or research, or for operational purposes are formulated in advance, to prevent foreseeable problems or the waste of time and money at later stages.

REFERENCES

Apelt, S., Gernert, H., and Koelzow, W. (1975). *Anwendung von Planspielen in der Aus- and Weiterbildung von Oekonomen.* Proceedings of the International Seminar on Simulation Games, 2nd, Berlin.

Assa, I. (1981). *Management Simulation Games for Educational and Research Purposes: A Comparative Study of Gaming in the Socialist Countries.* WP-81-18. International Institute for Applied Systems Analysis, Laxenburg, Austria.

Assa, I., Gevrenov, S., Kolarov, N., and Petrov, S. (1976). *The Management Game "Production Enterprise Economic Mechanism".* Proceedings of the International Seminar on Simulation Games, 3rd, Sofia.

Csaki, Cs., Mozes, L., and Zelko, L. (1975). *The General Management Game "Agricultural Game".* Karl Marx University for Economics, Budapest.

Doman, A. (1975). *Bericht ueber ein komplexes Unternehmensplanspiel, gennant DOENTS.* Proceedings of the International Seminar on Simulation Games, 2nd, Berlin.

Gallenmueller, O. and Wagner, W. (1979). *Anleitung zur Durchfuehrung des Planspiels BES-3.* Bergakademie Freiberg, Freiberg, GDR.

Gernert, H. and Habedank, M. (1980). *The Multilevel Game KOMBINAT.* Proceedings of the International Seminar on Gaming, 7th, Prague. (In Russian.)

Gernert, H. and Koelzow, W. (1973). *Ein betriebliches Simulationsmodell (BES-1).* Humboldt University, Berlin.

Machon, L. (1970). *Betriebsspiele.* INORGA, Prague.

NOTES

1. CMEA (also known as COMECON) stands for the Council for Mutual Economic Assistance.

2. The BES-1 game will be described in more detail in Section 4 of this chapter.

3. There is also a short presentation of some of the main features of IM-1 in Chapter IV:a of this volume.

4. The game *Economic Mechanism* (IM-1) can be expressed mathematically as follows:

$$Ax_e + Bx_z = c$$

where x_e is the vector of the endogenous variables, x_z is the vector of the exogenous variables, i.e., the decision variables, A and B are coefficient matrices, and c is a vector of resources.

5. The state vector x_e is obtained as follows:

$$x_e = A^{-1}(c - Bx_z)$$

Chapter V:c

TRANSFER OF GAMING TECHNOLOGY: A US-HUNGARIAN CASE STUDY

Myron Uretsky
Management Decision Laboratory,
New York University, New York (USA)

Laszlo Mozes
Management Development Center,
Karl Marx University, Budapest (Hungary)

Heber MacWilliams
Walthall and Drake, Cleveland, Ohio (USA)

1. INTRODUCTION

Computer technology is frequently claimed to be one of the most efficient and effective modes of technology transfer. In a similar sense, gaming technology is asserted to be an excellent mechanism for cross-cultural research. Unfortunately, although the result is desirable, practical problems have generally prevented the implementation of a systematic test of the hypothesis.

This paper describes an attempt to study the problems and benefits associated with the transfer of a business game from one country to another. Beginning in 1971, New York University (NYU), New York and Karl Marx University (KMU), Budapest initiated a project to transfer the NYU management game to Hungary. This project involved more than a simple movement of computer software from one location to another; it also included modifying the basic model to make it appropriate to its intended environment.

The overall project appears to have been a success, even though some errors were certainly made. At the same time, based upon the resultant utilization, the subsequent interinstitutional cooperation and growing efficiency in implementing later projects, all parties feel that the overall objectives of this project were achieved.

This chapter describes the activities that took place in this project, and begins by providing the reader with a brief overview of the NYU management game. Using the description as a starting point, it outlines the steps which took place in the transfer and the apparent results. It gives a brief overview of new Hungarian games initiated by the experience from the transfer of the NYU game. It also reviews how the revised NYU game was used for operational research purposes. Because the chapter is intended to assist future gaming specialists, we have attempted to go beyond the final results, to discuss the problems that were encountered along the way.

2. THE NEW YORK UNIVERSITY GAME—A BRIEF OVERVIEW[1]

The NYU management game is an environment-rich game used for training students who are in the second year of a graduate business curriculum. The game accomplishes this goal by providing the students with an operating environment that represents a careful balance between computer models and role players from the surrounding business community. This combination makes it possible to accomplish objectives that might otherwise be unrealizable, such as reflecting subjective factors that cannot be adequately modeled on a computer. More significantly, this same combination greatly facilitates the movement of the program from one social environment to another.

2.1. Team Structure

Students participating in this program are divided into twelve teams of eight players each. Each of these teams represents a US corporation that manufactures and sells consumer nondurables (at the time of this project, the specific product used was a detergent).

Groups of three teams each are divided into separate industries, each nominally selling the same product line in a competitive environment. Direct competition only takes place within a specific industry.

2.2. Role of the Computer

The computer model represents the operation of the factory, the market responses, and the firm's information system. In this sense, student teams make decisions covering a broad range of business activities (hiring, firing, purchases, shipment schedules, research and development, sales policies, etc.). The computer model evaluates the outcomes and provides the "results".

At the time that the model is run in the computer, the model has access to all of the decisions made within a single industry, so that direct competition is limited to intra-industry situations. Additional industries are simply the result of running the basic model again with three additional teams.[2]

It is possible to implement a wide variety of transactions and business agreements that go beyond the scope of the computer program *per se*. In this case, the transaction or agreement is evaluated outside of the computer and the results are implemented using a specially prepared "administrative adjustment" provision. This capability adds considerable power to the basic system, since it opens up the possibility for incorporating a wide variety of intercompany agreements without the simultaneous need for major computer model modifications.

2.3. The Game Environment

The computer model is complemented by adding many representatives from the business community who play themselves within the game environment. In brief, the following types of role players are incorporated within the game:

1. Each student company has a board of directors, comprising high-level executives from nearby businesses.[3] These executives play the role of "stockholder representatives" who are required to represent the interests of the owners in overseeing company operations. The business people meet regularly with the students to review company operations, advise on future plans, approve selected decisions which may have a major impact on future company operations, and provide feedback on activities of the student officers. These contacts take place during formal board meetings and during informal consultations.

2. All financing within the game environment is provided through contacts with nearby financial institutions. Student teams requiring additional finances are referred to loan officers or investment bankers at nearby firms, who counsel and react to proposals in the same manner that they do with their real customers.

3. The interests of the workers are reflected by a labor union. In this case, we have established a relationship with professional negotiators working with some of the unions in the New York community. A negotiation of working conditions and compensation rates is a major component in the simulated environment.

4. Each of the firms has access to lawyers who can advise on contractual obligations and, if necessary, represent them in legal cases.

5. The students are provided with access to a wide variety of consultants who enable a wide variety of experience to be incorporated within the simulated environment. Thus, for example, access is currently being provided to organization development specialists who can assist the students in dealing with interpersonal and communications problems.

In a very real sense, the rich environment is the most exciting and important component of the overall simulation. The benefits realized cover a very wide spectrum, thus enabling representation of many factors that otherwise could be presented only by developing very elaborate computer models. It permits the introduction of subjective factors that cannot be adequately reflected within computer models, and provides an automatic dynamism that enables the game to keep in line with changing economic, political, and social conditions. Finally, as in this case, it facilitates transfer of the gaming environment to other socioeconomic environments.

3. CHRONOLOGY OF THE TRANSFER PROCESS

Development of a Hungarian management game, based on the NYU game, represented a natural growth evolving out of an academic exchange program. The academic exchange program was designed to help develop a cadre of Hungarian management specialists who were familiar with US management methods. As part of this program, several Hungarian specialists came to the United States and worked with US academic colleagues. As a result of this intensive exposure, projects such as management games were identified to keep the cooperation alive after the initial study period was completed. This section of the paper contains a brief summary of the events that took place in one cooperative venture.

3.1. Initiation

The cooperation began in late 1970, when a Hungarian scholar from KMU came to NYU to study and to work with the management gaming group. This activity provided the opportunity for informal discussions that focused on continuing the cooperation after his return to Budapest. The possibility of developing a Hungarian equivalent to the NYU management game was a logical focus because it built upon the developed experience and collaboration, and because it provided a common dialogue for all participants. The necessary approvals and funding were obtained from authorities in both countries. Work on the project was initiated during the summer of 1971.

3.2. Mutual Familiarization

It was agreed that the first step in the project would have to be developing mutual familiarization regarding the two economic systems. Consistent with this objective, the US and Hungarian teams went to Hungary during the summer of 1971. A large number of interviews were carried out during this period. As an illustration of the breadth of this exposure, the following types of organizations and people were visited:

- Austrian branches of two multinational firms doing business in Hungary;
- Five manufacturing enterprises and one state farm;
- Three governmental branches--the Finance Ministry, the National Bank, and the National Planning Office;
- A prominent tax and accounting consultant to Hungarian industry;
- A well known management consulting firm; and
- Members of the KMU faculty.

While the agenda of each interview was modified to reflect the specific circumstances, the following points were generally covered:

- Discussion of the principal business activity;
- Organizational structure;
- Role and responsibility of principal managers;
- Marketing and pricing policies;
- Accounting and taxation rules;
- Production relationships;
- Labor utilization;
- The role of both central and enterprise planning; and
- The apparent value of the planned management game (as seen by the interviewer).

Each interview was used to collect data and to objectively validate previous interviews. Particular attention in the interviews was focused on the nature of the accounting and reporting requirements of the enterprises, because it was felt that while simulation/gaming might be new to future participants, the reporting structure incorporated within the game would be their base in reality.

3.3. Model Development

The interviews which took place during the summer of 1971 provided the basis for initiating redesign of several critical models--finance, accounting, and reporting. The remainder of the required changes were felt to be achievable through parametric changes and through the development of an appropriate Hungarian external environment.

The US team returned to New York, accompanied by Hungarian colleagues who could work on the required modifications. In general, the following changes were made:

1. The financial models were changed significantly. All items reflecting US specific financing, such as stock market financing, were deleted from the models. Additional models were developed to reflect the Hungarian approach to employee compensation, taxation, and allocations to investment funds.

2. All of the accounting models were modified to reflect the system then in use within Hungary. This modification was a major task due to the structure of the underlying computer program and due to the fundamental difference in accounting methods used in the two countries (the US system is based on French origins, while the Hungarian system is based on German origins).

3. All participant materials--players' manuals, decision forms, and reports--were translated into Hungarian. The player's manual was first prepared in English at NYU, based on preliminary specifications for the simulation, during the summer of 1971, and the translation was made in the fall of that year at KMU, while the program was being developed in New York.

4. Initial approximations were made to parametric changes that would bring production and marketing models into line with conditions in Hungary.

5. The marketing structure was modified so that it reflected sales to Hungary, the USSR, Western Europe, and the developing nations. This was in contrast to the US version, which assumed that sales were to four different regions of the United States.

6. Potential external business participants were identified, together with the roles that they would play. It was assumed that participants would be needed in the following categories: a board of inspectors (roughly the same as the US board of directors), representatives from the National Bank of Hungary, and representatives from the ministry controlling the simulated enterprises.

4. PRELIMINARY PROGRAM EVALUATION

4.1. Purpose of the Test Run

A two-week test run of the simulation game was conducted in January 1972 at KMU in Budapest. Since such a test run is a critical phase of the transfer process, and since many aspects of this game test also hold for the full implementation of the game, we shall describe this test run in some detail. The test run was intended to provide information to the developers on two levels.

First, with regard to the major goals of the project, a "live" test could give preliminary answers to the basic feasibility questions: (a) Was the program a reasonable simulation of the environment of managers of a Hungarian enterprise? (b) Could a program of this type be run in Hungary? (c) Would it be a useful tool for management education?

Second, on the operational level, four specific goals were set for the test run:

1. To test the available computer facilities and operational logistics to determine whether the program would run satisfactorily.

2. To test the overall realism and integrity of the simulation. This was a joint evaluation on the part of the participants, faculty, and research team.

3. To demonstrate the concept of large-scale management simulation to the participants and faculty. The use of computer simulation was not at that time a part of educational methodology in Hungary, and the usefulness of the technique in that environment had to be demonstrated.

4. To uncover particular program areas or models needing refinement or further development.

Throughout the preparations for the test, it was made clear to the participants that there was uncertainty connected with the design, implementation, and validity of the simulation, and that there would be no "success" or "failure" associated with the test run. This was necessary to ensure candor in the evaluation process and to gain cooperation from officials, faculty, and participants.

4.2. Computer Facilities

The management simulation program was written in FORTRAN IV and required 128 kbytes of memory on an IBM 360/40 or larger computer system. KMU did not have a computer with these capabilities, so facilities had to be found elsewhere in Budapest. IBM maintained a support center in Budapest, containing a 360/40 computer system with 256 kbytes of memory.

4.3. Background of the Participants

Three groups of participants took part in the simulation. Each group, hereafter called a "team", was composed of seven or eight individuals. Two teams consisted of managers from enterprises in the Budapest area, and the third team was made up of members from the KMU faculties of industry and of commerce who were interested in the educational possibilities of the simulation, both as a regular part of the curriculum and also as a device for professional development programs. Each of the teams included persons of varied management skills and positions in order to have the required range of talent for successful performance in the simulated enterprise. Nearly all of the managers had engineering degrees and had positions in upper-middle management.

4.4. Schedule of Play

The trial run began with an orientation lecture. After this session each team member was given copies of the output of the computer program which represented the most recent 12 months of history of their enterprises. Three days were allocated for the participants to study this output and to prepare a set of operating decisions for the next month of play.

The first four plays of the program consisted of one month of simulated operation of the enterprise. Since each play required approximately 350 decisions to be made (explicitly or implicitly) and the participants were also learning the responses of the simulation to various decisions, one day was considered to be the minimum time needed between plays. This single daily play was designed to provide opportunities for the group to organize, learn to operate effectively as a team, and experience the variety of interrelationships and dependent decisions made in a large enterprise.

The eighth and ninth days of the test required that the participants submit decisions for two months of operation; i.e., two sets of decisions were submitted and run together, but without an opportunity for the team to review the results of the first month before running the second. This placed a greater emphasis on planning and required a good understanding of the operation of the simulated enterprise. Decisions had to be made on the basis of overall strategy rather than as a reaction to the results of the prior month and the particular impact of the other enterprises in the industry.

The final day was planned as a general evaluation of the project including sessions with participants, faculty, administrators, and assistants to review the results and plan the steps required to implement a full-scale test of the program. Several observers from the ministry, bank, and exchange faculty from other East European universities were invited. The evaluation was not focused on the performance of individual teams, but on the overall nature of the simulation.

4.5. Participant Orientation

Participant orientation was a critical factor in the success of the trial run. The managers and faculty members participating in the experiment were important sources of criticism, and their ability to perform in the roles of both participant and evaluator was dependent on their perception of the nature of the simulation. Each had to be given some prior expectation of the nature of the task required, but the general orientation was given to explain (a) the purpose of the experiment; (b) the framework of the simulation; (c) the advantages and limitations of this method of learning; and (d) their role as evaluators of the simulation as a model of a Hungarian enterprise.

It was made clear that in this abbreviated test, full development of the "external environment" of real-world role players was not possible, but that such a system was the goal once the simulation program itself was thoroughly tested. Some of the external functions, such as the bank, would be available through specific members of the administrative committee acting in those roles.

Each participant was assigned to a management position on his team. These positions generally corresponded to the position of responsibility held by the participant in his real-world enterprise. Team organization was specified in order to assist the participants in adjusting to the simulation more rapidly and to facilitate the task of administering and evaluating the results of the test run. Ordinarily, team organization is not specified during the full-semester implementations because this allows more flexible organizational structures and permits internal changes in organization to occur more readily.[4]

As the simulation proceeded, there developed a healthy competition between the teams to achieve the greatest profit. Various strategies were chosen, including cost reduction measures, equipment modernization programs, and aggressive marketing campaigns. In the short period of play, few of the schemes came to full fruition, although several appeared to have been well formulated and seemed destined for future success. Generally the teams recognized that, in order to be successful, a coordinated plan had to be developed for the enterprise, and that overemphasis in one area usually resulted in serious problems in other areas.

4.6. Problems

The test of the program was carried out substantially as planned. During the period of play, many small and several major problem areas in the program were uncovered. The general problem areas were as follows:

Errors and omissions in the player's manual caused by changes in the program, the translation to Hungarian, or uncertainty in treatment of specific details resulted in many discussions with the participants over particular decisions.

A similar, but less troublesome, problem occurred in the translation of the text of the computer output. This resulted mainly from the absence of required Hungarian characters in the print chain.

One of the expected sources of possible problems failed to materialize. It had been anticipated that difficulties might occur in the adaptation of the participants to the structure and environment of the simulation, but the participants generally accepted the roles and burdens placed on them by the simulation and had little trouble associating with the processes involved in the simulated systems.

4.7. Participant Reaction

At the conclusion of the test run, each of the participants was invited to present oral and written comments on his impressions of the simulation and, in particular, what problems he saw in the design and implementation of the program.

The managers were generally optimistic regarding the possibilities of achieving a useful learning experience from participation in the simulation on a full-scale basis. Although their own experience was clouded by annoying technical problems, they were particularly impressed by the extent to which the simulation highlighted the interactions and mutual dependencies among the various functional disciplines in an enterprise.

A number of specific recommendations for improvements to the simulation program were offered. The suggestions showed an awareness of the complexity of the simulation and, at the same time, an appreciation of the possibility of serious involvement of professional managers and faculty in the operation of the simulated environment.

There appeared, however, to be one reaction to the simulation which was based on the background of the participants and the business environment. This was reflected in the nature of the questions and comments relating to the areas of production and marketing. The participants were evidently well trained and familiar with the technical problems of production, and were very critical of this area of the program.

Many suggestions were made which were intended to improve the realism of the production area, and these often seemed to be extremely technical. The impression was conveyed that there is preoccupation in the management of Hungarian enterprises with technical production details, perhaps due to the engineering and production backgrounds of many managers.

In contrast, very little fault was found with the marketing area, and comments about it were usually of clarification rather than of criticism. The participants seemed eager to learn as much as possible about marketing and distribution and apparently assumed that this part of the simulation was accurate, or that they were not qualified to judge the validity of the models.

4.8. Administrative Reaction

The involvement of the participants in the operations of the enterprises and the competitive reaction of the teams underscored the general satisfaction of the US and Hungarian administrators with the game. Most of the technical problems were solved, and the way seemed clear to prepare for full-scale implementation. The faculty members participating in the test were generally impressed by the scope and concept of the simulation, but were about evenly divided on the applicability of the program to the curriculum. The administrative committee and the president of KMU were satisfied with the concept of a large-scale simulation, and appeared ready to commit the necessary resources for a full-scale test.

Since a curriculum change at the university seemed to be a difficult obstacle, it was decided to attempt to run the simulation in the fall of 1972 as a professional development workshop for enterprise managers. The government was beginning to fund such programs to help speed the introduction of better management skills in industry.

5. FULL IMPLEMENTATION

The first full test of the simulation was held at KMU during the fall semester of 1972. This program included full use of the external environment that was previously discussed. The program ran for 14 weeks, and 24 periods of the simulation were executed. The full implementation of the program was planned, organized, and administered by a committee of the faculty at KMU. Technical advice and operational strategy formulation were provided through occasional transatlantic telephone conversations and one mid-semester visit to Hungary.

Use of the game has continued to the present time. The economics faculty at KMU continues to use the game for training around 300 management students annually, and a full support staff is in place. It is also being used by faculty and staff for research purposes (see below). Changes are continually being made to the game to reflect changing economic and management situations, and it is now in its fifth improved version.

The game is also in use at the Hungarian Management Development Center at KMU. In this case the audience comprises middle- and upper-level enterprise managers who are participating in postgraduate (executive development) courses. Although no formal studies have been carried out to determine concrete benefits from the use of this game, informal comments suggest that there are significant benefits associated with the pragmatic game context and the ease of transferring the newly learned techniques to a workplace context.

The game has also been used by the Danube Ironworks and by the Ministry of Heavy Industry and has been in operation there for internal training programs.

6. NEW GAMES INSPIRED BY THE ADAPTED GAME

Inspired by the success of the adapted NYU game, work on games of similar, but home-developed, conceptions were started. Thus the Hungarian Management Development Center at KMU developed the *Complex Enterprise Management Game* and the Computer Institute of the Ministry of Labor developed the game *Decide* (DOENTS). Work on both of these games was mainly done by people in some way familiar with the adapted NYU game.

Since these two new games, as well as the adapted NYU games, were all large, there arose at the KMU a need for smaller games that could be more readily integrated into the ordinary course program at the Management Development Center. Thus work started on smaller games, using both the experience from the playing of the adapted NYU game and the ideas of C. Csaki. This resulted in a smaller management game called *General Enterprise Decision Game* (1975) and in a *Decision Game for Agricultural Enterprises* (1976).

In 1981 a version of the *General Enterprise Decision Game* was introduced into the training program of the Hungarian Socialist Workers' Party.

Within the framework of collaboration between the socialist countries, the Lomonosov University of Moscow is using the *General Enterprise Decision Game* and the *Decision Game for Agricultural Enterprises*. In 1976 the Humboldt University in Berlin adapted the *General Enterprise Decision Game* and the game *Decision* (see Chapter V:b of this volume, by Gernert et al.). In 1978 the economics faculty of Novi Sad (Szabadka) University started to use the agricultural decision game. Thus the original US-Hungarian game transfer also had an indirect effect on the transfer of gaming technology to other socialist countries.

7. USE OF THE REVISED NYU GAME FOR OPERATIONAL RESEARCH PURPOSES

It should be mentioned that the adapted game has also been used as a tool for research on important practical problems. In 1974 the Hungarian Ministry of Finance commissioned KMU to use the game to carry out part of its research regarding the potential impact associated with changes in enterprise financing regulations. In particular, the ministry was interested in obtaining an early indication of how proposed financing changes would influence the behavior of practising enterprise managers.

Among changes contemplated were the following. Previously, enterprises had to pay a charge on assets on the basis of the *gross* value of a part of their fixed and circulating assets. The planned modification was that a higher charge (5% instead of 3%) should be paid on the *net* value of the assets. Another planned modification was that rates and taxes to be paid to the state after the wages paid would be raised by about 10% in order to stimulate enterprises to practise more economical labor management. The profits of an enterprise had previously been divided into (1) a fund to be distributed among the workers and employees, and (2) a development fund to be spent on the development of the enterprise according to a compulsory formula. The planned modification was that the enterprises themselves would have more freedom in the division of the profits between these two funds (for details see Mozes, 1980).

The aim and character of these planned modifications made it obvious that the new conditions would have different influences on the further development of enterprises with different capital compositions. Therefore, the three enterprises in the game were established in such a way that their capital compositions were also different. Relevant sections of the computer model and the players' materials were modified to reflect the proposed changes.

Practising managers were invited to participate in a gaming session based upon the modified game model. Enterprise leaders of high and medium level participated; the members of the board of directors were leaders of directing bodies; the bank was represented by real staff members of the Hungarian National Bank.

The game was thus used as a kind of "economic laboratory", i.e., as an experimental tool - a new use of gaming in Hungary. It was focused on planned modifications of the system of economic conditions, which had not yet been carried out in practice. In this way, these modifications could be tried out in advance. One could thus hope to get some early insights into possible enterprise reactions to the modified conditions, perhaps also finding out in advance some otherwise unforeseen deficiencies in the proposals. The game could also help in reducing the period required for the adjustment of management to the new conditions. Using the game, management could get acquainted with the new system in advance and hence learn to adapt themselves.

At the conclusion of the session, the game results were used to stimulate discussions regarding both the impact of and potential problems associated with the financing changes. From these discussions it appeared that the game had not given any new evidence that spoke strongly against the new regulations. The approach described above was certainly imperfect from a scientific viewpoint. At the same time everyone recognized the imperfections and it was felt that the game provided an artificial context that facilitated discussions and gave insights that might otherwise have been difficult to obtain. It should also be mentioned that certain behavior during the game later appeared to be verified when the new regulations were introduced in practice.

8. THE EXPERIENCE IN RETROSPECT

The overall experience of those associated with the development and implementation of the NYU-KMU management game has been quite positive. Since original development and testing activities in 1971-1973 there have been periodic informal reviews of the experience. In summary, we feel that the following identifiable benefits have been achieved:

For the Hungarian Side
- Access to an educational tool that had not been previously used on a wide scale within Hungary.
- Development of a model that was eventually used for research in connection with financial planning.
- Development of expertise regarding the operation of capitalist institutions.

For the US Side
- Development of expertise relating to Hungarian business methods. This information had a direct impact on courses being taught to foreign trade specialists.
- Development of expertise and experience relating to cooperation with socialist institutions. This experience greatly facilitated the conceptualization of similar projects with other socialist institutions.

For Both Sides
- Development of personal contacts that would facilitate the conceptualization of follow-on projects.
- Development of interinstitutional cooperation.

REFERENCES

Mozes, L. (1980). Management games in policy analysis and design. In I. Stahl (Ed.), *The Use of Operational Gaming as an Aid in Policy Formulation and Design*. CP-80-6. International Institute for Applied Systems Analysis, Laxenburg, Austria.

Uretsky, M. (1973). Management game: an experiment in reality. *Simulation and Games*, June: 221-240.

NOTES

1. A more complete description can be found in Uretsky (1973).

2. A version of this game currently being completed has the capability to represent a variable number of teams within a single industry. More significantly, the number of firms can be varied during execution of a play of the game. This capability permits the representation of situations involving the creation of new companies, or the merging of two already existing companies.

3. All role players are volunteers, who donate their time to help improve the educational program.

4. It is interesting to note that in the first full implementation, when the participants were free to set their organization, they each organized in a structure reflecting their actual real-world organizational relationships and professional duties.

PART VI

EAST-WEST INTERNATIONAL TRADE GAMES

Chapter VI:a

A US-USSR TRADE GAME[1]

Myron Uretsky
New York University, New York (USA)

1. PROJECT OBJECTIVES

This project was established to help accomplish several related
objectives:

1. To provide documentation of the steps involved during a typical
   trade negotiation between US corporations and Soviet organizations;

2. To document typical experiences that companies have had in
   such negotiations;

3. To identify differences in negotiating styles and approaches;

4. To identify typical problem areas, reasons for the problems,
   symptoms indicating a problem's existence, and alternative
   methods for resolving the difficulties; and

5. To develop tools that can be used to train people who are either
   about to enter US-Soviet trade negotiations or who must
   interact with people involved in these activities.

2. THE SCOPE OF THE PROJECT

This project was carried out under the auspices of the US-USSR Science and Technology Agreement. The US side was led by a team from
New York University and the Soviet side was led by a team from the Ministry of Foreign Trade, Academy of Foreign Trade. Both the US and the
Soviet participants agreed that they must limit the scope of the project
in order to ensure its successful completion. The following self-imposed
constraints were formulated to facilitate this process:

1. The work should be based upon actual technology transactions.
   The need was to inject theory into practice, and to provide tools
   that could significantly increase the volume of trade between
   the two countries.

2. The project was to center on the negotiating process, and not on the implementation of already concluded projects.

3. The initial activity was to focus on licensing transactions. License purchase and sale is becoming an increasingly large component in many East-West transactions because it is perceived to provide a partial solution to certain currency and technology transfer problems.

4. The project was *not* to transfer any national military or commercial trade secrets. Obviously, it is difficult to conceive of any licensing transactions that do not involve (or at least, appear to involve) some trade secrets. Nevertheless, both sides felt that the success of the project rested on maintaining a structure which assured participating firms or ministries that no trade secrets would be transferred.

5. The data and relationships which the working groups from either side exchanged could be modified to prevent disclosure of national or trade secrets. Similarly, either side had the right to rework the data so that its educational objectives could be more fully realized. The primary limitation was the requirement that the data and relationships must appear to be realistic and reasonable when reviewed by practising trade negotiators.

3. ANTICIPATED OUTPUT

The project was designed to provide trade-related cases and negotiating exercises which could benefit the US and Soviet academic and business communities. When completed, the following materials would be made available for use:

1. *Case studies* to be used to acquire an understanding of the steps pursued in typical transactions, the problems that arise, and their resolution. They would also form the basis for courses and training programs.

2. *A negotiation simulation* to be used to gain a sense of what it was like to participate in US-Soviet trade negotiations, and to anticipate common trade negotiation problems.

3. *A series of reports* would elaborate upon the negotiations process involved in US-Soviet trade.

4. OVERVIEW OF ACTIVITIES

All of the projected results enumerated above were encompassed within three major sets of activities:

1. *A case studies series* is being prepared to document how recent US-Soviet negotiations have generally proceeded. This documentation permits readers to observe:

(a) the troubles that arose;

(b) how problems were recognized;

(c) how the problems were resolved (if they were); and

(d) how the negotiations were concluded.

These cases are described more fully in Section 5.

2. *A simulation game* is being created to give participants greater insights into the negotiation process. This exercise involves two sets of participants: one set acting as US negotiators and the other as Soviet negotiators. The two groups of participants will have at their disposal background information regarding technology, industrial organization, company history, and financing. The actions taking place will simulate technical presentations and technical and commercial negotiations. This game is presented more fully in Section 6.

3. *Research* is being undertaken in order to acquire a greater grasp of the US-USSR trade negotiation process. These investigative efforts will permit both teams to observe such factors as: the role cultural differences play; personality characteristics of successful negotiators; and methods for making negotiations more effective.

5. CASE STUDIES

This part of the project deals with the development of cases describing the negotiations of technology-related transactions between the two countries. Development of these cases inherently involved overcoming operational difficulties, i.e., assuring participants that no commercial or government secrets would be transferred without prior approval. Most significantly, it was felt that the cooperation of outside organizations was dependent upon both the reality and the appearance of required safeguards. For this reason, three categories of cases were planned: single-company actual, composite, and parallel.

Single-company actual cases are exact descriptions of actual transactions. They are based upon specific transactions, and no attempt is made to disguise the company involved or other essential details. Each of these cases reviews the company or organization involved. A release must be received by the project team before the case can be released to the project team in the other country or to the general public.

Composite cases are designed to illustrate typical situations, and are not based upon any particular transaction or organization. Instead they are "armchair cases" that represent essentially accurate and realistic situations. Three of these composite cases have been completed. Provision is made to control the quality of these cases, since the protocol between the two project teams specifies that each case must be reviewable by professional trade specialists who must be willing to testify to the situation's plausibility. Composite cases are designed to accomplish two objectives. First, they permit focusing on situations where the specifics of company identification are not essential to the points being made.

Second, they facilitate progress in the case development effort. The latter point is particularly important. We have found that it is often difficult to get companies to participate in the development effort. This was to be expected, since the project's focus on licensing technology puts the project in the midst of issues relating to both national and company commercial secrets. The ability to develop composites permits the issues to be addressed and it provides illustrations of the project team's case approach.

Parallel cases are actual or composite cases that are intended to describe the same business transactions from US *and* Soviet points of view. They permit a detailed examination of the conflicts that arise because of differences in objectives or perspectives, and they show how these conflicts can be resolved. The development of parallel cases is inherently difficult because they deal with national and company commercial secrets on both sides. In addition, they sometimes deal with issues that the parties to the transaction would rather keep private. Consequently, implementation of this step assumes prior agreement by everyone involved in the process. At the time of writing, no parallel case based on actual transactions has been prepared. The closest current approximation exists in two composite cases developed by the US side. These cases were then given to the Soviet project team, who developed parallel composites reflecting a Soviet perspective.

6. THE TRADE NEGOTIATIONS GAME

The simulation game is intended to provide participants with an opportunity to experience trade negotiations. As such, it attempts to incorporate a large number of structural and interpersonal factors that appear to influence the outcome of such negotiations. This section serves five purposes:

1. It identifies the key groups associated with running the game;
2. It describes the overall game structure in terms of activities taking place;
3. It describes material given to the players;
4. It shows how subjective factors have been incorporated through the use of diary items and opportunity points; and
5. It explains the role of the computer in the game.

6.1. Groups Participating in the Game

US Players

Three to five persons play the role of the US trade negotiators. The materials that they will be given include:

- A case containing background information on the US company involved;

- A synopsis of the commercial issues at stake;
- An elaborate report on the US trade environment;
- A less detailed description of the Soviet trade environment, whose scope corresponds to that to which new US trade negotiators would normally have access; and
- A series of interactive computer programs to help prepare financial estimates, cost calculations, etc., for which US negotiators are normally responsible.

Soviet Players

Three to five people act as Soviet trade negotiators. The materials that they will be given include:

- A case containing background information on the Soviet organization involved;
- A synopsis of the commercial issues at stake;
- An elaborate report on the Soviet trade environment; and
- A series of interactive computer programs to help prepare financial analyses, cost calculations, etc., for which Soviet negotiators are normally responsible.

The Administrator

The administrator guides all game activities. His primary function is to periodically introduce "minicases" containing additional relevant data to appraise participants of the occurrence of such exogenous changes as marketing conditions, economics, organizational changes, prices, competition, etc.

6.2. Activities Taking Place

This section provides an overview of US-USSR trade negotiations game activities. The game covers every phase of a typical negotiation, from the initial interest in a license sale to a contract signing or negotiation breakdown. This overall process comprises several distinct stages in order to facilitate program execution:[2]

1. Background material is evaluated by each team;
2. Initial interest in negotiations is indicated by one of the sides;
3. A Moscow technical seminar is prepared by the US side;
4. The technical seminar is presented;
5. Technical negotiations are planned;
6. Technical negotiations are conducted;
7. Progress is reviewed by each team separately;
8. Commercial negotiations are planned;
9. Commercial negotiations are conducted;
10. A contract is drafted;
11. The contract is signed; and
12. The overall performance is reviewed.

Although these steps have been presented in their logical, anticipated sequence, the actual simulation may not have such clearly defined linear stages. For instance, if issues arise while drafting the contract, it may be necessary to revert to the negotiations stage again.

The game is planned to take place over a 15-week period (the duration of a normal university semester) although it can be adapted to nearly any time span. For instance, an administrator might decide to modify the game so that it could be used in a shorter (3-5 day) management development course.

The simulation terminates under one of two circumstances:

1. When an agreement is signed, or
2. When discussions have apparently collapsed.

The project does not extend into the implication stages.

6.3. Materials Provided to Participants

At the beginning of the game each set of players obtains three sets of basic reference materials:

1. Detailed descriptions of the operating environment and administrative procedures existing in their own country;
2. Abbreviated descriptions of the opponent's environment and administrative procedures; and
3. An extensive case study containing company background, organizational structure, team negotiation chronicle, and information about the roles being played. A series of minicases is interjected throughout the game, providing supplementary data about changes in the company's operating environment.

The negotiation simulation involves several rounds. When each period of simulated play concludes, the participants receive two documents: a formal report and a printed diary.

The formal report contains a description of the progression of the game with respect to its overall context. It is the more general of the two documents, containing information on budgets, time and resources expended, a listing of expected settlement terms, and a listing of agreed contract terms.

The diary is more specific in that it chronicles the events that have actually taken place. It introduces additional events (for instance, "back home" meetings, cultural activities, etc.) which provide participants with nonsimulated aspects of the East-West trade environment. It provides participants with opportunities (e.g., hosting delegations) which, if they capitalize upon them, could influence future negotiations.

By playing these three roles, the diary lends a richness to the environment by providing both a record of events and a flavor of the process. The diary specifically contains the following types of information:

1. *A record of joint meetings* between team representatives. These joint meetings include the actual game conference, as well as selected combined cultural events which can be referred to within the negotiations. A computer program automatically generates the latter items.

2. *A record of activities* in which the individual has been involved during the period. This includes, for example, planning meetings, review sessions, etc. These items are as detailed as possible, so that the participants may better internalize the activities transpiring.

3. *"Opportunity options"* which are diary options that a team may or may not exercise and that may or may not influence the outcome and timing of future events. Sample opportunities include: a US-USSR Trade and Economic Council membership invitation; the occasion to host delegations; and the opportunity to attend conferences.

The US and Soviet teams do not get the same diaries.

6.4. Computer Support

The US-USSR negotiations game utilizes three sets of computer programs: US team support models contain a set of financial analysis and monetary planning programs which enable participants to portray US business people. USSR team support models are a set of programs designed to aid participants playing Soviet trade representatives. Negotiations support models consist of a set of computer programs to assist the administrator to guide the progress of game activities.

The *US Team Support Models* contain two classes of computer programs that help participants to play US negotiators realistically:

1. *Financial planning computer programs* to generate current financial statements and key ratios. These interactive programs permit participants to incorporate assumptions regarding market size, share of market, etc., and subsequently generate financial projections consistent with these assumptions.

2. *Financial analysis computer programs* to generate the kinds of important ratios and reports upon which evaluations of the US-based firms are normally grounded.

As mentioned above, case studies giving background information on the US companies are supplied to the US participants. These documents contain several years of standard corporate-style financial data: income statements, balance sheets, sales-by-product and sales-by-geographic market segment, production costs, etc. These statistics are placed into a computer data-base, so that US participants can use them in tandem with the computer programs. Additional data are introduced in each period to reflect changes taking place during the course of the play. For example, another year's data are added when one year (in game time) ends.

The *USSR Team Support Models* include a series of computer programs to enable the Soviet players to act realistically. These models or programs, to be supplied by the Soviet side, are consistent with the protocol and approach being used for the US team support models. They should, among other things, be based on case studies that would be given to the Soviet players, and should be interactive.

The *Negotiations Support Models* are used to guide game activities; these activities should progress in the following manner. Both sets of players make decisions in the negotiation simulation. The decisions are handed to the administrator, who inserts them into the computer program. An "analyzer program" interprets these decisions and determines some of their consequences. This program tracks the flow of activities, accumulates resource utilization, determines timing and random events, and provides information to both the diary and the reporter programs mentioned above.

7. OVERVIEW OF THE PROGRAM

A considerable amount of progress has been made in bringing the US-USSR trade negotiations game closer to completion. Particular attention has been focused on developing broadly based interdisciplinary teams to ensure relevance to both academic and business communities. Major steps achieved include the following:

1. A joint US-USSR project team has been established. The disciplines represented within the US team include: computer science, model building, social psychology, gaming, and management. The parallel Soviet team includes specialists in the following fields: computer sciences, model building, and foreign trade management.

2. A broad network of Soviet trade representatives has been organized. We worked closely with the Soviet team to find a mechanism that would permit a nonbureaucratic flow of information to take place to offset the difficulties associated with our physical separation. In general, these specialists have been able to provide timely advice and/or information that would otherwise have been delayed due to the physical distance between the two countries.

3. An academic/industrial advisory panel has been established to review work on the project and to assess its relevance to the intended audience.

There have been a number of exchange visits by each team. These meetings have permitted the teams to become familiar with the operating environment, to collect data, and to interview specialists. Most significantly, each of these visits has included extensive consultation with representatives from outside organizations. Efforts have been divided along lines of comparative advantage, with each team taking responsibility for those development activities with which they have the most expertise. Thus, the US team is taking the responsibility for defining the US trade and company environment, while the Soviet team is taking responsibility for defining the Soviet environment.

The following activities have been completed thus far in the project:

- A complete overview of the game has been prepared and agreed to by both teams.

- A series of working papers has been prepared describing the functions that are to be included in the game.[3]

- A case has been selected as a basis for building the US company environment. This case is now being modified and enhanced to make it relate to the specific objectives of this project.

- Specifications for role player guides, player instructions, and administrator's guide have to be completed.

- The Soviet side has produced the description of a foreign trade game. The characteristics of this game have been incorporated into the overview referred to above.

- The Soviet side has produced a mathematical summary of activities taking place within the trade negotiation process.

- The Soviet team has provided books describing the Soviet foreign trade environment and approaches to planning and managing trade negotiations. These books are being translated into English.

Although the project is currently inactive due to the world political situation, all materials have been stored in a manner that will permit project completion and expansion at an appropriate future time. Much of the material could also provide the basis for similar international trade games.

NOTES

1. Work on this chapter has been funded in part by New York University and by the National Science Foundation, under grants MCS-76-16601-A02 and MCS-76-17325.

2. This scenario description is written from the US viewpoint. Information regarding USSR activities is being prepared by the Soviet group.

3. These are available from Professor M. Uretsky, The Management Decision Laboratory, New York University, 100 Trinity Place, New York, NY 10006, USA.

A GDR-UK TRADE GAME

Hans R. Gernert
Humboldt University, Berlin (GDR)

James P.A. Conlan and Anthony Pope
*School of Management, Buckinghamshire College,
High Wycombe (UK)*

1. INTRODUCTION

Management simulation games (MSGs) provide the opportunity to combine features of several disciplines, such as management theory, simulation methods, game playing, etc. The intersection of these disciplines is of special interest for developing efficient MSGs for educational or operational purposes. It is this complexity that enables MSGs to reflect real management problems better than simple games on specialized economic topics.

The MSG described here represents the joint work of three authors in constructing a computer-based, international business simulation. Initially, the contacts between Humboldt University in Berlin and the School of Management at High Wycombe were merely part of the teaching programs of the two institutions. Quite independently, H. Gernert and W. Koelzow, staff members of the Department of Statistics at Humboldt University, had developed a computer model of a manufacturing unit, whilst at High Wycombe business games of a variety of types had been developed. The next stage involved combining this experience for a quite specific, common research purpose. Meanwhile, contacts had also developed with the Administrative Staff College at Henley, Oxon, UK, where B. Aston was developing other types of international simulations. His comments have been very valuable to the development of this project.

2. OBJECTIVES OF THE GAME

The main objectives of this joint venture may be described as follows.

The exchange of ideas and experience on the development and use of different kinds of games. This transfer of game-playing methodology shortens the time needed to develop the game. The original viewpoints of the authors were, to start with, by no means identical. Gernert and Koelzow have used the computer as a means of simulating the complexity of industrial organizations. In contrast, Pope and Conlan have always regarded computer assistance in operating games as only necessary under exceptional circumstances.

The elaboration of a rigid-rule large-scale MSG. This game is a tripartite exercise which purports to represent a UK manufacturer of sophisticated, robot-like, production devices, supplying a GDR car manufacturer, who, in turn, supplies a UK concessionaire. The game constructors gain insight into complex and different approaches to East-West trade. The participants in the simulation runs will also be able to study certain parts of the vertical structure of the centrally planned socialist economy of the GDR and both the managerial behavior and the market mechanism operating in the British economy.

The comparison of game-playing behavior in the GDR and in the UK. It is planned to play the game with participants from Berlin and from High Wycombe. The annual exchange of students between the two institutions even provides the opportunity of playing the game with internationally mixed teams. Because of the very different social systems built into the game, any differences in the behavior of the decision makers will soon become obvious.

One further objective in developing the international simulation game described here is to illustrate the different approaches to management in the socialist GDR and in the capitalist UK, and to demonstrate the mutual advantages of international trade between countries having different social systems.

The areas of management responsibility covered by this MSG can be listed as follows:

- Optimizing a given production-marketing situation.
- Planning all the arrangements required to open up a new market.
- Conducting international negotiations as necessary to supply that market.
- Budgeting for the capital investment necessary to increase production whilst reducing unit costs.
- Striking a balance, under conditions of constrained supply, between the demands of several differing foreign markets.
- Solving the entrepreneurial problems of supplying a new product to an existing market.
- Establishing an importing agency and conducting fruitful negotiations with the potential supplier.

This research project has shown that individual constructors of MSGs, even those coming from such diverse economies as the UK and the GDR, are quite able to develop useful joint games.

The modular arrangement of the three parts of the game allows it to link very different types of models without undue difficulty. Details of the individual models can be developed almost independently: given the distance between Berlin and High Wycombe, this has played a large part in making the project feasible. The authors' relatively rare direct discussions largely center on the task of specifying correct interfaces between the various models.

3. STRUCTURE OF THE GAME

As illustrated in Figure 1, the game will be operated by three teams, representing

- A UK company (UKS) manufacturing and selling production equipment suitable for vehicle manufacture;
- A car manufacturing company (Kombinat) situated in the GDR; and
- A UK company (UKD) expressly established to import Kombinat cars into the UK and to act as an exclusive distributor.

During the game a period of about three years will be simulated, results being declared by the umpires, where appropriate, at six-month intervals.

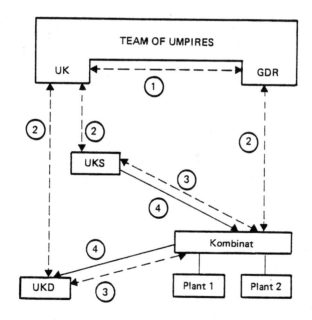

Figure 1. The structure of the game. The meanings of the numbered arrows are as follows: (1) Coordination in controlling the game, elaborating the strategic aims of the simulation, and evaluating the results. (2) Information on national economic developments, trends, and events, the issue of the plan targets and the allocation of resources (*from* the team of umpires); reports on the actual economic developments during the periods simulated (*to* the team of umpires). (3) International trade negotiations between the teams concerned. (4) Flow of products.

3.1. The UK Supplier

We will examine first the UK equipment-manufacturing model. This part of the simulation feeds the second (GDR) model.

The UK production model has two parts, one essential and one optional. The essential part simulates the structure of the pre-existing markets for the production-automation devices. These markets are of varying size and profitability. They are designed in such a way that the initial situation for the UK producer is viable but not particularly profitable.

The GDR market can be introduced into the set of markets already supplied by "abandoning" the least profitable of the existing markets.

Alternatively, the UK producer can attempt to achieve economies of scale, increasing total production and sales, by the addition of the GDR market to existing commitments. Either way, profitability will be enhanced, even at prices and volumes that may seem superficially not to be very attractive. This enhanced profitability will, however, only be achieved at a reasonable volume of business.

The optional part of the model would be a production simulation, similar to but less elaborate than the GDR production model. Such a model of the UK production company has not yet been constructed and, initially at least, this part of the total simulation is represented only by a price/volume relation, subject to some degree of uncertainty concerning delivery from the factory. The remaining, essential part of the UK model, is therefore portrayed as the international marketing subsidiary of the parent production company.

In summary the team responsible for managing this UK supplier company must find a favorable strategic concept, enter into negotiations with the team of the GDR Kombinat, and run the game in such a way as to maximize the profit margin on all sales of equipment.

3.2. The GDR Producer

The GDR team acts as the top management of the industrial combine Kombinat, being responsible for producing and marketing private cars.

The team activities aim at showing how

- The planning system is realized in a socialist economy;
- The macroeconomic interdependence of various factors is taken into consideration;
- Import and export transactions are initiated and realized; and
- Import-export business on the basic principle of mutual advantage can stimulate the production of high quality goods on very efficient production lines.

There are several stages in the decision-making process in the game for the GDR team:

(a) Elaboration of a market analysis. Background papers show the team members how the market for private cars is likely to develop in the forthcoming periods (2-3 years). There are three market areas: the internal market, the socialist currency area, and the nonsocialist currency area. The market research for the nonsocialist currency area is provided in this game by the team representing the UK distributor. This area is therefore identical with the UK market for private cars from Kombinat. The market analysis will show the necessity of increasing production in order to meet the higher demand.

(b) Business policy and the planning of the production process. The first step is an assessment of the balance between existing production capacity and the given supply targets. At the beginning of the game there is insufficient capacity available. Because there is full employment in the GDR and labor is relatively scarce, the business policy must take into consideration alternatives such as:

- Increasing the level of technology on existing production lines;
- Improving research and development;
- Devoting more resources to manpower training; and
- Investing in new and very efficient equipment.

In realizing the planned targets, the team members have to allocate funds to the first three of these measures in accordance with data provided by the KOMBINAT simulation model.

In order to implement investments, special negotiations have to take place because the necessary equipment has to be imported from the UK supplier company. This stage involves activities such as:

- Asking for a tender;
- Taking the decision to import after having established that this is feasible as regards the balance of foreign currency;
- Awarding the contract; and
- Delivering and installing the equipment.

(c) The simulation process. The simulation is implemented using the computer program package KOMBINAT-2 (see Gernert and Messerschmidt, 1982). This model was developed in the Department of Statistics, Section of Economic Science, in cooperation with the computer center, at the Humboldt University, Berlin. So that it could be included in the international simulation discussed here, the existing BES-1 model (see Chapter V:b in this volume) had to be altered and adapted to fit into the economic framework of the joint game. Some parts of the algorithm of the BES-1 model were also used in the new program. The KOMBINAT-2 model is able to simulate the behavior of an industrial combine consisting of two or more plants. The decisions taken at the level of the Kombinat management concern production, turnover, investment, research and development, raw material purchases, manpower, working conditions, profit appropriation, etc. The Kombinat team has to disaggregate the proposed plan targets and reconcile them with the available resources of the individual plants.

The model is programmed in FORTRAN either for batch processing or for interactive use of display terminals. The simulation output shows how successful the team has been in fulfilling the given task: namely, increasing efficiency in producing more private cars for all markets.

After the simulation run, the GDR team has to negotiate the delivery of cars to the UK distributor. These three stages of the game are repeated for any further period.

3.3. The UK Distributor

The starting position of the second UK team is that contact has already been made with the Kombinat in the GDR. The team is provided with a short market survey indicating a possible niche for the GDR cars in the UK market, together with some fairly vague sales forecasts. The report recommends the setting up of a concessionaire in the UK. Information is also given about dealer mark-ups, desirable levels of spares, stocks, and so on. (During the first stage of the game there is only *one* UKD company. It is possible to enlarge the scale of the model in later stages to include alternative distributors.)

The internal details of the UK concessionaire model cover product design and quality, the recruitment of dealers and measures of their varying effectiveness, delivery reliability, the availability of spares and servicing, and finally, the stocks of the cars themselves.

The model generates demand data, using relevant parameters from the results of the trading and financial negotiations conducted with the GDR suppliers.

3.4. The Interface Between the Models

There is always a danger that computer-based business games may be seen by the participants, at least to some extent, as games against the computer. However, the skill or "gamesmanship" element of this particular exercise is actually deployed at the *negotiation* interface. The three models themselves play more of a background role.

It can be seen, of course, that the correct quantification of the interfaces between the models is crucial to making the whole exercise work. However, because of the modular arrangement of the models, the physical connection between the three teams can be established on paper. The participants elaborate their own strategic concepts and then have to carry through their various business policies into decision making, after negotiating with the other teams and with umpires representing the national economic environments in the UK and the GDR.

4. EXPERIENCE GAINED IN DEVELOPING THE GAME

From our experience of the development of this game, combined with the accumulated insight of several years of elaborating and using MSG, we can outline the following criteria for the successful development of such games:

- The process to be simulated should relate to a real-life problem, which may constitute a crucial problem area in the economy of the country concerned. The demonstration of the problem and its solution in practice become the main goals of the exercise.

- The subject of the game has to be modeled realistically in its full complexity, and the modelers must draw on expertise from many fields of knowledge (economics, managerial techniques, management accountancy, computer science, etc.).

- The structure of the model has to be flexible so that the game can be adapted easily to a changing economic environment.

- The description of the economic process simulated in the game may be generalized to a certain extent so that other institutions can also use the game successfully.

- Games with educational aims must clearly be in harmony with the educational philosophy of the institution involved.

- The level of complexity of the model must be a function of the time available to develop the game. Limited resources and time constraints can obviously limit the achievable degree of complexity of the game.

- Most of the MSGs are at least partly based on computerized simulation. Thus the technical specifications and availability of the hardware and software used must be taken into account in developing games which aim at wide usage.

REFERENCE

Gernert, H. and Messerschmidt, K. (1982). *Planspiel KOMBINAT 2*. Humboldt University, Berlin.

PART VII

GAMING FOR FUTURES RESEARCH
AND SCENARIO GENERATION

THE USE OF GAMING IN FUTURES RESEARCH AND PUBLIC POLICY MAKING[1]

Jan H.G. Klabbers
Department of Education, University of Utrecht and
Futures Research Unit, University of Leyden (The Netherlands)

1. INTRODUCTION

We will direct our attention to futures research on social systems, i.e., organizations, institutions, and societies. In this context we see futures research as the development and application of a methodology that will lead to better insights into possible (and desirable) future social systems and ways to reach them. Two aspects are central in this description: a view of the future, and an ability to shape the future.

Amara (1977) distinguishes the following characteristic features of the futures field. It is *visionary:* integrative and strategic, with a temporal focus seldom less than five years ahead, and usually twenty years or more in the future. It is *analytical:* multidisciplinary and methodological, with special emphasis on explicitness in forecasting, modeling, scenario building, and related activities. And it is *participatory:* problem- and implementation-oriented with particular attention paid to the social and political aspects of planning.

Subsequently he describes five basic functions in the futures field that combine the three features:

1. Goal Formulation. This function includes issue or problem definition, creation of future images, and generation of alternative futures. It is directly related to the visionary component of the futures field.

2. Method Development. This function includes the development of a body of explicit knowledge for surveying the future. This function stems from the analytical or research component of the futures field (together with applications).

3. Applications. One of the practical objectives of the futures field is to provide inputs to planning and decision-making processes by helping to expand the range of useful alternatives, evaluate consequences of such alternatives, and structure programs of intervention or action. This function may or may not involve the application of formal methodologies.

4. Coupling. This function is related to the assimilation of results of futures research by intended users - individuals, groups or organizations. The objective is to influence perceptions, attitudes, and behavior.

5. Implementation. This function includes the interventions and actions carried out to realize the objectives of a plan. At the same time it provides feedback, which may lead to adjustment of goals, development of new methods, or initiation of modified programs of action.

For our purposes we will perceive these five functions as the main steps in problem-oriented futures research of social systems. They form a cycle in which research is part of a broader process of social change. This cycle represents the accumulation, although not linearly, of knowledge, skill, and experience within the scientific community. If one adds to the five functions the subsequent phases of a policy-making process, the *Macro-cycle* of policy-oriented research is obtained (Figure 1).

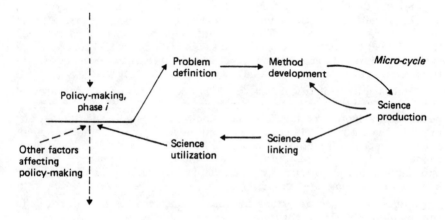

Figure 1. The macro-cycle.

It is reasonable to assume that, at each of the six steps in this macro-cycle, different people will contribute to its progress. They differ with respect to motivation, knowledge, skill, experience, and responsibility.

Between Method Development and Science Production, it is possible to distinguish another cycle, which includes the processes of abstraction, deduction, and realization. This cycle, the *Micro-cycle*, represents mainly basic and applied research.

We will start discussing the micro-cycle to show the underlying principles and to point out conditions for the successful application of research in the policy-oriented macro-cycle. The central theme in discussion of the micro-cycle is the development and use of simulation and gaming to improve the interface between research and policy making and to improve the policy-making process itself.

2. THE MICRO-CYCLE

2.1. Introduction

The micro-cycle consists of: (1) abstraction; (2) deduction; and (3) realization (Figure 2).

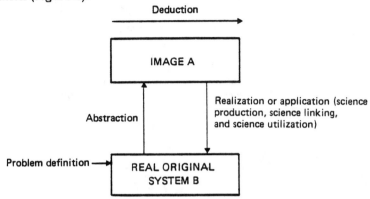

Figure 2. The micro-cycle.

During the development of a model, an image A is designed from the original B. Depending on the problem definition, particular variables and relationships can be mapped into the image system. This procedure of choosing the relevant variables is defined as *abstraction*. After the model or image system has been constructed, it can be manipulated and analyzed so that conclusions can be drawn. This stage is called *deduction*. The next stage is to verify the conclusions. This stage is called *realization* or *application*.

A rule of correspondence has to be established between the original system B and the image system A. This implies that important characteristics of the social system involved have to be included in the image system. Two features of a social system have to be taken into account: complexity and uncertainty.

Complexity results from the large number of aspects that have to be considered, their interrelationships, and the many ways in which the system can be described.

Uncertainty is a consequence of our lack of knowledge about the system, of the unpredictability of specific future events, and of factors such as value judgements and political actions. To deal with these factors, models of social systems should be open to influences both from the environment and from within, caused by decision-making (policy-making) processes. Uncertainty about the behavior of a system arises partly from its complexity, partly from environmental conditions.

2.2. Hierarchical Approach and Interactive Simulation

The hierarchical approach is a suitable way to deal with complexity. The system is divided into subsystems, which will be described and analyzed subsequently. Partial solutions of subsystem problems are integrated (coordinated) according to a hierarchy of decision problems in order to reach a general description and a general solution.

Generally, three different strata are distinguished in the hierarchy: a causal stratum, a decision-making stratum, and a norm stratum. The causal stratum is related to that system of activities through which the input-output processes, e.g., material flows, are accomplished. In the decision-making stratum several layers can be distinguished, e.g., goal, policy, strategy, and implementation layers. Finally, the norm stratum is related to norms and values and the way these govern decision-making. Higher levels in the hierarchy deal with global and long-term decisions, while the lower levels deal with more specific and short-term decisions. Both the decision-making and the norm strata define the purpose of the system and consequently how the system responds to influences from the environment and from within. The causal stratum and part of the decision-making stratum can be described by mathematical models, which can be simulated on a computer.

To deal with uncertainty, the system described in a hierarchical way can be embedded in an "interactive simulation". The way the strata are mapped into an interactive simulation is shown in Figure 3.

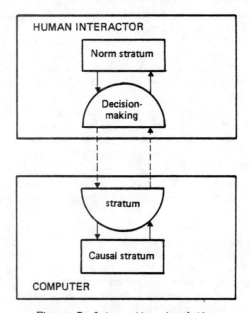

Figure 3. Interactive simulation.

The most interesting characteristic of interactive simulation is that man and computer cooperate during the evolution of the system. The interactor, who can choose from a number of alternatives, observes the system behavior that results from his decisions and the structure of the causal model. After each time increment the behavior is evaluated and, if the system does not respond as desired, decisions are adjusted for the next increment. Interactors integrate available knowledge, adapt to changing conditions, and make decisions based on their knowledge, skills, norms, and values. The computer performs the logical numeric operations in a fast and efficient way. In the integrated set-up of interactive simulation, man and computer represent the model of the real system.

In policy-oriented futures research on social systems it is important to realize that planning decisions result from complex interactions among several groups of actors. These groups have different objectives, different modes of organization and operation, different perceptions of reality, and different degrees and kinds of power to shape events (Hall, 1980).

Because of this quality of social systems we thought it appropriate to integrate interactive simulation with gaming simulation. Gaming simulation has proven to be a flexible approach in dealing with groups of people engaged in very divergent activities. With regard to the hierarchical approach, gaming integrated with interactive simulation assists the development of multi-level structures of social systems. It brings the characteristics of the image system closer to reality. Against this background we would like to stress that interactive simulation integrates all-computer simulation, with strong emphasis on a rational and calibrated approach, and gaming, which is more susceptible to an intuitive approach.

3. AN INTERACTIVE SIMULATION/GAME FOR THE MICRO-CYCLE

An interactive simulation/game is developed in three stages (Figure 4):

1. Development of the simulation model.
2. Embedding of the simulation model in an interactive simulation.
3. Embedding of the interactive simulation in a game.

Each stage provides a product that can be analyzed in its own right. Stage-specific goals are listed below.

1. Goals of all-computer simulation are related mainly to analysis of social systems at the technoeconomic level, emphasizing the quantitative aspects.
2. Goals of man-computer simulation incorporate the previous goals but also include more qualitative aspects of individual human behavior such as transfer of information and skills of interaction with the dynamic elements of the simulation model, the study of individual values and norms, and exploration of how to cope with complex phenomena.

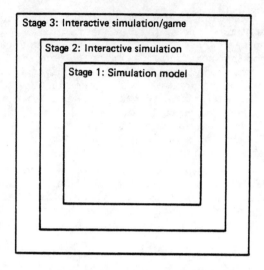

Figure 4. Structure of an interactive simulation/game.

3. Goals of gaming incorporate the previous goals but are also related to interaction within and between groups, to human organizational aspects, and to communication, social learning, and policy formation.

The development of an interactive simulation starts with identification of the problem (problem definition) and finishes with an interactive simulation/game. This instrument can be used to make deductions at the level of the simulation model, of the interactive simulation, and of the interactive simulation/game. With this instrument it is possible, in a participatory mode of policy formation and planning, to engage all persons involved in policy dialogues, which are supported by research. A policy dialogue is a discussion about policy problems, causes, impacts, and options (Klabbers et al., 1980).

Using these ideas about the micro-cycle, we can now connect the micro-cycle with the macro-cycle.

4. EMBEDDING THE MICRO-CYCLE IN THE MACRO-CYCLE

4.1. Introduction

When the link between Methods Development and Science Production (Figure 1) is considered from the point of view of design and use of simulation and gaming, in dialogue with a client system, we have a flexible and powerful tool to embed in the policy-oriented macro-cycle. This is especially useful in important policy matters affecting a nation as a whole, to be dealt with by upper-level policy makers.

In this regard simulation/gaming is able not only to provide specialized scientific knowledge, but also, in particular, to suggest collaborative arrangements compatible with the nature of utilization of knowledge and with the existing systems of inquiry used to obtain and process information.

A series of simulations/games, with participants representing all groups involved in the policy formation process, will create situations that mirror the complexities of the actual situation, will indicate to policy makers what they have to know, and will help them understand which decisions should be made using data and which ones should be made on the basis of non-research knowledge (because they depend on value judgements or political prerogatives, for example).[2]

Simulation/gaming is able to enlighten problem solving, policy formation, and policy making through the new concepts that it either provides or stimulates. We realize, however, that the potential of this methodology has only partly been explored and used for these purposes.

4.2. Level of Policy Making and Type of Gaming

Now we will direct our attention to some general notions about policy making and social systems to provide a frame of reference for embedding the micro-cycle in the macro-cycle.

Starting the macro-cycle with Problem Definition, we have to realize that the level of policy making is crucial to the issues involved and the way knowledge will be used, i.e., either instrumental or conceptual utilization. We assume that upper-level policy making mainly deals with long-term issues. Over the long term, social systems are ill-defined and poorly structured.

Middle-level, bureaucratic policy making, dealing with issues over a shorter term than upper-level policy making, tends to be narrower in scope. Caplan states that the application of knowledge at this level "involves the use of data ordered by the end user, produced by the user's agency and most often applied with a view of improving management of the agency's internal operations".

As the time horizon for policy making decreases, the structure of the social systems becomes better defined. Policy makers concentrate more on improving management of internal operations and thus try to reinforce or even optimize the parameters of the existing structure. High-level policy making, in its turn, tends to be less inward-looking, and is more open to information from the environment of the social system and thus more apt to establish new structures to cope with changing conditions.

Let us assume that a research project is set up to provide information for use by policy makers. It will be clear, from insights gained from the links between research and policy making, that it is important to know for which level of policy making the results (instruments) will be suitable. The content and meaning of Problem Definition will depend on the level of the policy-making process. As a consequence, the design of an interactive simulation/game and the final product will be influenced by this level, and the linking and utilization of knowledge will follow a certain route. However, the methodology dealing with the micro-cycle provides the flexibility to take into account and adjust to these circumstances.

Let us first look at the case when the macro-cycle starts with Problem Definition at the *middle level* of policy making. It seems reasonable to assume that the structure of the social system is set. Because of the ongoing administrative and information processes, many decisions tend to become more routine. As policies and programs are rather well defined within that structure, the interpretative context is also established fairly well. In terms of the strata mentioned earlier, it is also reasonable to assume that the causal stratum and part of the decision-making stratum are well defined.

An interactive simulation/game based on such a system follows fixed procedures for designing and conducting the game, in agreement with the real situation. Such an interactive simulation/game will be classified as a rigid-rule game. The aim of a rigid-rule game in general is to improve or reinforce the existing social structure, independent of whether the game is used for educational, research, or practical purposes.

Let us next assume that the macro-cycle starts with Problem Definition at the *upper level* of policy making. At this level the structure of the social system is assumed to be poorly defined. Policy making at this level establishes notions of acceptable structures and arranges procedures and conditions for society in the future. The interpretative context is only vaguely known, and, therefore, so are the "ins and outs" of the system.

An interactive simulation/game based on such a situation follows a more open procedure for designing and conducting the game, also in agreement with the real situation. Such an interactive simulation/game will be classified as a free-form or frame game. The aim of a free-form game is to establish a satisfactory structure, independent of educational, research or practical purposes of the game. With the use of such a game the interpretative context of the social system for the long term may be established.

In both situations mentioned above, the systems approach and the method of interactive simulation are methods of inquiry rather than tools *per se*.

4.3. Phases of Policy-Making Process and Types of Gaming

We next consider the use of an interactive simulation/game at different phases of the policy-making process. Mitchell (1980), in discussing an empirical study of social science utilization among state legislators, distinguishes four phases of decision making:

- Articulation
- Aggregation
- Allocation
- Oversight

(The macro-cycle (see Figure 1) is connected to each of these phases.)

During the articulation phase, social science serves primarily to conceptualize the policy issue (enactment) and define subgroups within major interest groups. Utilization of social science during the aggregation phase is more concerned with problem solving and coalition building. During the allocation phase, the main impact of social science is related to evidence assessment and persuasion. Finally, when the legislative oversight phase starts, social science is mainly involved in evaluation and criticism.

During the articulation phase, the macro-cycle should provide knowledge to enhance the conceptualization of the problem. In this respect, free-form games seem most appropriate. During the aggregation phase, when groups focus on problem solving, rigid-rule games seem to be more suitable. In both cases the gaming aspect, i.e., communication within and between groups of policy makers, is most important. When a policy-making process enters the allocation phase, rigid-rule games will be useful, but emphasis may be placed more upon the simulation part of the game, for example, to perform cost-benefit analysis. If simulation/gaming is applied to policy making, it seems most suitable during these three stages.

4.4. Gaming and the Gestalt of the Situation

One of the main results of systems research in general, and of simulation/gaming in particular, is that the research team develops a systems view, or gestalt, in which the relationship between state description (structure) and process description (function) can be articulated well. A major problem is how that systems perspective can be communicated to the user, who normally lacks the time, skill, or motivation to become familiar with the image system, i.e., the model and its behavior.

In this regard, interactive simulation/gaming is not only an instrument for analysis, but is at the same time an instrument for communicating a systems perspective in a client-oriented rather than a method-oriented mode. In an interactive simulation/game participants become directly involved in simulating reality. In doing so, they not only use cognitive skills, but also exchange experience and knowledge that are based, to some extent, on intuition and beliefs. While interacting with the computer, participants also communicate with each other, within and between groups. Every participant and every group develops an image of the system, relying both on instrumental and conceptual information.

Because of social interaction during the game, an individual's image of the system is much richer than it would be after reading a technical report of the research, for example. There is no guarantee that the user, having read a report, has gained experience in using the particular information, or that he knows how to translate the results into long-range policies or daily decisions. Therefore, in this context an interactive simulation/game is more suitable. At the middle level of policy making, it leads to better insight into the qualities of the existing structure of the social system. At the upper level, it gives a better insight into the qualities of new structures and their possible consequences for members of the system, e.g., citizens, professional policy makers, and action groups.

The body of knowledge of social systems consists of both common sense and scientific knowledge. Interactive simulation makes it possible to confront one with the other. The more fruitful this confrontation is with respect to social problem solving, the more effective will be the linking process.

5. SUMMARY

The main ideas of the paper can perhaps be summed up in the following ten statements.

1. The aim of middle-level policy making is more concerned with optimizing the parameters of the existing structure, while the aim of upper-level policy making is directed more to establishing new structures.

2. Simulation/gaming should take into account these levels of policy making. A rigid-rule game is more suitable for middle-level policy making, while a free-form game is more suitable for upper-level policy making.

3. A client, i.e., a policy maker, usually lacks the time, skill, or motivation to become familiar with the model and its behavior.

4. An interactive simulation/game is not only an instrument for analysis, but is also an instrument for communicating a systems perspective in a client-oriented rather than a method-oriented way.

5. There is no guarantee that the policy maker, having read a technical report, has gained experience in using the content of the report, or that he knows how to translate its results into long-range policies or daily decisions.

6. Policy making and planning are processes of continuous, although not linear, incremental learning, evaluation, and modification. Policy makers are willing to take advantage of scientific knowledge of social systems to improve the policy-making process.

7. Synthesis of knowledge from sub-disciplinary research into an integrated body of knowledge is lacking. The way scientific research is budgeted reinforces this situation. It hampers the progress and utilization of the social sciences in particular.

8. The interface between research and (public) policy making, and thus communication between representatives of both groups, is inadequate.

9. Problem definition improves with a growing awareness of the characteristics of the system. The more explicit the assumptions underlying the interactive simulation/game, the better the instrument is able to stimulate discussion of problem definition, future images, and so on.

10. Interactive simulation/gaming facilitates the mixture of analytical and interactive problem solving. It enlightens problem solving (policy making) through the new concepts that it either provides or stimulates.

REFERENCES

Amara, R. (1977). The futures field: functions, forms and critical issues. In W.I. Boucher (Ed.), *The Study of the Future.*

Caplan, N. (1981). *Social Research and Public Policy at the National Level.* Invited paper for the SVO-Workshop on Educational Research and Public Policy Making, 20-22 May 1981, The Hague.

Hall, P. (1980). Great planning disasters. What lessons do they hold? *Futures,* 12(1): 45-50.

Klabbers, J.H.G. (1975). General system theory and social systems: a methodology for the social sciences. *Nederlands Tijdschrift voor de Psychologie,* 30: 493-514.

Klabbers, J.H.G. (1979). The process of model building and analysis of social systems. *Progress in Cybernetics and Systems Research,* IV. Hemisphere Publications Corporation, Washington, D.C.

Klabbers, J.H.G. (1982). Futures research and public policy-making. In D. Kallen et al. (Eds.), *Social Science Research and Public Policy Making: A Reappraisal.* NFER-Nelson Publishing Company, Windsor, United Kingdom, pp. 94-126.

Klabbers, J.H.G., Van der Hyden, P.P., Hoefnagels, K., and Truin, G.J. (1980). Development of an interactive simulation game: a case study of DENTIST. *Simulation and Games,* 11 (1): 59-86.

Mitchell, D.E. (1980). Social science impact on legislative decision making: process and substance. *Educational Researcher,* 9 (10).

NOTES

1. This chapter is a condensed version of an article (Klabbers, 1982) published in D. Kallen et al. (Eds.), *Social Science Research and Public Policy Making: A Reappraisal,* and appears here by permission of the publisher, NFER-Nelson Publishing Company. See also Klabbers (1975, 1979) and Klabbers et al. (1980).

2. By stressing the versatility of simulation/gaming from rigid-rule to free-form games, we have paraphrased certain conditions of knowledge utilization mentioned by Caplan (1981).

GAMING AS AN INSTRUMENT FOR FUTURES RESEARCH

Ryszard Wasniowski
Futures Research Center, Technical University of Wroclaw,
Wroclaw (Poland)

1. INTRODUCTION

A growing awareness that many of the decisions taken today will have very long-term consequences makes it increasingly necessary for society and individual decision makers to consider and plan for their future responsibilities. At the same time, a number of these decisions assume large-scale and sweeping socioeconomic and technological changes will take place; moreover, the pace of changes which directly impinge on individuals and society is accelerating. As a result of these developments there is an increasing need for the integration of knowledge concerning social and sociotechnological systems and for better tools for policy formulation and implementation.

In this chapter we shall first discuss the potential of "futures research" for fulfilling this need and next examine the use of gaming within this field. We shall then discuss some work in progress at Wroclaw's Futures Research Center (FRC). Here an interdisciplinary research team is studying and analyzing systems of different natures, with special emphasis on decision-making processes, in order to assess and improve long-range planning and strategy formulation. Within this context we will discuss futures research using gaming in two specific areas: regional development and the computer industry.

2. FUTURES RESEARCH

Futures research is a relatively new field, about which there exists considerable confusion. It has gained widespread publicity during the last decade in the course of producing a number of much-discussed "world models", but the term "futures research" still leads to some misunderstanding. In the sense that we understand it, futures research means an attempt to foresee the future development of a given system. The aim of systematic research on the future is to make statements about possible real future developments on the basis of presently available concrete data.

The results of futures research can be applied in many areas of life. Usually, futures research is undertaken for a specific client. We are personally interested in the use of futures research results for planning. Here the most direct effect is usually on normative planning, which in turn influences strategic, tactical, and operational planning (see Figure 1).

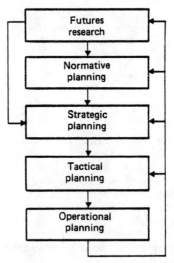

Figure 1. The role of futures research in the planning process.

In the last few decades several important books have appeared which attempt to delineate a methodology for futures research. The literature in this area deals with several aims: these include setting general goals for futures research, outlining methods to be used in futures research, and providing frameworks within which futures research can be carried on. Helmer (1966) argues that the future can be investigated systematically through a three-step process:

- Constructing forecasts delineating obvious major changes;
- Constructing more imaginative projections of presently unanticipated changes; and
- Determining which forecasts are most compatible with dominant social values and preferences.

For this school of thought, then, the purpose of futures research is not merely to predict the future but to help to create it.

3. GAMING IN FUTURES RESEARCH

Just as the field of futures research itself is difficult to define, not much consensus exists on how to describe and categorize the tools and approaches that are used in the field. The most useful tools are those that permit us to include the human factor in the research. This is the reason why *gaming*, in which human players work with a representation of a system and make choices based on perceived or expected outcomes, has been introduced into the basic methodological approaches (see Table 1).

Table 1. Three types of methodological approach (after Amara, 1981).

Perceptual	Structural	Participative
Selecting	Connecting	*GAMING*
Eliciting	Relating	Role playing
Distilling	Modeling	Conflict resolving

The three types of approach distinguished in Table 1 concern different, though related, aspects of futures research: affecting people's perceptions of the future, analyzing the structure of problems and alternative choices, and participating in decision making.

The term "gaming" has many different connotations. In order that the following discussion be precisely understood some introductory definitions[1] must be made. We define the "game situation" as one involving at least two decision makers (players) whose choices noticeably influence each other. The "game" is defined as the model of a game situation and the term "game playing" is reserved for the manipulation of this game by at least two independent players. The term "interactive", which is very relevant to our interests, means that each decision maker supplies his decisions several times, in most cases after having received feedback on the effects of earlier decisions in the game. Gaming, finally, is understood here specifically as interactive game playing.

As regards futures studies, we see gaming as a class of participative methods of involving people in experimenting with alternatives, so as to understand them more fully before making choices or implementing alternatives. We will discuss later why we regard gaming as one of the most important tools for futures researchers, describing gaming situations in which human players work with a representation of a system in which choices are made in response to perceived or desired outcomes. Gaming is then a form of role playing by a group of individuals who represent different interests as well as a joint problem-solving and mediation technique for reconciling differences in the desired outcomes.

Gaming is used in such situations to stimulate the interest of various "actors", and also

- To provoke discussion aimed at better recognition of future possibilities and consequences;
- To deliver more complete information to decision makers about the potential consequences of their decisions; and
- To develop alternative strategies.

In this connection it should be stressed that the futures research process is not a mechanical, unidirectional progression from problem formulation through logical steps to analysis and conclusions, but rather a complex process of feedback and reconsideration. During the course of the research unexpected constraints may be discovered, or new opportunities opened up that lead to new approaches or a redesign of research methods. In practice, futures research involving gaming consists of the steps outlined in Figure 2.

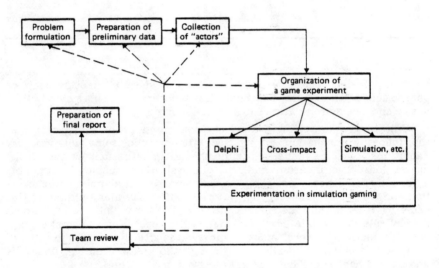

Figure 2. The main elements in futures research using gaming.

4. COMPUTER-AIDED GAMING FOR REGIONAL DEVELOPMENT

As an example of the use of gaming in long-range planning, we will examine a game developed for the Jelenia Gora area, not far from Wroclaw. The game was initiated by the Jelenia Gora Regional Planning Agency and its aim was to aid decision makers in the formulation of strategies for regional development. More specifically, the object was to confront the participants with possible future events influencing regional development, thereby generating discussion leading to recognition of future needs and opportunities and formulation of alternative courses of action.

The game has usually been played by four groups, each having between three and seven players. The players have mainly been middle-management staff from regional planning organizations. One group plays the role of "society", i.e., the people of the area concerned. The other groups, the "sector teams", play the roles of major regional development sectors, e.g., agriculture, industry, and tourism. The players also interact with the game director who represents the outside world. Prior to the actual game, the participants (planners and managers) are given an overview of the issues facing the Jelenia Gora region; they are thus better prepared for participating in the game and interpreting its results.

The game director initially provides the players with an intentionally but realistically incomplete description of the regional development prospects for Jelenia Gora over the next two decades. The "society team" gets more information than the "sector teams", which must analyze the information and try to build a better picture by discussion with the "society team" and the game director. This enables the "sector teams" to identify possibilities and to allocate the funds available in each period accordingly. In addition, they may choose to implement a variety of different development policies. Most of the requests for information, as well as decisions on allocation of funds, etc., are input to a computer model. The computer calculates the effect of the players' decisions and these effects are then assessed by the society team.

Although the game in its full form is dependent on minicomputer support, it can, with some constraints, also be played manually. The game, covering 4 periods of 5 years each, takes roughly 2.5 hours to play. It was developed in 1979 and has since been played several times at seminars in the region. In view of the favorable response from planners the gaming activity has continued.

To extend the possibilities for studying regional development problems still further we have developed a generalized simulation system which can work symbiotically with other methods for futures research, such as Delphi and cross-impact techniques,[2] and which functions interactively by getting the "players" into the act.

The gaming experiment was regarded as an instructive experience with regard to strategic planning by the regional planners and researchers involved. The use of gaming by experienced practitioners permitted very rapid, yet in-depth coverage of a complex subject area. The participatory nature of the technique ensured that a high degree of group consensus was maintained for successively more complex game runs. This last point is of particular interest for the field of regional development, which requires numerous ideas, attitudes, and viewpoints to be taken into account.

5. CROSS-IMPACT GAMING FOR THE PERSONAL-COMPUTER INDUSTRY

For a mature industry, such as those producing shoes or steel, it is often sufficient to extrapolate current trends to forecast the future. A more sophisticated analysis may take into account foreseeable changes that could have an impact on the industry, such as demographic changes. Such simplistic approaches are not, however, adequate for a dynamic, emerging industry such as that producing personal computers (Gray, 1980). We shall now briefly describe the approach used during 1980 at the Futures Research Center to evaluate the future of the computing industry, in particular as regards personal computers.

In addition to attempting to predict the future, gaming should, according to our philosophy, play a part in designing a desirable future. Managers responsible for various parts of the organization studied should therefore participate in the gaming activity. Emphasis is then placed on the *process of planning* rather than on the resulting plan. The process adopted for developing alternative futures involves three main activities:

- Generating an information base;
- Generating alternative futures for the external environment perceived by the organization; and
- Generating alternative futures for the organization itself.

This process is illustrated in Figure 3.

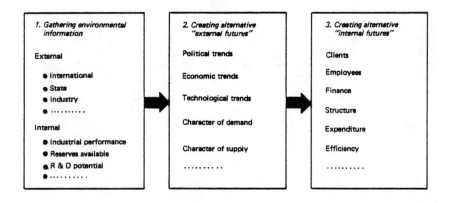

Figure 3. The process of developing alternative futures.

The purpose of our experiment was to guide governmental policy makers in Poland, and in particular those concerned with the computer industry in Wroclaw, through developing a number of alternative strategies for the future development of the industry. We also had a number of more research-oriented goals: learning to apply various techniques of futures research (including gaming) and attempting to integrate these techniques to construct a research tool for strategic planning.

At the beginning of our work we identified a number of issues and policy areas for consideration, including education, business, trade, implications for telecommunications, etc., by a process of literature searches and lectures from experts in various fields.

Next, a Delphi inquiry[3] was carried out among 60 Polish scientists and engineers working on computer development; the inquiry, involving some 50 questions, went through five rounds. The Delphi inquiry resulted in the generation of various scenarios as regards computers in the year 1985, of the type presented in Table 2.

Table 2. Examples of Delphi scenarios for personal computers in 1985.

Area	Scenario 1	2	3
Hardware cost ($)	1,000	500	250
Sales (units)	300,000	8,000,000	18,000,000
Programming	Basic	Precoded	Precoded
Memory (kb)	64	512	1,000
Major use	Hobby, education	Business	Business, home
Interface	Keyboard	Keyboard	Keyboard, light pens
Mass storage	Cassettes	Floppy disk	Floppy disk

The Delphi inquiry also generated a list of possible events and trends. From this our research team selected, for the next stage of the gaming, a set $(e_1, e_2, \ldots, e_n)$ of possible *events* and a set $(t_1, t_2, \ldots, t_m)$ of *trends*. In this way, we compiled a starting list of events:

- A large company entering the personal computer (PC) market;
- The CMEA entering the PC market;
- European companies entering the US PC market as major competitors; and
- Governments in various important countries requiring registration of PC designs and imposing annual license fees; etc.

and a similar list of starting trends:

- Cost of the mid-range PC;
- Expected sales of PCs;
- Number of PCs used in education;
- Number of homes using PCs; and
- Number of jobs created by the PC industry, etc.

We then formulated a starting list of actors (including the United States, the Soviet Union, the CMEA countries, Japan, etc.) and their respective objectives. We next organized a cross-impact gaming experiment with ten specially selected experts.[4] The important part of the experiment is the establishment of the coefficients in the cross-impact matrix which had the following format:

	e_1	e_2	.....	e_n	t_1	t_2	.....	t_m
e_1								
e_2								
⋮		P_{ij}						
e_n								
t_1								
t_2								
⋮								
t_m								

p_{ij} is an example of a coefficient representing the impact that the occurrence of the event e_i has on the occurrence of the event e_j in the next time step. The idea is to link together those events which have some kind of causal relationship. If one event occurs, the likelihood of certain other events soon occurring may increase. For example, how will the entry of a major computer manufacturer, like IBM, into the PC market affect the likelihood of later European entry into the US PC market? Probably negatively, implying a negative value for p.

The cross-impact experiment consisted of the following steps:

- Presentation of collected data to the participants;
- Assessment of the coefficient in the cross-impact matrix by the participants;
- Assessment of the effects on the game of random changes in the probabilities of certain events and trends;

- Discussion of the results of a given step in the game;
- Return to previous steps; and
- Preparation of an overview of the complete experiment.

As a result of these gaming experiments using the cross-impact technique, the research team generated various divergent scenarios. Some examples are as follows:

Scenario A. Japan, making use of its achievements in the field of microcomputer chips, is conquering the world computer market. The US government undertakes action aimed at encouraging West-European countries to advance their computer technology too, in order for the US to gain partners for cooperation.

Scenario B. The Soviet Union, recognizing that the development of personal computers is an important strategic task, makes rapid progress in this field so that the competitiveness of its products on the world market is developed.

Scenario C. Taiwan, South Korea, Singapore, Brazil, and Mexico enter the personal computer market. As is already the case for TV sets, they produce high-quality products at competitive prices.

Scenario D. The US government, acknowledging the importance of having an advanced PC industry, takes specific protective action for this industry.

These and several other scenarios were used to provide background information for discussion of strategy formulation in a research institute associated with a major computer company, and also within the board of directors of the company itself. Several board members regarded this material as helpful.

REFERENCES

Amara, R. (1981). The futures field: searching for definitions and boundaries. *The Futurist*, February: 25-29.
Dalkey, N. and Helmer, O. (1963). An experimental application of the Delphi method to the use of experts. *Management Science*, 9.
Gray, P. (1980). *Using Futures Research Methods to Assess Policy Implications of the Personal Computer*. University of Southern California, Los Angeles. (Mimeograph.)
Helmer, O. (1966). *Social Technology*. Basic Books Inc., New York.
Helmer, O. (1978). *Cross-Impact Gaming Applied to Global Resources*. RM-78-4. International Institute for Applied Systems Analysis, Laxenburg, Austria.

NOTES

1. Here we try to follow the terminology used in Chapter III:a of this volume.

2. These two techniques are discussed below in connection with the game on the computer choice.

3. The Delphi method is a procedure for eliciting quantitative but subjective opinions from various experts. The procedure aims at some degree of consensus by feeding back others' opinions and allowing group members to reassess their initial judgements. The method depends upon anonymous judgements, feedback indicating the degree of opinion diversity, and a willingness of people to compromise on opinions not strongly held. For details, see Dalkey and Helmer (1963).

4. For a brief review of the cross-impact gaming methodology see Helmer (1978).

THE ROLE OF GAMING AND SIMULATION IN SCENARIO PROJECTS

H.A. Becker
University of Utrecht, Utrecht (The Netherlands)

1. INTRODUCTION

1.1. Background

Imagine a policy maker who is confronted with a tricky problem in some social system. It is obvious to him that the elimination of this problem will demand a lot of time and effort. He suspects that there are a number of solutions to the problem, each with its own advantages and disadvantages. He also suspects that the behavior of the social system will contain a lot of surprises. In a situation like this, the policy maker could use *scenarios* to prepare the discussion that will ultimately lead to a policy decision.

Scenarios are the outcome of a *scenario project*. In the example just given, a scenario project would examine the following questions:

1. What exactly is the social problem involved, and what brought it into existence?
2. How did the social system involved behave in the past, and what is its most likely behavior in the future?
3. How does the policy maker want the social system to behave after the problem has been eliminated?
4. What are the strategies that could lead to the elimination of the problem? What are the costs and benefits of each strategy?
5. Which of the strategies is the optimal one? How could this strategy be implemented?

In theory, a policy maker could provide the answers to all of these questions himself, and if a small problem is involved, this may well be what happens. However, in practice most problems are quite complicated and a different approach must be adopted. In this case, the policy maker asks one or more social scientists to do the necessary groundwork and to draw up a set of scenarios for him. This type of work has now become a professional activity for social scientists, who use examples of past projects, literature on methods for designing scenarios, and previous experience accumulated in working with scenarios as the basis of their professional expertise.

In this paper four *questions* are examined: (a) What are the main characteristics of scenarios and of scenario projects? (b) What are the main phases in a scenario project, and what do they demand from the social scientist? (c) Where and how could gaming and simulation be used in each of these phases? (d) What will be the future of gaming and simulation within scenario projects?

This paper illustrates the answers to these questions with a project carried out by a team of social scientists working at the Department of Planning and Policy Studies at the University of Utrecht in The Netherlands. The project consisted of an evaluation of the methodological aspects of scenarios, the development of a "manual" for designing scenarios, and the execution of a number of experiments in scenario design. The scenarios studied were all concerned with possible developments in The Netherlands during the coming decades.[1]

1.2. Characteristics of Scenarios

The *Shorter Oxford English Dictionary* defines a scenario as "(a) a sketch of the plot of a play, giving particulars of the scenes, situations, etc., (b) the detailed directions for a cinema film". This definition adequately describes the early history of scenarios, which were originally confined to the realm of the theater and later adopted by the motion picture industry.

The military world was the next to take over the concept. Institutes like the Rand Corporation in Santa Monica were commissioned by the Defense Advanced Research Projects Agency and other authorities in the military field to develop methods for designing military strategies and determining which to choose. Military authorities have since used scenarios on quite a large scale. H. McIlvaine Parsons (1972) has described many of these models, defining scenarios as "verbal simulations", and contrasting them with computer simulations.

The fourth stage in the history of scenarios is again a civilian one. Scientists who had worked on military projects put their experience to use in designing scenarios for society in general, governments, business corporations, and voluntary organizations. An example of this stage is *The Year 2000* by Kahn and Wiener, published in 1967, which provides "a framework for speculation on the next thirty-three years". Kahn and Wiener define scenarios as "hypothetical sequences of events constructed for the purpose of focusing attention on causal processes and decision points. They answer two kinds of questions: (i) precisely how might some hypothetical situations come about, step by step? (ii) what alternatives exist, for each actor, at each step, for preventing, diverting or facilitating the process"?

Kahn and Wiener designed a *standard world*, starting from "surprise-free projections" of the past. They compared this standard world with three *canonical variations*. These are:

- A more *"integrated"* world (a relatively peaceful, relatively prosperous, relatively arms-controlled world with a relatively high degree of consultation among nations, and political coordination or even integration among all, or almost all, the major and/or minor powers);

- A more *"inward-looking"* world (almost as peaceful and prosperous as in the first variation, but with little arms control and general coordination);

- A world in greater *"disarray"* (a relatively troubled and violent world, but one in which no large central wars have occurred).

The approach of Kahn and Wiener is still used quite widely. In the French tradition of scenario design, for instance, a "standard world" is called a "trend scenario". Variations (canonical or more radical alternatives) are called "contrast scenarios". More recently, scenarios have been designed mainly by scientists from nonmilitary backgrounds and the method has lost most of its military associations.

As a second example we shall consider *Facing the Future*, the report of the INTERFUTURES project, which was published by the OECD in 1979. This publication, with the provocative subtitle "mastering the probable and managing the unpredictable", first puts forward a number of physical limits to growth up to the year 2000. This is followed by a description of four main scenarios, which may be summarized as follows:

Scenario A: collegial management of conflicts in the developed countries; increased free trade; increasing Third World participation in world economic exchanges; sustained economic growth in the developed countries, but no rapid changes in values.

Scenarios B1, B2, B3 assume the same as Scenario A as regards the nature of relations between developed countries, between developing countries, and between the two groups. On the other hand, the developed economies will experience only moderate growth, with other differences described by three alternative scenarios: B1 assumes rapid changes in values, B2 assumes convergence of the relative productivities of different countries, while B3 assumes divergence linked to social and institutional disparities between the various developed countries.

Scenario C was introduced in order to analyze the implications of a North-South confrontation. It assumes that a majority of developing countries choose to break their links with the developed nations.

Scenario D: disintegration of the developed-country group and mounting protectionism, with the emergence of zones of influence centered around three poles: the United States, the European Economic Community, and Japan.

Our third example is the report *Energy in a Finite World* (1981). The project first analyzes the dynamics of the global energy system over the past hundred years and then explores the limits of different primary energy sources over the next half century and beyond. Finally two "benchmark scenarios" labeled the "high scenario" and the "low scenario" are presented, together with three supplementary cases that are variations of the benchmark scenarios. The high scenario leads to a 2030 level of global primary energy consumption which is slightly more than four times the 1975 level of energy consumption, while the low scenario yields a global primary energy consumption in 2030 a little less than three times the 1975 level. In the IIASA report, scenarios are not "verbal simulations" (compare McIlvaine Parsons) but quantified policy alternatives within a computer simulation model.

In the Utrecht project mentioned earlier, a scenario was defined as "a description of (a) the present state of society (or some part of it), (b) feasible and desirable future states of that society and (c) sequences of events that could lead from the present state to the future states". This is a very broad definition of the term "scenario", which is often used in a more restricted sense that includes only elements (b) and (c). The manual developed in the Utrecht project contains a *typology* of scenarios that can be summarized as follows:

Degree of authenticity. Some scenarios are prescriptive, in that they provide us with ideas about a feasible and desirable course of action. In contrast to these "real" scenarios are the so-called *quasi-scenarios*, which represent situations quite different to those currently found in the real world - doomsday scenarios, for instance. Of the examples already given, the canonical variations of Kahn and Wiener, the INTERFUTURES scenarios, and the IIASA scenarios are all real scenarios. In the French tradition, quasi-scenarios are called "scenarios de l'inacceptable": these "scenarios of the unacceptable" are not meant to be realized in practice but are intended to shock and to provoke action (see Julien et al., 1975).

Scope. Scenarios range from *micro-scenarios* (dealing with a small community or small organization) through *meso-scenarios* (for a medium-sized community or medium-sized organization) to *macro-scenarios* (covering a whole country or an international system). All three examples given in this paper deal with macro-scenarios.

Degree of complexity. Scenarios may be either *multi-sectoral* (Kahn and Wiener, INTERFUTURES) or *mono-sectoral* (IIASA energy scenarios).

Perspective. Some scenarios are *projective*, looking from the present towards the future; good examples are the scenarios of Kahn and Wiener. Other scenarios start from a point in the future, and look back towards the present time; this *prospective* approach is sometimes described as an "inverse decision tree". The INTERFUTURES and IIASA scenarios belong to this category.

Degree of experimentation. Here we distinguish between scenarios that follow a *dominant* trend (such as the standard world of Kahn and Wiener) and scenarios that are at least partially *exploratory* (for example, Kahn and Wiener's canonical variations, and the INTERFUTURES and IIASA scenarios).

Degree of public support. Here we divide scenarios into two categories based on their degree of popular support. A *preferential* scenario is one that is supposed to be generally in harmony with public opinion (for instance, Kahn and Wiener, INTERFUTURES B, and the IIASA energy scenarios); all other scenarios are assumed to be based on *a priori* ideas conceived by the scenario builders or some other small elite group (INTERFUTURES C and D).

This short, preliminary typology only gives a rough idea of the ways in which scenarios can be classified. Scenario building is still a very young field, and clear-cut, stable categories cannot yet be defined.

2. PHASES OF A SCENARIO PROJECT

This section gives a rough *model* of a medium-sized scenario project, based upon the Utrecht manual mentioned earlier. Three main phases can be distinguished: an *initial phase*, a *main phase*, and a *rounding-off phase*. The subsections below describe the most important activities carried out by the scenario team during each phase, with particular emphasis upon the types of *gaming* employed. Table 1 provides an overview of this process. It should be realized that this is very much an idealized description; in reality steps may have to be duplicated, omitted, combined, executed in a reverse order, and so on.

2.1. Initial Phase

The basic groundwork is done in the first or initial phase of the project. This phase may also include a preliminary exploration of the design problems facing the team, and is quite often carried out as a *pilot project*.

Analyzing the Social Problem and Defining System Boundaries

The first task of the scenario designer or the scenario team is to analyze the *social problem* that has to be solved by the policy maker. Finsterbusch and Motz (1980) define a social problem as "a situation that many people consider adverse or intolerable in its effects on a large number of people over a long period of time"; they consider that social problems demand constructive change.

They continue by noting that social problems involve conflicting interests and cognitive disagreements. Because there is little unanimity among the various groups as to what the problem is and how it should be solved, the mitigation of social problems is a very complex process. According to Finsterbusch and Motz, administrators would be more effective if they were:

- Knowledgeable about the situation for which change is advocated;
- Aware of the conflicting groups, their different value judgements, and their aims;
- Free from any personal or official stake in the conflict or its resolution and thus able to see both the wood *and* the trees;
- Informed about the relationship between the *target population* (that is, the people whose lives are most directly affected by the social problem) and the conflicting advocates of change;

Table 1. Activities and types of gaming taking place in each phase of a scenario project.

Phase	Activity	Type of gaming used[a]
Initial	Analyzing the social problem and defining system boundaries	Brainstorming
	Preparing the project	
	Baseline analysis and analysis of possible futures	Delphi procedures
	First round of designing	Heuristic gaming
Main	Review of earlier steps	
	Second round of designing	Morphological analyses (heuristic gaming again)
	Comparison of the scenarios with the results of baseline analysis and analysis of possible futures	
	Third round of designing	Evaluative gaming
Rounding-off	Review of earlier steps	
	Reporting the results	Workshops with potential users
	Evaluation of the project	

[a]In this table gaming is interpreted in its broadest sense to include nonsimulation games such as "brainstorming". Most of the terms used here are explained in detail later in the text.

- Able to set priorities, recommend policies, and anticipate their potential impacts.

Parallel to defining the problem to be solved by policy action, the scenario team has to define the *target system* and its *systems environment*. Defining the problem and the system boundaries can only be done in a preliminary way in the initial phase; redefinition may prove to be necessary later on.

Preparing the Project

The next step is for the team to decide upon the type of scenarios that should be constructed. This choice may have many consequences. For example, if multisectoral scenarios are required, the project team should as a rule be multidisciplinary.

Most projects propose a number of scenarios and subscenarios, although sometimes only one scenario (for instance, a doomsday scenario) is given.

Baseline Analysis and Analysis of Possible Futures

The scenario team now executes a *baseline analysis*. This covers the historical developments in the target system and its environment that may have some relevance to the problem under study. A baseline analysis generally involves the analysis of time series data, *ad hoc* empirical studies to supplement the information from these data, and the theoretical interpretation of the past behavior of the target system and its environment. An *analysis of possible futures* is also carried out, looking at developments to come. These may be predictable enough to make highly reliable forecasts feasible, although more often a speculative exploration of the future is the only possible approach.

Initially, the suggested developments are simply spatial or temporal *projections* of observed behavior or trends. However, this is not generally sufficient for our purposes - we are also interested in the limits to development and the ways in which different types of development can be redirected or combined. A *sensitivity analysis* could be used to provide this additional information.

First Round of Designing

The initial phase also includes the preliminary design of *alternative futures* in which the social problem envisaged by the policy maker has been eliminated. These alternative futures are based mainly on *guiding images*. A guiding image is an aim that the policy maker and the other parties involved should try to achieve. Alternative futures may also include pictures of situations that are unavoidable or that can be tolerated. These *circumstantial images* may, for example, describe certain aspects of tension, conflict, or under-development that may have to be included in the image of the future.

By using *alternative* futures and *alternative* guiding images in this way, a rigid approach to analysis is avoided. Scenarios are not blue-prints of the future - on the contrary: they constantly invite the reader to view the future as a challenge and remind him that the future can be predicted in only a very restricted way. A doomsday scenario seems at first sight like a very rigid prediction of disaster, but a closer look reveals that it is in fact a prescriptive scenario "in disguise". The reader is supposed to lift the veil of pessimism to uncover the prescriptive message that lies beneath.

The next problem is to determine the pattern of developments that might lead to each of the proposed alternative futures. In a scenario project these developments have to be made explicit, if only to show that the guiding images are feasible. Some of these development processes may be *pre-plans*, preliminary outlines of policy measures that might be taken to make the guiding image reality. Others may be *circumstantial* processes which accompany the development of the target system but which cannot be manipulated by the policy maker in order to translate his guiding image into reality.

2.2. Main Phase

Review of Earlier Steps

The main phase starts with a review of the results obtained in earlier steps. In this review we generally find that:

- The problem has to be reformulated, possibly because it has become necessary to sharpen its focus;
- The system boundaries have to be redefined - as a rule they have to be specified more clearly;
- The project has to be redesigned;
- Comments concerning the preliminary scenarios have to be acted upon.

Second Round of Designing

How is it decided which scenarios to build? How many scenarios should be presented? As a rule, publications dealing with scenarios are not explicit about how the set of scenarios was arrived at. Kahn and Wiener do not explain why their canonical variations are the most interesting alternatives. INTERFUTURES and the IIASA energy books are also silent on this issue. It has become a tradition to present one optimistic scenario, one "business as usual" scenario, and one pessimistic scenario, but is this the best approach? A *morphological analysis*, discussed further below, can help the group to choose their scenarios more carefully.

The process of design is not discussed in most scenario projects. Is it possible to give rules for the combination of art and science that is scenario design? Teams that want to strengthen the design process are advised to adopt the technique of the "mental experiment". The first step is "thinking away". This involves taking each component of the situation or process involved, and asking yourself what would happen if the component were absent. The second step is "thinking in terms of analogies". Are there any other situations comparable to the target system? What are the parallels in other countries, other organizations, other periods? The second step normally leads to the generation of a great number of alternatives. The third step involves "critical thinking", in which all the alternatives that are neither feasible nor desirable are eliminated. These three steps are usually repeated a great many times.

The second round of designing should also include some *heuristic gaming*, i.e., gaming focussed on the generation of *new ideas*. This heuristic gaming should involve players from outside the scenario team, who must however be sympathetic with the general aims of the group in order to protect the team from too cold a shower of criticism at this early stage of the project.

Comparison of the Scenarios with the Results of Baseline Analysis and Analysis of Possible Futures

How closely should the scenario follow the observations made of past developments and the predictions made about the future? It is probably wise to design a number of dominant scenarios and a number of experimental scenarios in order to be able to compare and choose between them.

The comparison in this step also generally leads to changes in baseline analysis and the analysis of possible futures. More data will be needed, and these data will have to be more specific. Certain areas will not be covered by empirical data, however, and in these cases only a conceptual analysis will be possible.

Third Round of Designing

The preliminary scenarios are revised once again, and a new round of designing is initiated. Parallel sessions of smaller teams are held, and members of "critical audiences" invited to take part.

2.3. Rounding-off Phase

Review of Earlier Steps

Has the team strayed too far away from the original problem? Is the "fit" between baseline analysis, forecasts of the future, and scenario design optimal? This is the last chance the team has to take these issues into account.

Reporting the Results

Different audiences are interested in different aspects of the study and therefore multiple reporting is necessary. Executive summaries provide policy makers with a quick overview, while a more elaborate version of the report gives the reader a chance to "play" with the results on a more sophisticated level. Technical reports give fellow scenario designers the background information they need to evaluate the project and adapt it for their own use. The group could also hold a workshop to acquaint potential users with the results of the project.

Evaluation of the Project

The project is evaluated at the end of each phase (formative evaluation) and also at the end of the whole process (summative evaluation). During the latter we should consider questions such as: Should a subsequent project be carried out in the same way? What does the project contribute to the methodology of scenario design in general?

3. THE CONTRIBUTION OF GAMING AND SIMULATION

3.1. Contribution to the Initial Phase

The initial phase of a scenario project will probably involve a considerable amount of *brainstorming*. This term describes a loosely structured discussion in which participants are invited to come forward with ideas as uninhibited as possible. The results of the brainstorming are immediately written down on a blackboard visible to the group as a whole, and the results are later analyzed and collated. In the Utrecht project a number of brainstorming sessions were often held simultaneously. Some small groups would discuss the same subject independently and their results would be compared afterwards. By this means it was hoped to reduce any bias in the results of the brainstorming sessions.

A more structured type of gaming can be useful in baseline analysis and the analysis of possible futures. Martino (1975) explains that a group of experts can exert strong social pressure on its members - pressure, for instance, to agree with the majority, even when the individual feels that the majority view is wrong. This is especially true when a group is asked to produce a joint forecast, since the results depend not on facts but only on informed opinions. One member of the group may well give up presenting certain relevant factors if the remainder of the group persists in taking a contrary view.

Experiments with small groups have shown that it is frequently not the validity but the number of comments and arguments for or against a proposed position which carries the day. Since the group takes on a life of its own, the issue of reaching agreement frequently comes to be considered of greater importance than the production of a well thought-out and useful forecast. The members of the group may come to have vested interests in certain points of view, especially if they have presented them strongly at the outset.

The Delphi procedure, originally developed by researchers at the Rand Corporation, now makes it possible to retain many of the advantages of group interaction while eliminating most of the disadvantages of less structured methods such as brainstorming. The Delphi procedure is characterized by three features which distinguish it from other methods of group interaction. These are (a) anonymity, (b) iteration with controlled feedback, and (c) statistical group response. *Anonymity* here means that the group members are not made known to each other. The interaction of the group members is handled in a completely anonymous fashion through the use of questionnaires. As a result, the originator of an opinion can change his mind without publicly admitting that he has done so, and thereby possibly losing face. Group interaction takes place through responses to questionnaires (*iteration with controlled feedback*). The individual serving as forecaster is thus informed only of the current collective opinion of the group and the arguments for and against each point of view. The group will produce a forecast which contains only a majority viewpoint (a *statistical group response*). There may also be a minority report if the remainder of the group feels sufficiently strongly about the issue.

A Delphi procedure is conducted in a number of rounds - in a "classic" or "pure" Delphi procedure about four rounds are normal. Evaluation of the results of this method has shown that, especially in the field of "almanac"-type forecasting, the level of intergroup consensus is quite high and the accuracy of short-term forecasts is often quite good (Martino, 1975). However, the costs of the Delphi procedure are also relatively high, and therefore all kinds of *quasi-Delphi procedures* have been developed.

In the Utrecht project, quasi-Delphi techniques were used on quite a large scale and proved to work reasonably well in practice. Experts are willing to volunteer much valuable information, and to spend a lot of time in answering questions. However, the scenario team still has to analyze, systematize, and supplement the information received, and this requires a huge amount of highly skilled labor. In addition, the scenario team has to devise procedures for the resolution of points on which there is dissent between experts in the Delphi rounds.

Both baseline analysis and the analysis of possible futures may benefit from computerized *analytical simulation*, which may or may not be interactive; simulation by human analysts alone is not generally an appropriate way of studying dynamic phenomena. As stated before, projection and sensitivity analysis may also prove to be necessary at this stage.

Heuristic gaming is needed to structure the design process and stimulate new ideas. In the Utrecht project the preliminary scenarios went through twelve stages of design and revision, a number of which took place at workshops and involved gaming. Parallel small groups proved to be particularly productive in scenario design. Heuristic gaming should be used only when the members of the team are in good condition both physically and mentally, for example, following a holiday.

3.2. Contribution to the Main Phase

How can we ensure that our set of chosen scenarios is more than a haphazard collection of possibilities? One answer is to carry out a *morphological analysis* of the problem. According to Martino (1975), the use of the morphological approach in scenario projects is derived from the ideas of Zwicky. In this approach, a system or problem is broken down into parts which can be treated independently, and as many solutions or approaches as possible are devised for each part. Some of the solutions can be rejected immediately on the grounds of feasibility, while others can be rejected because of conflicts with other solutions. One is finally left with a set of solutions from which the final choice has to be made on normative grounds. Because of this, Martino classifies the morphological approach as a "normative method" of forecasting for decision making.

Martino believes that the strength of normative methods is that they tend to organize and structure the problem. By systematically displaying the structure of a problem, they can assist in the generation of new alternatives, helping to ensure completeness by making certain that no promising solutions are overlooked. Even if all of the alternatives uncovered with the use of normative methods prove to be inferior to those already known, it inspires greater confidence that the method chosen is indeed the best that could be found.

Since one of the claimed advantages of normative methods is their completeness, it might be asked whether there is any guarantee that a normative model is complete. The answer, of course, is that there is not. There is no formula or procedure that will guarantee that the constructor of a morphological model has not omitted something. The technique of drawing relevance trees is closely related to the morphological approach.

In the Utrecht project morphological analysis was used in the spirit of Martino's caveats and staged as a game. Competing teams worked on the reduction of alternatives (of which 81 were considered), firstly eliminating possibilities on logical and empirical grounds and then using normative arguments to reduce the number of alternatives still further.

Critical gaming may prove to be a useful technique in the main phase of the project. At this point the preliminary scenarios are put to the test in gaming sessions involving both critical and sympathetic participants. The game involves two sides, one of which represents the policy maker or designer in defending the preliminary scenarios, while the other side tries to demolish them. If the participants are likely to be too polite, this second role may be staged as a "devil's advocate". Critical gaming should take place a number of times with different teams, and the results compared systematically. Only in this way can future criticism of the scenarios be adequately foreseen.

3.3. Contribution to the Rounding-off Phase

It has already been noted that "multiple reporting" is necessary to present the results of a scenario project to a number of different audiences. One of the reports prepared should be suitable for *instructive gaming* in a *workshop*. The idea here is that potential users of scenarios should be invited to play with them in a gaming setting that mirrors the real situation as exactly as possible. Parliamentary debate, decision making in a board meeting, etc., can be simulated in such a way that participants are trained in working with the scenarios, defending them where appropriate, and learning about their weaker points. If the potential user restricts himself to reading the scenario reports, he will probably obtain only a superficial impression of the ins and outs of the policy alternatives involved. Workshops are also necessary if the scenario reports are meant to help support staff or other persons outside the inner circle of policy making.

4. PERSPECTIVES

The future use of scenarios in policy analysis will depend largely on whether their advantages are seen to outweigh their disadvantages. Let us first look at their strong points:

1. Scenarios are suitable for designing and analyzing alternative policies in problem areas that demand complicated, long-term, and adaptive actions.
2. Scenarios are suitable for discussing complicated, long-term, and adaptive policy alternatives with both specialists and laymen.
3. Scenarios can prepare the ground for detailed *ex ante* evaluations (cost-benefit analysis, multidimensional analysis, simulations, etc.).
4. Scenarios provide an overview of progress during an actual policy campaign.

The present weak points of scenarios are the following:

1. The analysis of the practical problem involved is often inadequate, mainly because "problem analysis" is not sufficiently well understood in the social sciences in general.
2. Baseline analysis and analysis of possible futures require more time-series data than are normally available, while the development of social indicators is still at a very early stage: much time must therefore be spent on *ad hoc* fact-finding missions.
3. The theoretical basis of social problem analysis is in many ways still inadequate.
4. Ways and means of implementing the results of scenario projects are still being developed and tested; only a small number of policy makers actually "play" with scenarios prior to a major policy decision.
5. The use of scenarios in the discussion of practical problems with large audiences has not been sufficiently tried and tested to make it a technique that can be used with confidence.

This paper treats scenario generation as a major technique for policy analysis, and gaming and simulation simply as auxiliary techniques that could be used in a scenario project. Of course, other approaches can be adopted to deal with this type of problem and it is quite possible for the roles to be reversed, with scenario generation playing a minor part in a gaming project.

REFERENCES

Finsterbusch, K. and Motz, A.B. (1980). *Social Research for Policy Decisions*. Wadsworth, California.

IIASA Energy Systems Program Group (1981). *Energy in a Finite World* (in two volumes). Ballinger, Cambridge, Massachusetts.

INTERFUTURES Project (1979). *Facing the Future: Mastering the Probable and Managing the Unpredictable*. OECD, Paris.

Julien, P.A., Lamonde, P., and Latouche, D. (1975). *La Methode des Scenarios*. Paris.

Kahn, H. and Wiener, A.J. (1967). *The Year 2000: A Framework for Speculation on the Next Thirty-Three Years*. Macmillan, New York.

Martino, J.P. (1975). *Technological Forecasting for Decision-Making*. Elsevier/North Holland, New York. (To be reprinted in 1983.)

McIlvaine Parsons, H. (1972). *Man-Machine System Experiments*. Johns Hopkins University Press, Baltimore, Maryland.

NOTE

1. The project was coordinated by H.A. Becker, P. Thoenes, and H. de Vries, and was financed by the Rijks Planologische Dienst at The Hague. The results were published (in Dutch) in 1981 and an English translation of the manual is in preparation.

PART VIII

GAMES WITH SPECIAL PURPOSES
IN SPECIFIC AREAS

Chapter VIII:a

GAMES FOR THE CONTROL OF LARGE CONSTRUCTION PROJECTS

V.I. Rybalskij
Kiev Building Institute, Kiev (USSR)

1. INTRODUCTION

The multicontractor method of construction is frequently used in large projects to cut down overall production time and to achieve planned completion dates. Controlling the implementation of such construction projects and programs is a complicated and important problem. Finding the most appropriate solution involves integrating the efforts of all those engaged in the projects and directing their activities toward effective implementation of the program developed.

Switching over to multicontractor methods of construction requires proper training of the management staff, engineers, and technicians involved. They should possess skills in team decision making with due regard for the many variable factors that can affect building production. Such skills can be obtained by participating in a series of specially prepared business games.

In the past few years, construction management games developed by the Kiev Building Institute have been played at production organizations and higher-education establishments in Moscow, Leningrad, Kiev, Kharkov, Dnepropetrovsk, Vladivostok, Tashkent, and other Soviet cities, for training purposes and for improving the control of various large projects. Thousands of engineers, lecturers, and students have taken part in these games, which have been favorably accepted and of great practical benefit. The business games have had wide application and have also led to more effective decision making by planners.

2. AN EXAMPLE OF A CONSTRUCTION MANAGEMENT GAME

The Kiev Building Institute has developed about ten different construction management games. Here we shall present first one of these games, known as SPUSK, in greater detail; this is because SPUSK is the basis for more complicated games, including the game KROSS, to be discussed later. Both SPUSK and KROSS deal with network planning and the control of construction complexes, i.e., the application of the PERT[1] method to construction problems.

The playing of SPUSK is preceded by a study of PERT methods. It is also assumed that the game participants are fairly well versed in the problems of technology, management, and economics in the construction industry.[2]

2.1. Game Participants, Their Purposes and Functions

The simplest version of the game involves a small group (10-15 persons) working under the guidance of a game director, and the group is distributed as follows.

The management of the construction project consists of one or more persons. The goal of the management in every stage of the game is to achieve the completion of the project and its operation on time. The Network Planning and Control (SPU) system service attached to the management consists of between two and four persons; its goal is the same as that of the management.

In addition there are supervisors, each of whom is responsible for the completion of a certain set of operations in the project (e.g., the project groundwork and foundation laying). The goal of the supervisor is to ensure the meeting of scheduled deadlines as regards this specific set of operations. This also means ensuring normal conditions for the operation of individual teams and sections, full use of machinery and installations, good quality, low cost, and a low percentage of accidents.

It should be noted that the interests and goals of the management and the supervisors are not identical. The supervisors have a definite interest in extending the time allowed for the completion of their specific set of operations, whereas management wants to reduce the time for each such set of operations.

The umpire, a role usually exercised by the game director, issues decisions made by higher authorities (e.g., directives on the project schedules) to the management, acts as a generator of problem situations, solves controversial questions, controls gaming conditions, and assesses the activities of all the participants in the game.

2.2. Interests and Criteria

The quality of decisions made by each player is evaluated by the sum of points collected during the game. Each participant, in cooperation with others, tries to amass as many points as possible; it is possible to get a negative score. The careful awarding of points ensures a fairly objective and comprehensive assessment of the positive and negative contributions made by each participant.

2.3. The Four Stages of the Game

Stage 1. Preparation

During this stage "the management", appointed by the game director, studies the documentation and the system service available. It also
outlines some general features of the project (separation into sites, flow-
process priorities, etc.). The umpire controls the work done by the
management; if necessary, he suggests that work be repeated and penalizes the incompetent management by deducting a certain number of
points in accordance with a penalty scale. All decisions made by the
management are relayed to the participants. The participants are also
informed about the rules of the game and the initial data.

Stage 2. Initial Planning

This stage consists of six steps.

During the *first* step the system service specifies the tasks to be
handled in the initial PERT models. The specification list contains the primary resources and the alternative durations (maximum, average,
minimum) allowed for each task. The probability of timely fulfillment is
also specified. Naturally, this probability increases with the length of
time allotted for fulfillment.

During the *second* step the supervisors in charge, after being
informed about the task, construct initial PERT models and hand them
over to the system service. The system service checks these models and
the accompanying specification lists, and if there are any errors imposes
corresponding penalties and insists on the models being reconstructed.

During the *third* step the system service assembles the initial PERT
models into an integrated model of the whole project, using data on forthcoming events presented by the supervisors. The system service also calculates time parameters for the overall integrated PERT model. If the
networks involved are extensive, a computer is required for these calculations. The management controls the proper fulfillment of this work and,
if necessary, penalizes the system service and requires the service to perform its tasks again.

During the *fourth* step the system service analyzes the results of its
calculations and prepares preliminary suggestions for changes in the
individual PERT models.

During the *fifth* step the management convenes a meeting of all
supervisors who do not have enough resources for the completion of their
tasks by the specified deadlines. The system service also takes part in
this meeting. The management, having decided on the total amount of
points to be used for the timely completion of the whole project,
announces how many "bonus" or incentive points it will distribute for
speeding up the work and meeting the project deadline. Then the various
supervisors inform the management, in written form, on how many days
they are ready to cut from the time initially allotted for completion of the
tasks under their control if they receive a certain number of these points.

The management, after familiarizing itself with all the suggestions, decides which of them should be accepted. If none of the suggestions is suitable, all the players are informed and a new amount of points to be used for the completion of the project on schedule is announced. This procedure continues until the management can make a final decision. If necessary, the management charges the system service with the task of checking the feasibility of the decisions under consideration by repeated calculation of the integrated PERT model.

During the *sixth* step the system service introduces changes into the integrated PERT model and controls the introduction of similar changes into the initial PERT models constructed by the supervisors.

Stage 3. Control of the Operation

Each cycle at this stage, corresponding, for example, to the 20th or 40th day of operation, consists of six steps.

During the *first* step the umpire informs the management about the decisions made by higher authorities. The umpire furthermore introduces random values characterizing the state of each operation, for example, the number of days delay in the work. Thus, the unpredictable variations affecting the construction process are reflected.

During the *second* step the supervisors, having received information about their "own" operations, decide whether the expected delay could or should be eliminated in order to avoid penalties. The decisions include changing the topology of the PERT network, transferring resources from other operations, etc. In the latter case it is conventionally agreed that the supervisors can speed up the work delayed at the expense of other work proceeding in parallel and requiring the same resources.

Other measures that require outside resources are penalized. An example is the transfer of resources from a long-term task to one with a shorter duration; in this case, a number of penalty points are transferred to the management "bonus" fund. One player can also "buy" a reduction in the time of a particular operation from another player who must simultaneously prolong one of his own operations requiring similar resources.

Then the supervisors submit operating information to the system service in the form of work progress reports, reflecting all their activities during the second step.

During the *third* step the system service checks the reports of the supervisors. If there are errors it makes suggestions for the reorganization of plans and imposes penalties. The system service then records all the changes that have taken place in the integrated PERT model and recalculates the time parameters of the integrated model. After this calculation it becomes clear which operations overran their allotted time during the cycle in question, and the system service imposes penalties accordingly.

The fourth, fifth, and sixth steps are then similar to the respective steps implemented in Stage 2.

In order to improve operational management skills it is recommended that Stage 3 be repeated several times.

Stage 4. *Calculation and Analysis of the Results*

During this stage the number of points per section is recorded. At the end of the game the results are calculated and general comments are made by the umpire. It is advisable to conduct the game simultaneously with several groups using initial data from the same project since it is often useful to compare the results obtained by each group.

3. EXAMPLES OF OTHER GAMES

The business game SPUSK described above is comparatively simple. After it has been mastered, more complicated versions can be studied. These latter games involve the participation of specialized organizations and the integration of a number of projects into a complex optimization of PERT models with regard to cost, labor, and resources.

A number of these games have been developed at the Kiev Building Institute. For example, there are the games OSKAR, concerned with minimizing the cost of a complex under conditions of automatic control, and OPTIMUM, concerned with optimization in a game reflecting assembly-line methods of construction, etc.

There is also the DISPUT business game for the planning and management of a "building trust", i.e., a large construction corporation with many projects. This requires 25 to 30 participants. The basic differences between this game and SPUSK are that DISPUT embraces not just a single construction project, but all the projects of the building trust. Moreover, DISPUT is not only concerned with the completion of the construction projects by the scheduled dates; it also combines the work carried out at all the construction sites into a production-line process and shares the work between the component units.

Our most effective business game is KROSS, dealing with both management and control of construction. As mentioned earlier, it can be regarded as a more advanced version of SPUSK. The main purpose of KROSS is to enable participants to acquire skills in decision making for the implementation of a multicontractor construction program covering a number of important complexes (for example, chemical or metallurgical plants in a large industrial region). During the game the participants practise exercising control over a large multicontractor program at all levels--from supervisors to the heads of building agencies and ministries.

The game requires at least 150 participants and the total playing time is around 20 hours. Each group, consisting of 20 to 25 participants, "constructs" a single complex consisting of three or four component units. The game participants perform the functions of head of the construction complex, heads of separate construction units and building organizations, supervisors of work, and staff of data processing services. A number of participants act as the management of the entire construction system, responsible for all the complexes to be erected and representing various organizations involved, for example, institutes involved in design work, companies delivering precast concrete or building machinery, etc.

A properly thought out incentive system allows us to simulate conditions closely resembling actual production situations. The participants are encouraged to make decisions that benefit the whole scheme and also to produce objective assessments of the contribution made by each participant to the multicontractor system.

The elements of the business game KROSS have been used in practice in a number of large building organizations. It has been played mainly by middle management in the organizations involved with some top management also taking part. KROSS, in different versions, has been played about 80 times.

In particular, it should be mentioned that KROSS was used when developing the system for controlling the multicontractor construction work for the 1980 Olympic Games in Moscow. The results obtained were later used for more exact specifications of some documentation of the PERT model system used in the actual construction of these facilities.

During the design stage, the organizational structure of the system and the information flow were specified. Very early in the development process, a special version of KROSS featuring the basic principles of the future system was prepared and played with the staff of the client building organization. The engineers of this building organization thus had the opportunity to go deeply into the system being developed and to make concrete proposals concerning further developments and improvements of the system. These proposals were taken into account when preparing detailed designs for the construction system. At the same time, the special version of KROSS was being continuously improved; a second version of the game was developed so as to make the game as close as possible to the real-world system. This improved version was then played once again prior to the beginning of commercial operation.

REFERENCES

Gidrovich, S.R. and Syroezhin, I.M. (1976). *Game Modeling of Economic Processes: Business Games*. Economica, Moscow. (In Russian.)

Komarov, V.F. (1979). *Management Simulation Games and Automized Management Systems*. Nauka, Moscow. (In Russian.)

Rybalskij, V.I. (1980). *Systems Analysis and Objective Management in Civil Engineering*. Strojizdat, Moscow. (In Russian.)

Rybalskij, V.I. et al. (1980). Business games in management and civil engineering economics. *Vishcha Shkola, Kiev*. (In Russian.)

Vetrov, Y.A., Litvinenko, E.A., and Rybalskij, V.I. (1981). Main part of the modern education system. *Vestnik Vishchej Shkoli, Kiev*, 4. (In Russian.)

Yefimov, V.M. and Komarov, V.F. (1980). *Introduction to Management Simulation Games*. Nauka, Moscow. (In Russian.)

NOTES

1. The term PERT is used here to represent a critical path network analysis of the Program Evaluation and Review Technique type. The critical path concerns those activities for which any delay will lead to a corresponding delay in the final completion date of the whole project. The PERT technique uses the computer to deal with the problem of uncertainty in the activity time estimates. Instead of using a single estimate for the duration of an activity, both optimistic and pessimistic time estimates are used.

2. All terminology and information used in the game completely coincides with the Basic Provisions for the Development and Application of Systems of Network Planning and Control (SPU) approved by the USSR State Committee for Science and Technology.

GAMES FOR MODEL TESTING: THE CASE OF
WATER COST-ALLOCATION METHODS

Ingolf Stahl
*International Institute for Applied Systems Analysis,
Laxenburg (Austria)*

1. INTRODUCTION

This chapter deals with the use of gaming for testing other types of models, with examples drawn from an operational research game on methods for allocating costs in joint water projects.

Although the testing function is relevant for experimental, research, and operational games[1], we shall focus here on operational games, including the important special group which we have called operational research games (see Chapter III:a, Section 7), i.e., games designed to provide a decision aid, but not focused on a specific decision.

The models to be tested here are thus models whose ultimate purpose is use as various kinds of decision aid. The idea of testing by gaming is first of all to discover whether it is reasonable to use the model for the intended purpose. The costs of using an inappropriate model can be very high, while gaming experiments are relatively inexpensive. If gaming experiments can stop the use of inappropriate models this would in most cases more than pay for the gaming activity.

The models we are testing here are complete models in the sense of Chapter III:a; they contain both institutional and behavioral assumptions and therefore provide solutions. The models deal with game situations, and thus mainly with the theory of game playing,[2] in most cases rational game playing. Our main concern is therefore the testing of game-theoretical models.

The testing concentrates on the behavioral assumptions of the model, since we try to use the same institutional assumptions in the gaming model as in the complete model to be tested. The questions to be answered are either "Do people behave as described by the behavioral assumptions of the model?", focusing the testing on the *predictive* aim of the model or, "Do people *want to behave* as described by the behavioral assumptions of the model?", focusing on testing the *normative* aim of the model.

We will illustrate the testing of both the predictive and the normative aims by testing a number of methods, based on game theory, for allocating costs in a joint water project applied to a real case in Southern Sweden. We will also report on how the game was played with professional water planners, as well as students, in Sweden, Italy, Poland, and Bulgaria.

2. THE WATER COST-ALLOCATION SITUATION

We begin with some background information on the particular cost-allocation exercise we will use later for illustration.

At the beginning of the 1970s, municipalities in southwestern Skane, in Southern Sweden, were planning for a predicted large increase in water demand during the coming decade. The question facing most municipalities was to what extent they should try to solve their water supply problem on their own, rather than joining together with other municipalities to do it more cheaply. Although there are a total of eighteen municipalities in this region, it was found practical, from a research point of view, to group these into six groups for which it appeared reasonably realistic to build separate water facilities. Due to "economies of scale", there were in most cases predicted to be further cost savings if these groups joined together, and the "grand coalition", consisting of all six groups, would lead to the lowest total costs. The symbols A, H, K, L, M, and T used below for these groups denote the main municipalities in each group; for example, L denotes the university town of Lund, and M, Malmö, the largest city in the region (for details, see Young et al., 1980).

On the basis of real cost data for the situation in Southern Sweden, a cost table was computed for each of the 63 possible coalitions that these six groups or parties could form. The results are given in Table 1, where costs, as in the following text, are specified in millions of Swedish Crowns (one Crown was at that time approximately equal to US$0.20). The table shows the costs of providing water supply facilities for each party separately or for each of the possible coalitions.

The question is now, how these costs should be allocated. The cost-allocation problem arises from the fact that there is no unique way in which a proportion of the fixed costs of construction can be assigned to each party. One can only propose various principles on which such allocation should depend (Young et al., 1980).

The first principle adopted is that the parties form the most efficient overall arrangement, namely, the grand coalition. The theory then focuses on how the parties should divide the costs associated with this arrangement.

One division procedure would be to allocate costs in proportion to water demand. With the total costs of the grand coalition amounting to 83.82 and M being responsible for 34% of the demand, M would then have to pay 28.48. Alternatively, if M stayed out of the coalition and produced all its own water, it would, as seen in Table 1, only have to pay 20.81. Hence M would have a strong motive for leaving the final coalition if costs were allocated in this way. Hence we rule out the Demand-Proportional

Table 1. Total cost of providing water facilities for each possible coalition (millions of Swedish Crowns).

A	21.95	AHK	40.74	AHKM	60.25
H	17.08	AHL	43.22	AHKT	62.72
K	10.91	AHM	55.50	AHLM	64.03
L	15.88	AHT	56.67	AHLT	65.20
M	20.81	AKL	48.74	AHMT	74.10
T	21.98	AKM	53.40	AKLM	63.96
		AKT	54.85	AKLT	70.72
AH	34.69	ALM	53.05	ALMT	73.41
AK	32.86	ALT	59.81	HKLM	48.07
AL	37.83	AMT	61.36	HKLT	49.24
AM	42.76	HKL	27.26	HKMT	59.35
AT	43.93	HKM	42.55	HLMT	64.41
HK	22.96	HKT	44.94	KLMT	56.61
HL	25.00	HLM	45.81	AKMT	72.27
HM	37.89	HLT	46.98		
HT	39.06	HMT	56.49	AHKLM	69.76
KL	26.79	KLM	42.01	AHKMT	77.42
KM	31.45	KLT	48.77	AHLMT	83.00
KT	32.89	KMT	50.32	AHKLT	70.93
LM	31.10	LMT	51.46	AKLMT	73.97
LT	37.96			HKLMT	66.46
MT	39.41	AHKL	48.95		
				AHKLMT	83.82

method on the basis of the principle of "individual rationality": no party shall pay a higher cost than it would have to pay if it were to fulfill its water needs completely on its own.

A method specifically developed in the United States for practical use in water resource planning is known as the Separable Costs Remaining Benefits (SCRB) method.[3] From Table 2, we see that H, K, and L will, according to the SCRB method, pay 13.28 + 5.62 + 10.90 = 29.80. If they have to pay this much together, they would collectively have an incentive to leave the grand coalition and instead form the three-party coalition HKL, which, as can be seen in Table 1, has a total cost of only 27.26. Hence, SCRB is rejected here on the basis of the principle of "group rationality": the sum of payments made by the members of every coalition which is smaller than the grand coalition should not be larger than the cost of the coalition working on its own.

Game-theoretical methods were then investigated. Probably the best known method in this area is the Shapley Value. The grand coalition is formed step by step; first one party joins together with another party to form a two-party coalition. Then one more party is added to form a three-party coalition, etc., until finally the grand coalition is formed. There are many orders in which such a procedure can take place, depending on which party "signs up" first, and which "signs up" next. For

Table 2. Allocation of the total costs of the grand coalition (83.82) using six different methods (millions of Swedish Crowns).

Method	A	H	K	L	M	T
Demand Proportional	13.07	16.01	7.30	6.87	28.48	12.08
SCRB	19.54	13.28	5.62	10.90	16.66	17.82
Shapley Value	20.01	10.71	6.61	10.37	16.94	19.18
Nucleolus	20.35	12.06	5.00	8.61	18.32	19.49
Weak Nucleolus	20.03	12.52	3.94	9.07	18.54	19.71
Proportional Nucleolus	20.36	12.46	3.52	8.67	18.82	19.99

each such sequence, a party joining a coalition is considered only to pay the incremental costs. The Shapley Value for each party is that party's *average* payment, computed over *all* sequences of coalition formation. However, the Shapley Value was also rejected since in this situation it also fails to fulfill the principle of group rationality.

Since the above-mentioned principles of individual and group rationality were regarded as theoretically essential, the area of solution concepts was now restricted to those known as Core methods, where the Core is the set of all cost allocations for the grand coalition fulfilling these two rationality principles.

The most common Core concept is the Nucleolus. The Nucleolus was, however, regarded as inappropriate for this game, for the following reason: if there were a cost overrun for the grand coalition of 4 million Crowns (ie., 87.82 instead of 83.82), then party K would actually pay *less*, namely 4.51 instead of 5.00.

Hence two other Core concepts were studied, the Weak Nucleolus and the Proportional Nucleolus. These two concepts do not have the problem mentioned above in cases of cost overrun. The Proportional Nucleolus was in this case preferred since it, in contrast to the Weak Nucleolus, fulfilled yet another principle: a player who never contributes to any cost savings when joining with other parties or coalitions should *not* realize any cost savings above his costs of "going it alone".

Having singled out the Proportional Nucleolus as a theoretically appealing solution, the question arises as to whether one would really want to suggest this cost-allocation method for practical use.

3. THE MAIN PURPOSE OF THE TESTING ACTIVITY

Before going into details of how to use gaming to test such models as game-theoretical models, we must look at the purpose of such testing.

The broad question which we would like to answer is as follows: "is the theoretical model valid for decisions in reality?" The use of gaming in testing cannot give a full general answer, but does provide certain critical steps towards such an answer. To explain this in greater detail, Figure 1 illustrates the position of game testing in a larger framework: the relationship between the *model* and *reality*. The three relationships R_1, R_2, and R_3 in this figure can also be seen as a measure of the degree of correspondence between each pair of components involved. We shall write $R_i \sim 1$ if there is a high degree of correspondence, and $R_i \sim 0$ if there is a low degree of correspondence.

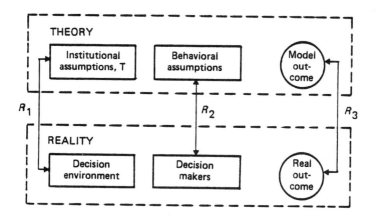

Figure 1. Relationships between theory and reality.

The game-theoretical model can be divided into institutional and behavioral assumptions (see Chapter III:a, Section 4). The interaction between these types of assumptions will generate a model outcome, in other words, a solution.

In the specific case of the water cost-allocation game, the institutional assumptions are mainly the costs (shown in Table 1) of the 63 different coalitions, the rules controlling communication, and the rules governing the formation and breaking of any of these 63 coalitions. The behavioral assumptions would, for the case of the proportional nucleolus, mainly consist of the following principles: individual rationality, group rationality, no benefits from cost overruns, and no part of savings if no contribution.[4]

The real decision process takes place in a complex environment. This environment would, in the present case, include the eighteen municipalities, which could form the six municipality groups, as well as the real data on water demand, the investment costs, etc., and the uncertainty associated with these data. The decision makers would involve a hierarchy of the municipal councils and municipal water boards, as well as key politicians and administrators responsible for making decisions on water issues and negotiating with other municipalities.

The real outcome of the cost negotiations is the ultimate concern of the game-theory model. This outcome concerns firstly, the question of which coalition is ultimately formed and secondly, how the joint costs are distributed.

Looking at the relationships in Figure 1, we are *ultimately* most interested in R_3, in particular as regards *future* applications of the model. This relationship R_3 can involve two main sorts of correspondence, predictive/descriptive or normative. In the predictive/descriptive case the model outcome would have direct relevance without the decision makers knowing about the theoretical model. In the purely predictive case the game-theory model would, *prior to* the actual event, forecast the outcome. In the descriptive case, the model would, *after* the event, possibly generate a similar outcome. In the normative case the model outcome would have relevance for the real outcome by influencing the decision makers to reach an agreement close to the model outcome.

In our cost-allocation case the focus was clearly normative, i.e., it was intended that the cost-allocation methods would influence the decision makers. It was hoped that development of the method would ultimately help water planners to reach agreement more quickly.[5]

When applied to a specific decision situation, the main question is whether the results (e.g., a cost distribution) suggested by a model on the basis of some specific behavioral assumptions (e.g., those behind the proportional nucleolus) would be acceptable to the decision makers. However, since we are generally interested in a broader application of the model situations with different arrangements of the institutional assumptions, the focus shifts from relationship R_3 to R_2, i.e., the relationship between the behavioral assumptions of the model and the way actual decision makers will (or will want to) behave. The question of importance for the normative aim then becomes: do the decision makers want to behave in line with the behavioral assumptions of the model?[6] In the case of the predictive/descriptive aim the question can be stated as: "will the parties behave (or have they behaved) in line with the behavioral assumptions of the model?" It is in answering this type of question that gaming comes into the picture.

4. THE SPECIFIC ROLE OF GAMING

By introducing gaming on an intermediate level between game theory and reality we obtain the framework shown in Figure 2.

The gaming activity consists of a game, i.e., a model of the game situation (with only institutional assumptions) and the players. In the Skane case the game consists of the rules, as summarized below, together with the table of costs (Table 1), as well as information on the water demand facing each of the six municipality groups. The players included professional water planners, as discussed below. The main points of the rules are as follows:

- 217 -

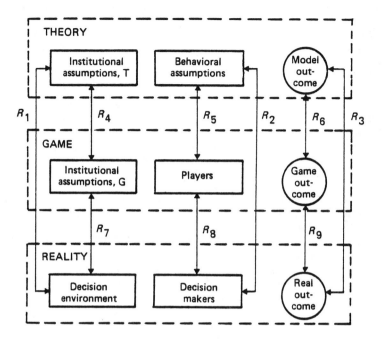

Figure 2. Relationships between theory, game, and reality.

There are six players in the game. By drawing lots, each player is assigned the role of representative of one of the six municipality groups. Each player will try to solve his water supply problem as cheaply as possible by entering into a coalition with another player or players. Should a player not enter into a coalition with any other, he will pay that sum in Table 1 which represents what he would have to pay if acting alone. By acting skillfully both during the formation of coalitions and during the allocation of the total costs within the coalition, a player can get away with a considerably lower payment than if acting alone. When forming a coalition, the players reach an agreement on how much each of the participants in the proposed coalition shall pay of the total cost facing the whole coalition.

As soon as a coalition has been formed and an agreement has been reached as to the allocation of the total costs of this coalition among its members, they register the coalition with the game leader. A coalition does not come into force, however, until 15 minutes have elapsed since its registration, and then only provided that none of its members has been registered in another coalition during this period. A player can also leave one coalition and join another. A coalition dissolves when any member registers a new coalition. Once a coalition has come into force, each of its members "pays" the game leader the amount agreed upon at the time of the registration. The game continues in this way until all participants are members of one or other coalition which has come into force (with the possible exception of a single "leftover" participant). Should the game continue for more than 90 minutes it will automatically end and all coalitions registered but not broken at that time will come into force.

What gaming can do is to test the relevance of game theory for game playing. As mentioned above, we are mainly interested in estimating the value of R_2 (ultimately, in order to determine R_3). R_2 is in turn dependent on R_5 and R_8. If, by suitable choice of players in the game, one can get a high degree of correspondence between the players and the real decision makers, one can hope for $R_8 \sim 1$. In this situation the relevance of R_2 would hinge on R_5. Since, as mentioned earlier, one can make the IA_C (Institutional Assumptions in the Game) very similar to the IT_A (those of the theory), i.e., make $R_4 \sim 1$, R_6 can be used to check the value of R_5. We therefore examine the degree of similarity between model outcome and game outcome to determine the similarity between the behavioral assumptions of the model and the way the players behave or want to behave in the game.

Thus, in order to test the relevance of the theory for decisions in reality, we want to check how relevant the theory is for the playing of the game. For the relationship between *theory and reality* we distinguished between predictive, descriptive, and normative aims. When trying to test these aims by examining the relationship between *theory and game playing* we assume the relationships in Table 3 to hold.

Table 3. Relationship between testing a model for reality and testing in a game.

Purpose of theory for reality	Predictive	Descriptive	Normative
	↓	↓	↓
Test using gaming	Predictive	Predictive	Normative or special predictive

The model's predictive capability in reality is estimated by testing its predictive ability in the game. Its ability to describe a real situation can only be estimated by testing its predictive powers in the game. It seems appropriate to construct the model *prior to* running the game; otherwise model-building could become merely an exercise in "curve-fitting". The test of the model's normative relevance for reality is more complicated and requires further discussion.

5. TESTING A MODEL'S NORMATIVE VALIDITY BY GAMING

5.1. Definition of the Term "Normative"

The term normative is frequently used in connection with models of game situations, particularly game-theoretical models. Therefore, it is important to be quite clear what is meant by the term. The word normative will here be used in the sense of being normative for a specific type of decision situation and normative for one specific party, the decision maker.

A model fulfills its normative purpose if the party concerned, after being thoroughly informed about the characteristics of the model and the mode of behavior recommended by the model, decides to follow this recommended mode of behavior, at least to a significant extent. Our definition is hence operational. The fulfillment of the normative purpose can be tested directly by seeing whether the party wants to follow the advice of the model. More concretely, the important ultimate question concerning "normative validity" as defined here is as follows: would decision makers such as corporate executives and senior civil servants want to act in accordance with the behavioral assumptions of the "normative" model in real situations that are important (e.g., involving substantial amounts of money) and for which they have considerable time for deliberation?

It should be stressed that when we use the word "normative" we focus on the advice given to *one* specific decision maker. In this way the term "normative aim" can be distinguished from the connected terms "mediation aim" and "arbitration aim".

"Mediation aim" refers to models, mainly of negotiations, used for giving advice simultaneously to at least two parties, for example to induce them to reach agreement earlier. The parties are free to accept or reject the advice given by the model. This definition is also operational and allows for testing. The mediation aim is fulfilled if the parties concerned decide to follow the mode of behavior recommended by the mediation model.

"Arbitration" refers to the process by which a third party *imposes* a settlement on the parties in the game situation. Since the parties involved in the game cannot reject the solution of the arbitration model, gaming can only test the validity of an arbitration model with regard to whether "arbitrators" want to use the arbitration model or not. Obviously problems arise here regarding the choice of "arbitrator" in the game. However, we will not explore arbitration models any further here.

There does not seem to be any agreement in the literature on the definition given above for a "normative model". The word "normative" is often used in a more general sense than that given above, namely as "normative for the rational economic man", without really considering the application of the model to any specific type of decision situation or any specific decision maker. This type of model only prescribes how persons should act, if they obeyed certain assumptions. Whether or not there exist any persons who would wish to obey these assumptions is, from the point of view of these models, irrelevant. This kind of validity cannot be the object of any kind of empirical testing, e.g., using gaming, and we would prefer to say that this sort of model is for "basic research purposes". A model's value in this regard depends mainly on the extent to which it inspires other theories.

5.2. Methods for Testing the Normative Purpose

Having now defined "normative" and "mediation" purposes and established that these purposes are testable by gaming experiments, we shall proceed to discuss how such testing can take place. We shall deal mainly with the normative purpose and only briefly (in the next section) discuss tests of the mediation purpose.

Let us first examine the traditional idea of a "normative model". First one tries to discover the behavioral assumptions[7] according to which the party wants to act. The model constructor will then help the decision maker to deduce which decisions follow from these behavioral assumptions. The main contribution of the normative model is in helping the decision maker with the *deduction* (and computation) of the solution. In line with our discussion above, the model should not *force* behavioral assumptions[8] on the decision maker. Testing the validity of the model for normative purpose should hence consist only of finding out whether the decision maker says that he wants to follow the stated behavioral assumptions. There are, however, two significant problems with such an approach:

1. It appears that the behavioral assumptions cannot be tested *"in vacuo"* one by one. Presented one at a time to decision makers, they appear in many cases as meaningless abstractions[9].

2. Even if a decision maker is able to establish that he wishes to behave according to the behavioral assumptions, it is by no means certain that he, therefore, wants to act in accordance with the model. One cannot rule out the possibility that he distrusts the deduction of the model. There are at least three reasons for such behavior:

   — He believes that the deduction or computation are erroneous. In many cases, such fears may be justified!

   — He believes that the deduction of the solution implicitly involves other assumptions to which he fears he would not subscribe.

   — He feels generally uncomfortable about relying on a procedure which he, and possibly also his trusted collaborators, do not understand.

Because of these problems it appears that other methods of testing the normative aim of a model must be used. In line with our definition of the normative purpose one might then focus on the following question: would decision makers want to use the game model, if they had been properly introduced to it, and would they, after having used it, want to use it again?

One way of testing a normative model experimentally is therefore to have the game leader instruct the players about the normative model and then let the participants play the game to see if they would use the model. There is, however, at least one important difficulty with such an approach, namely the problem that conforming to higher authority may over-ride other considerations in the experiment. If players do not gain or lose considerable amounts, they are likely to accept the advice of the game leader, since they do not want to appear "stupid".[10]

In order to avoid such effects, one could in principle present several normative theories and allow the gaming participants to be "free" (i.e., uninfluenced by authority) to choose any one. A problem with this approach is that the presentation of several models in a sufficiently detailed manner in one experiment might be time consuming and perhaps also confusing. It is, furthermore, reasonable to assume that the order in which one presents the models plays some role. The participants are more likely to remember the first and the last of the models presented.

One might instead choose to run only *one* model in each experiment, with a new experiment and new subjects for each model, or to run two models at a time, in a kind of tournament. However, both of these methods would require more gaming experiments and hence more time.

Another way of running the experiments is to supply different models to each player. Here each player obtains information on one specific model, preferably a model that is particularly favorable to the player concerned. The information could be in the form of a "consultant's report" containing different arguments for using this particular model.

Another possible way to test the normative value of a model is to use a robot, i.e., a computer program that behaves according to the model. One can then study whether the human players will be inspired to play like the robot, i.e., more in line with the theory (Stahl, 1982a).

A completely different approach to normative testing is to run the test mainly in a predictive way without any normative influences of the types described above. One advantage of such an approach is that one avoids the mentioned "authority" effects. The whole idea is based on the view that the only differences between the normative and the predictive aims are differences of degree and not kind. The differences in degree can take the form of certain measures to increase the likelihood that the parties will behave according to the behavioral assumptions. For example, when these assumptions reflect assumptions of rational behavior one can use the following approaches:

1. Select players more carefully to ensure proper levels of intelligence and education.

2. Increase the time allowed for playing.

3. Supply the players generously with calculators and other types of computing equipment.

4. Increase the incentives, for example, by giving higher monetary rewards for successful playing.

5. Allow the players to learn by playing several games. It is important, however, that in each game each player faces a completely new set of "coplayers" or opponents. Several games played with the same players would imply a "super-game" which might have different implications for playing than the single games it contains.

6. Suggest that the game leader asks the simple questions: "Do you want to play like this?" or "Does everyone agree to this?" to encourage extra reflection when some player is about to make a move clearly in violation of the behavioral assumptions of the model.[11]

7. Make the parties look several periods ahead by asking them to define strategies for the playing of several future periods.

8. Focus the attention of the players on issues that might induce them to follow the behavioral assumptions by providing specific information or tasks.

Even with these devices, there is in many cases the problem that the normative model is based on such sophisticated deduction that it is unreasonable to expect any of the gaming participants to be able to establish a desirable solution on their own. One way to overcome this problem is to present initially very simple versions of the model, for example with very few strategies and very few periods. Deductions might then be very simple. Whether or not the person will follow the model will then be more a function of his acceptance of the behavioral assumptions than of his deductive capacity. In this simpler model one might, however, be unable to test the whole set of behavioral assumptions. It might, therefore, be appropriate to continue to present successively more and more complicated versions of the game. This would also allow for some learning, permitting somewhat more complicated deductions on the part of the players.

5.3. Testing the Mediation Purpose

The mediation purpose can be tested in two different ways. The *first* way focuses on the question of whether a skilled mediator can get the parties to agree on the terms suggested by the model. For example, the experiment leader could assume the role of mediator. In order to measure the suitability of a model for the mediation purpose--and not the experiment leader's ability to persuade--it is particularly important in this case that other models should also be tested in the same way as the model studied.

The *second* way of testing the mediation ability of the model is to test whether an experimental subject, instructed to act as a mediator, will want to use the model when presented with it. In this instance it is also appropriate that the model should compete with other models to see which model will be most readily adopted by the party acting as mediator.

6. TESTING IN THE WATER COST-ALLOCATION GAME

We now present some results of the testing of the Water Cost-Allocation Game. The game has been played 16 times. Twelve of these games focused on testing the model's ability to *predict* the outcome.[12] By choice of players, supply of calculators and on some occasions, asking simple questions (see point 6 above), we tried to exert a slight influence, in order to make behavior more rational.

The four remaining games were focused more on testing the model's *normative* ability, i.e., its ability to influence the playing in the game. In three games the players were, before playing, given a one-hour lecture on the game-theoretical analysis presented above. In two of the three games each player furthermore received a "consultant's report", suggesting that he should argue for one specific method (out of those listed in Table 2) and outlining the main arguments for this method. Each player got a different one-page report generally arguing for that method which happened to be the most favorable for him: for example, the Shapley Value for player H, the Proportional Nucleolus for player K, etc. In the two remaining games, the parties had to specify their distribution of two cost levels for the grand coalition, namely 83.82 and 87.82 million Crowns. This was done in order to focus the attention of the players on the principle of "no benefit from cost overruns", which, as noted above, played an important role in the game-theoretical analysis.

In order to compare how well the theoretical methods predicted the game outcomes, we used three simple statistical measures, namely (1) the sum of the absolute differences (between the theoretical prediction and the actual outcome for each player), (2) the sum of the squared differences, and (3) the sum of the relative squared differences, i.e., of the squared differences after dividing each difference by the theoretical value. For every game we calculated these measures for each of the six methods of distribution presented in Table 2. For each game we also ranked the methods, regarding one method as "better" than another if it had a lower value for at least two different measures. We then gave the best method rank 1 and the worst rank 6.

The findings from all sixteen games are summarized in Table 4, in which we present the average difference measures as well as the average ranking values.

The most striking result to be seen in Table 4 is how far away the actual performance is from allocations strictly according to demand.[13] The reason is not that the planners ignored the information on water demand given: in fact, in many games there were strong efforts to base the cost distribution on water demand. However, such allocations violated the principle of individual rationality, i.e., that a municipality group will not accept higher costs than the costs of "going it alone", which thus appeared to be a very valid principle.

The second thing to be observed in the table is that, among the game-theoretical methods, the difference measures are larger for the methods which were favored in the game-theoretical analysis mentioned above. The Proportional Nucleolus preferred in this analysis is at the bottom among these methods, while the Shapley Value, which is not even in

Table 4. Average ranks and difference measures from sixteen games.

| | Rank | Difference measure[a] | | |
		1	2	3
Shapley Value	1.75	7.26	13.67	1.06
Nucleolus	2.00	7.97	17.26	1.69
Weak Nucleolus	3.31	8.74	21.65	3.01
SCRB	3.62	9.99	23.12	1.80
Proportional Nucleolus	4.31	9.93	25.74	3.96
Demand Proportional	6.00	32.90	244.86	15.00

[a]1, sum of absolute differences; 2, sum of squared differences; 3, sum of relative squared differences (see text).

the Core (see earlier), is at the top, slightly ahead of the Nucleolus, which although in the Core violates the principle of no benefits from cost overruns.

In fact, the solution was outside the Core in 10 of the 16 games. Of the six games with the solution in the Core, three were the games for which the players had obtained information about the game-theoretical analysis *prior to* playing. One might, therefore, hypothesize that the Core concept is more valid as a normative concept than as a predictive concept.

Even in these three "normative" experiments, the Shapley Value fared better than the Proportional Nucleolus. The question then arises as to why the players did not play more in line with the game-theoretical "best" solution. One important reason seems to be the fact that in *none* of the sixteen games did the parties form the grand coalition directly without first forming some smaller coalition(s). In many games, a two- or three-party coalition was first formed, followed by a four- or five-party coalition, before the grand coalition was established. The actual coalition-formation procedure was thus more in line with the Shapley Value, implicitly assuming a step-by-step build-up of the grand coalition, than with the Core solutions, which do not take any gradual coalition formation into account.

7. INTERNATIONAL GAME-PLAYING COMPARISONS

Another interesting aspect of the game playing involved comparisons of playing by local and regional planners in the water field from four countries: Sweden, Bulgaria, Italy, and Poland. We were interested to see, not only if there were differences between the countries, but also if there were detectable differences between planners from countries with different social systems. The game was also played with doctoral students and scientists in Sweden, Bulgaria, and Poland, as well as at IIASA (in Laxenburg, Austria).

The main point of interest to report is that we found *no* significant differences as regards the playing of the game with the planners from the four different countries. In fact, the prediction that a planner in one country would play like a planner in another country proved to be more reliable than any of the six methods discussed earlier![14] The difference between planners and students in the *same* country was considerably larger. The marked differences in behavior that appeared to exist between, for example, the planners and students with little experience of this kind of problem, indicate that it might be well worth the extra cost to utilize as far as possible "real decision makers" when one wants to use gaming as a test of models ultimately aimed at aiding real decisions.[15]

8. CONCLUSIONS FROM GAMING TESTS

Suppose that one has tested a model by game playing, for example in the way described in the preceding sections: what conclusions can then be drawn? In order to try to answer this question we return to the discussion of Figure 2 in Section 3.

Using gaming we have tested relation R_5 by looking at R_6, in a situation where $R_4 \sim 1$. We shall here distinguish between two main cases: (A) the positive case, when the game outcome is similar to that of the model (i.e., $R_6 \sim 1$) and (B) the negative case, when the game outcome is different from that of the model (i.e., $R_6 \sim 0$).

A. Model Outcome Supported by the Game

Let us look at the possibility of drawing conclusions when $R_6 \sim 1$. We first have the problem that, even though $R_6 \sim 1$ and $R_4 \sim 1$, it is not certain that $R_5 \sim 1$, i.e., that the players behave in accordance with the model's behavioral assumptions, since it is quite possible that another set of behavioral assumptions, taken together with IA_T, would lead to the same model outcome. In order to be certain that $R_5 \sim 1$ we must:

1. Analyze the model structure to see whether other behavioral assumptions could possibly lead to this outcome, and/or

2. Study the whole game process to see whether the players seemed to behave in line with the model.

Both of these tasks are of course very difficult. One cannot study all possible behavioral assumptions and models often deal with implicit thought processes.

Let us assume, however, that through such analysis we have become reasonably certain that $R_5 \sim 1$, i.e., that the players behave in the same way in the game as in the model. Only in the very special case where $R_7 \sim 1$, implying that the institutional assumptions of the game map very closely onto reality, could one be reasonably confident in applying the model in the real world.

In the more probable case of $R_7 \sim 0$, there would still be the problem that the decision makers might behave differently in the more complex reality than they behaved in the game. Several factors suggest that people are less likely to follow behavioral assumptions that are focused on rationality (as in game theory) in reality than they are in a game.

We note in particular the following points:

1. There are in reality more players than in the institutional assumptions. In the water game, for example, there was not just one player per municipality group but several.

2. In real life, information is incomplete and decision making takes place under some degree of uncertainty, with the various players at best being able to assign subjective probabilities to various events and outcomes. The computational requirements for finding a solution in a game-theoretical model are far greater than in a model with deterministic information (see Harsanyi, 1967). This greater computational requirement reduces the likelihood of full rationality (see Cyert and March, 1963). In the real water cost-allocation exercise, the demand conditions in particular were extremely uncertain.

3. Free and instantaneous communication between *all* players is an institutional assumption fundamental to much of cooperative game theory. Such communication did not seem to occur in the real water situation. Limiting communication limits information further and works against game-theoretical "rationality".

4. In reality there is often a lack of symmetry as regards size and payoff functions for the various players. Such symmetry, which is often assumed in experimental games, would be conducive to game-theoretical rationality (see Johansen, 1981). Although the water game was not itself especially symmetric, there was, in the real situation with eighteen municipalities of greatly varying sizes, even less symmetry.

Hence, a positive result in a game would very seldom allow us to draw the conclusion that we could with confidence apply the model in reality. At best, we might revise our subjective assessment of the model's probable applicability in the real world. Depending on the cost of gaming relative to the cost of making a mistake in applying the model, we might in this situation proceed to further testing of the model.

B. *Model Outcome Refuted by the Game*

The conclusion that $R_8 \sim 0$ implies that $R_5 \sim 0$, i.e., that the parties did not follow the behavioral assumptions of the game. To analyze the implications of this further we shall distinguish between two cases in terms of how well the institutional assumptions of the game represent the real decision environment, i.e., whether (a) $R_7 \sim 1$ or (b) $R_7 \sim 0$.

a. Institutional Assumptions Correspond to Environment. Assuming that, as in the water games played with the planners, we have obtained $R_8 \sim 1$, i.e., the players are "decision maker similar", we can conclude that $R_5 \sim 0$ implies that $R_2 \sim 0$, i.e., that the behavioral assumptions of the model are *not* valid in reality. This is the most clear case for using gaming as an acid test. If the gaming in the case refutes the model, then there is no reason to try to apply it to the real situation.

b. Institutional Assumptions Differ from Environment. In the case of $R_7 \sim 0$, we cannot draw strong conclusions. Even if $R_8 \sim 1$, i.e., the players are "decision maker similar", their behavior might be different due to the fact that $R_7 \sim 0$. One cannot, without further investigation, rule out the possibility that decision makers would behave differently in the generally more complex real environment. It is of particular interest to note that one cannot rule out the chance that they might then, in reality, act *in accordance with* the behavioral assumptions of the model. One must therefore look more closely at R_7, to see in what respects the IA$_G$ (the Institutional Assumptions of the Game) differ from the real environment and to what extent this could possibly lead to changes in behavior.

Let us illustrate this by reference to the Water Cost-Allocation Game. Here, as already noted, the players in most games violated the behavioral assumptions underlying the Core method, and in particular those of the Proportional Core. As shown above, the IA$_G$ provided a very simplified model of the decision environment. The question is then whether it is reasonable to assume that because the environment is different, real water planners will, in the real situation, behave in an entirely different way. One should generally try to see through the different factors underlying the institutional assumptions and assess whether differences really would make decision makers more likely to act like the model in reality than in the game.

There seem to be two main factors that could work in this way: time compression and incentives for decisions. Decision models based on assumptions of rational behavior implicitly further assume that there is plenty of time for very careful deliberations. Furthermore, institutional payoff assumptions, explicitly or implicitly, concern very substantial sums of money. On the other hand, the main simplification in the game is the "time compression", since in most cases, for practical reasons, one cannot involve qualified persons in a game for more than a very limited time, for example, one evening (see Chapter X:a). In addition, the money paid out to the game participants is generally small for budgetary reasons. Real situations may involve millions of dollars, while in the game situation this sum is scaled down to only a few dollars. If a model has been refuted in a series of experiments, it is therefore wise to question whether the failure might have been due to the fact that the players had too little time for their decisions and too little economic incentive to play "well".

One way to check these factors would be to make the institutional assumptions more "realistic" by increasing monetary payoffs and available decision time. Of course, one cannot make any drastic changes in the game for the reasons mentioned above. In the water game we varied the monetary payoff by roughly a factor of 10. The amounts involved were, of course, still insignificant, with a maximum total payoff of $20. As regards the time for the game, we varied this by a factor of two. (The maximum game length is 90 minutes: in some games agreement on the grand coalition was already reached within half that time.)

These changes did not appear to have any noticeable effect on behavior. We can, then, perhaps at least refute the hypothesis that "the outcome of a game is a strictly monotonous function of time for decisions and monetary payoffs". We cannot, however, rule out the possibility that behavior might change if there were a very drastic change, for example, in monetary payoffs. The only indication we have that this was not the case came from discussions with water planners, who assured us that they would not have played differently even if the payoffs had been much higher.

On the other hand, we must remember that in Section 8.A we presented four factors that suggested the opposite, i.e., that decision makers are more likely to act like the model in a game than in reality. In the water game it appears that these four factors are stronger than the two mentioned above. In such a situation one would, on the basis of a negative outcome in the gaming experiment, have a somewhat more sound basis for the hypothesis that the model is *not* valid for real use. We would then suggest that one should *not* go ahead and directly apply the game-theory model in reality.

Summing up, testing by gaming mainly has the function of an "acid test"; i.e., it should be used as a screening process for models that one wants to use for real decisions. Models can be rejected as regards their validity for real applications by not being successful in the gaming experiments. Being successful in the gaming experiments is, however, far from sufficient to ensure successful real-world applications. Rather, success in gaming experiments is equivalent to a "green light" for continued testing of the model.

9. REVISING THE MODEL ON THE BASIS OF GAMING TESTS

It should finally be stressed that the rejection of a model through a negative outcome in the game need not mean that the model should be "scrapped" altogether: it is often more a case of "back to the drawing board". Then one would try to change the model on the basis of the experience gained from the gaming experiments.

Here we encounter another important function of gaming, namely, gaming as a generator of ideas for constructing new or revised theoretical models. These new theoretical models may not be based on the same types of assumptions of unlimited rationality as the game-theoretical models, but may be part of a more general theory of game playing. In other cases, the new behavioral assumptions might still be in the realm of fully rational game playing but the focus may be different.

As regards the water game, we concluded that a major reason for the predictive weakness of the core methods was that the methods did not allow for the formation of the grand coalition through a step-by-step approach (although this actually occurred in *all* the games). This inspired us to construct an alternative model for cost allocation in situations of the type described.

The main idea is that each new coalition is formed by only two parties, be they single players or already existing coalitions of players. The formation of the grand coalition will therefore, in the six-player game, always involve five coalition-formation steps. In this regard the new theory is similar to the coalition-formation process of the Shapley Value discussed in Section 2. The difference, however, is that in each step we choose the *most likely* coalition. This is defined as follows. Each of the remaining parties (i.e., six parties in the first step, five in the second step, etc.) name the party with whom they prefer to form a coalition, because it will give them the highest cost savings. The two parties forming a coalition split the total cost savings equally.[16] If two parties have each other as preferred parties, they form a CCP (Coalition Candidates Pair). If there is only one CCP, the parties of this pair will form a coalition. If there are several CCPs, the one leading to the highest cost savings will turn into a coalition. If in a particular step there is no CCP, the game will continue for a while. In a dynamic game, with the parties incurring certain time penalties (an early agreement is worth more than a late agreement), a CCP will generally evolve after some delay and will then form a coalition.

For the Water Cost-Allocation Game this theory leads, under the assumption of equal time penalties (interest rates) for all parties, to a solution, which for the difference measures mentioned above fares better than any of the six original methods. We cannot, however, claim any predictive value for our method, since the model has been constructed *after* the playing of the game. (We hesitate to talk even of a descriptive value at this stage.) The model's predictive value must now be tested in new game runs, preferably ones with different numerical values than those which inspired the new theory.

More generally, after reconstructing a model in the light of gaming tests, it is necessary to perform new tests. Hence the use of gaming in testing is only one link in an iterative process of model construction, testing, revision, and further testing, leading step by step to a model that is more valid for real applications.

REFERENCES

Allais, M. and Hagen, O. (Eds.) (1979). Expected utility hypotheses and the Allais paradox: contemporary discussion of the decisions under uncertainty with Allais' rejoinder. *Theory and Decision Library 21.* Reidel, Dordrecht.

Cyert, R.M. and March, J.G. (1963). *Behavioral Theory of the Firm.* Prentice Hall, Englewood Cliffs, New Jersey.

Friedman, M. (1953). The methodology of positive economics. In *Essays in Positive Economics.* Chicago University Press, Chicago, Illinois.

Harsanyi, J.C. (1967). Games with incomplete information played by "Bayesian" players. *Management Science*, 13(2): 80-106.

Johansen, L. (1981). *On the Status of the Nash Type of Non-cooperative Equilibrium in Economic Theory*. Memorandum. Institute of Economics, University of Oslo.

Stahl, I. (1980). *Cost Allocation in Water Resources--Two Gaming Experiments with Doctoral Students*. WP-80-134. International Institute for Applied Systems Analysis, Laxenburg, Austria.

Stahl, I. (1982a). *Six Games for Research and Education*. Internal Discussion Paper. International Institute for Applied Systems Analysis, Laxenburg, Austria.

Stahl, I. (1982b). Gaming: a new methodology in the study of natural resources. In W. Eichhorn, R. Henn, K. Neumann, and R.W. Shephard (Eds.), *Economic Theory of Natural Resources*. Physica Verlag, Wuerzburg.

Young, H.P. (1980). *Cost Allocation and Demand Revelation in Public Enterprises*. WP-80-130. International Institute for Applied Systems Analysis, Laxenburg, Austria.

Young, H.P., Okada, N., and Hashimoto, T. (1980). *Cost Allocation in Water Resources Development--A Case Study of Sweden*. RR-80-32. International Institute for Applied Systems Analysis, Laxenburg, Austria.

NOTES

1. As defined in Chapter III:a.

2. As defined in Chapter III:a.

3. The marginal or "separable" cost for a party is the marginal cost of being the *last* to join the *grand* coalition. "Remaining benefit" is the difference between the cost if the municipality goes alone and its marginal cost. The party pays its marginal costs *plus* its share of the nonallocated costs, where this share is proportional to the party's share of remaining benefits.

4. Although these last two principles were first stated as desirable properties of a solution, they can be reworked into behavioral assumptions by stating that "a party will not agree to any cost division that would violate these principles".

5. Although the Skane study began with something of a direct operational purpose, namely to help with the decision on increased water supply for the 1980s in Sweden, it turned out during the study period that, due to the economic setback in Sweden after 1973, the original demand forecasts were much too high and that a much smaller increase in water supply was called for. The cost data were, however, still reasonable. The study hence became much more focused on using these data for developing better cost-allocation methods. For this reason the gaming activity acquired the character of an operational research game.

6. This does not mean that it is absolutely *necessary* to get correct behavioral assumptions. Quite often a model can, e.g., make good predictions without the behavioral assumptions being a good replication of the actual behavior of the players (see Friedman, 1953). However, unless the behavioral assumptions in some way capture the essence, i.e., the most important properties of the behavior, the model's predictive ability under certain institutional assumptions might be purely coincidental and one would then be hesitant to use it for situations with very different institutional assumptions. It should be stressed that our method of testing by gaming does not focus on the direct observation of the behavioral assumption.

7. Among the behavioral assumptions, one should include what in many models are referred to as axioms, often concerning desirable properties of the solution.

8. Except (possibly) assumptions regarding deductive and computational ability by providing deductions and computational facilities. In this section we shall therefore exclude assumptions regarding deductive and computational ability when we talk about behavioral assumptions.

9. Look at the assumptions in Chapter III:a, Section 6. How does a decision maker answer the question: "Do you want to act as if you have correct expectations concerning the expectations of the other parties?".

10. This has, for example, been critical for many experiments testing utility theory (see Allais and Hagen, 1979).

11. For an example, see Stahl (1980, p.7).

12. In one of these twelve games the parties played, prior to the game described here, a sealed auction bid game (Young, 1980), the outcome of which could possibly be used as a reference point for the later game. In this game another model (not one of those discussed earlier) was also tested.

13. Allocations according to population would lead to even greater differences.

14. For instance, in the games with planners in Sweden, Italy, and Poland the outcome of any game in the other three countries was the best predictor, and in the game with the Bulgarian water planners the games in the other countries were the second-best predictors, only slightly behind the Shapley Value (Stahl, 1982b).

15. This is discussed in more detail in Chapter X:a, Section 2.2.

16. This equal split is derived from basic game-theoretical assumptions.

Chapter VIII:c

OPERATIONAL GAMING OF CATTLE BREEDING

Sandor Somogyi and Istvan Kisimre
Institute of Management Sciences, Subotica (Yugoslavia)

1. INTRODUCTION

In many countries, the agricultural sector is organized in the form of large agroindustrial complexes. However, the size of these complexes increases, in turn, the associated problems of planning, decision making, and coordination. Methods from operational research are often helpful in planning and decision making but they usually cannot satisfactorily take into account all the complexities of large systems and the dynamics of their behavior. The very precise "optimal" solutions provided by these methods are often unnecessary and serve only as broad guidelines.

With this in mind, we started research into methods that imitate the dynamics of complex agroindustrial systems. Experience in setting up and using simulation models has shown that they can handle the complexity and dynamics of these big systems, and the rapid generation of a great number of possible solutions permits an effective choice of suitable solutions to be made.

Our first attempt at developing simulation models was made after study of the agricultural operational gaming efforts of the Hungarian scientists Csaki and Mozes (1976) (see also Chapter V:c of this volume). We began by trying to adapt their game to our requirements, but it soon became apparent that the needs of our users were very different from the possibilities inherent in the original game, so that we had, in essence, to change the whole game. Using the experience obtained from that game, we then developed our own simulation model of general farming.

Our next step was the development of a simulation model specifically for cattle breeding. The need for such a model has long been felt by agricultural planners in Yugoslavia and our work was widely supported. We developed this model completely on our own. The result of the work is a well-documented simulation model (see Somogyi and Kisimre, 1981). To make the model more accessible, we developed it in three different versions, with different degrees of complexity.

In this chapter we shall briefly describe this operational game. We begin with a description of the cattle farm viewed as a manufacturing system, then move on to an outline of the simulation model of cattle breeding. This is followed by a short review of the operational gaming effort, and the chapter closes with a discussion of the practical experience acquired by using the game.

2. THE CATTLE FARM AS A MANUFACTURING SYSTEM

Within large complex systems for food production, cattle breeding plays an important role because less valuable plant products are converted into highly valuable animal products. In Yugoslavia, cattle breeding has tended to be organized more and more in large specialized units. These cattle breeding farms are specialized economic complexes equipped with buildings, equipment, energy supplies, certain categories of cattle, and manpower.

The cattle breeding farm may be viewed as a manufacturing system which transforms fodder into various products. It involves constant *transformations* of the state of the system: these transformations are the results of the mutual interactions of work, biological processes, fodder, money, energy, information, and surroundings.

If we analyze the transformation processes occurring in a cattle breeding farm, we can differentiate the following components:

- Biological components, i.e., the cattle, as the bearers of genetic potential and the capability for converting fodder into highly valuable products.
- Fodder, which is effectively transformed into cattle.
- Manufacturing and nonmanufacturing services, which are necessary for the continuing development of the production process.
- Investment, which is necessary for the functioning and development of the farm.
- Energy, for manufacturing and nonmanufacturing purposes.
- Work, i.e., manpower, as the driving force behind the production process on the farm.
- Environment, i.e., those factors which influence the functioning of the system described above.
- Data, i.e., information about the state and behavior of the system and its environment.

3. A SIMULATION MODEL OF CATTLE BREEDING

Simplified models of complex systems, which more or less faithfully imitate all the essential characteristics of the systems, have an exceptional significance in planning, decision making, and business management. Such models permit the rapid testing of the consequences of a variety of possible decisions using a computer. The task of the simulation model is to simulate all the essential transformation processes of the system and thus to represent the possible behavior of the system.

Experience has shown that, in order to arrive at a valid simulation model, it is necessary to perform the following tasks:

- Study the behavior of the system to be simulated.
- Determine the transformation processes of this system.
- Define the system's inputs and outputs and the relation between them.
- Outline the approximate logical structure of the system in a model.
- Write and test the computer programs.
- Write the instructions for using the models and programs.

Our simulation model of cattle breeding was developed along these lines. After studying cattle breeding as a manufacturing system, we began to consider the various transformation processes. On the basis of these transformations we defined the transformation formulas, i.e., the mathematical descriptions of these processes. These formulas were based on empirical data. The user of the simulation model can either be informed about these formulas, or use them as a "black box". When necessary, the transformation formulas are left "open" for the user who can, optionally, modify them by specifying the corresponding parameters in the form of input data.

The simulation model of the cattle breeding farm system comprises the following significant components:

- State of the system at the beginning of the period to be examined.
- Input into the system during the period.
- Characteristics of the transformation processes during the period.
- Output of the system during the period.
- New state of the system at the end of the period.

If the initial state of the system and the inputs during the simulation period are quantified and estimates of the transformation processes are made, the corresponding output of the system can be computed. This simulation will not, as a rule, supply a unique optimal solution but only one of several possible solutions. The results obtained should be analyzed and examined bearing in mind the main goals of the system. In the case of the cattle breeding farm, for instance, the goal is generally to reach a higher level of production with a favorable rate of conversion of fodder, thus realizing a level of economic operation that can cover the current needs of the farm as well as providing for expanded future production.

With every simulation model it is of course important to define the time period to which the simulation refers. The simulation of cattle breeding is generally performed for a period of one calendar year.

4. INPUT-OUTPUT PARAMETERS OF THE SIMULATION MODEL

The most important input data for the simulation model fall into three main groups:

1. *Initial State of the Farm*
   (a) Cattle stock
   - Number of head of cattle (at the beginning of the year) according to category.[1]
   - Weight per head according to category.
   - Value (price per kilogram).
   - Age structure according to category.
   - Percentage of milk cows and heifers in breeding stock that are pregnant.
   - Weight structure of cattle for fattening, etc.
   (b) Buildings and equipment (only total values given)

2. *Direct and Indirect Inputs of Cattle During the Year*
   (a) Input of cattle
   - Number of cattle bought according to category.
   - Average weight at purchase.
   - Average purchase price.
   - Percentage of cows and heifers that are pregnant at purchase, etc.
   (b) Input of materials (raw materials and semimanufactures)
   - Fodder (kind, quality, quantity, price).
   - Auxiliary material, energy, and services (only total values given).

3. *Inputs Related to the Transformation Formulas*[2]
   - Weight of calves in breeding stock.
   - Increase in numbers according to category.
   - Number of calves born per pregnant cow.
   - Proportion of male calves in the total.

Many external factors or disturbances influence the functioning of cattle breeding. The directions and intensity of their effects in any subsequent period are very difficult to estimate. However, it is necessary to try to predict their net influence and to include this in the model. If the disturbances are of a stochastic nature, random-number generators can be used. A number of such random factors are included in our model, relating mainly to disease, enforced slaughter of cattle, and so on.

The simulation of a given period ends with the attainment of the new state. The parameter values characterizing the new state are generated by the simulation process. The most important output tables concern the following:

- Turnover (measured in head of cattle).
- Records of the weights, increase in numbers, and values of each category of cattle.
- Record of milk production.
- Survey of the need for fodder.
- Daily feeds required for the various categories of cattle.
- Manpower plan.
- Overall economic results of the cattle breeding.
- Indicators of the successful functioning of the cattle breeding farm.

Information on the new state of the cattle breeding farm is thus obtained after each period of simulation. The data describing this state can be used as input for simulation of the next period: this is useful when we wish to simulate the behavior of the farm over many years.

5. SHORT DESCRIPTION OF THE OPERATIONAL GAME

Cattle breeding is a complex process, so the simulation model of the process is correspondingly complicated. Therefore manual simulation on the basis of the model described above would be very tedious and the calculation of the model's output on the basis of several different sets of input data would be almost impossible. However, simulation models only really make sense if it is possible to test many cases in order to find the combination of input data that gives the most acceptable results. It is therefore necessary to implement the simulation model on a computer; this permits rapid simulation, together with the possibility of successively changing decisions in order to find the most suitable solution. If the user uses a simulation model in this way, then, *according to our definition*, he is playing an operational game. In this case he is termed a *player*, and the internal logic of the model constitutes the rules of the game. The physical output and financial indicators are measures of the degree of success achieved by the player in the game.

The basic version of our cattle breeding operational game is a general simulation model of the cattle breeding farm. The player starts the simulation by inputting data on the initial state of the system. If necessary, he modifies some of the transformation formulas. He then defines the input decision variables for the simulation period. The computer performs the simulation and provides results in the form of tables, which the player examines. On the basis of these tables he makes decisions about possible changes in the initial state of the system, the transformation formulas, or the decision input data. The gaming is planned in such a way that some intermediate results can be considered, and so that decision making is possible, not only at the very beginning of the simulation, but also at various so-called control points.

It is important to note that the general simulation model of the cattle breeding farm is formulated so that it enables the use of data from *real* farms. The initial state of the system and other data can be taken from a specific farm and the future behavior of that farm can be simulated under different conditions and on the basis of various management policies. In fact, the primary purpose of the operational gaming effort is just such an application to the real conditions of cattle breeding farms.

An important feature of the cattle breeding game is the possibility for *competition* between the players. The physical and financial indicators, which are obtained as output at the end of the simulation, can be used as measures of the success of the various players. The initial state can be defined in advance and all players can start from the same state. Their results can then be compared at the end of a specific period, so that the skill of each player can be evaluated. This feature is particularly useful for educational purposes.

The game is intended to be used by players from different professions, interests, and occupations, ranging from students to highly skilled workers and experts in cattle breeding. In order that all categories of users derive the maximum benefit from the game, three versions are available.

In the *simplest version* of the game, the players calculate only the turnover and the growth of the herd and the milk production. All the transformation formulas are fixed. On the basis of relatively few data, indicators of turnover of the herd, milk production, increase and growth in the number of cattle, and total income of the farm are calculated. This version of the game is mainly intended for students.

The other two versions use the complete simulation model of cattle breeding. They enable all data related to the state of the system and changes and modifications of the transformation formulas to be input. In the *medium version*, the players input the data on daily feeds for the cattle.

In the *most difficult version*, the players input only the available quantities of different kinds of fodder, indicating also the nutritional ingredients and price of each and the special dietary needs of some categories of cattle. The feeds themselves are calculated by means of linear programming.[3] This complex version requires the players to have nutritional knowledge and is mainly intended for the simulation of real (existing or foreseen) cattle breeding systems. The players in this case should be groups of experts with a wide range of professional backgrounds and this version is used for business decisions later to be applied in actual practice.

6. THE USE OF THE CATTLE-BREEDING GAME

This operational game relies completely on the use of a computer. The player has two main options:

1. To input all data concerning the state of the farm and changes during the examined period for computer processing in batch mode and, after the processing, to analyze the results obtained.

2.   To input the data interactively using a terminal, in order to be able to examine all intermediate results obtained as a basis for decisions about the next task.

The flow diagram for the most difficult version of the operational game is presented in Figure 1; the simpler versions use only a part of this procedure. The game proceeds as follows.

At the beginning of the game, the player inputs the data on prepared forms, thus defining the state of "his" cattle breeding farm at the beginning of the simulation period. If necessary, he modifies the transformation formulas by specifying various parameters and defines the input data for the period. The forms are structured in a way that helps the player to define the input data more easily and effectively.

Some input data are related to the purchase of cattle. If the player, for the time being, does not have all the data necessary for making decisions about purchases, he first simulates the turnover of the herd based only on the reproduction of his original herd. After analyzing the results obtained, he repeats this part of the simulation if necessary, now including his decisions about purchases of cattle.

On the basis of the initial state of the system and the input data, the first part of the simulation projects the turnover of the herd, milk production, and growth in the number of cattle, and also gives some financial indicators, such as the value of the cattle produced. The simplest version of the game finishes at this point. The player can repeat the simulation many times with changed data or perform the simulation for succeeding periods by using the data obtained to define the initial state for the next period.

In more difficult versions of the game, the data on feeding the herd are given *after* the "control point" at which the results of herd turnover are considered. If the player wishes to establish total fodder needs on the basis of optimization of the daily feeds he inputs the following information:

- Nutritional requirements of the cattle;
- Nutritional content of fodder;
- Quantities of fodder available;
- Prices of fodder.

On the basis of these data the optimal structure of daily feeds for each category of cattle is calculated by means of linear programming. If the player does not want to utilize the optimization procedure, he must himself specify the structure of the daily feeds.

In both cases, the final results of this part of the operational gaming are indicators related to the feeding of the cattle (fodder requirements, daily feeds, costs of feeding, etc.). Having studied these results, the player can decide to repeat just this part or the whole procedure from the beginning in order to improve the results by changing the data. In the most difficult versions of the game, we have found that it is very often necessary to change the input data related to feeding, because the first runs are usually insufficient for specifying feeds of the required quality and quantity.

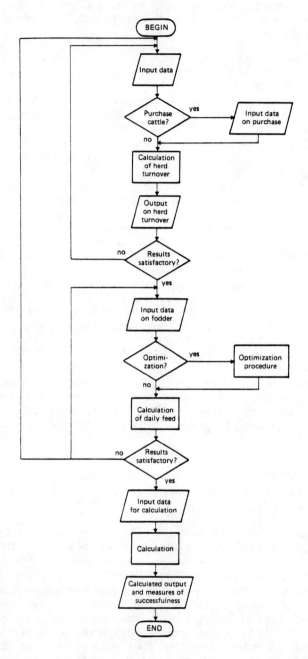

Figure 1. The flow diagram of the cattle-breeding game.

7. PRACTICAL EXPERIENCE WITH THE CATTLE-BREEDING GAME

The simulation model and the corresponding computer programs were developed at the Institute of Management Sciences in Subotica on a UNIVAC 1100/20 computer. The programs are written in FORTRAN, and the standard programming package FMPS (Functional Mathematical Programming System) is used for the optimization of daily feeds.

From the flow diagram of the game (Figure 1) it can be seen that there are three separate programs corresponding to the three stages of the simulation. These programs are connected by the job control language of the operating system. On average, the programs consist of 700 lines of code. They are written according to the block principle, where every block has a clearly defined and separate function. Therefore, adaptation for new requirements (e.g., changing transformation formulas or producing output tables in other languages) and the transfer of the program to some other type of computer are relatively simple.

It is also quite easy to teach the use of the game. If the player does not want to work interactively with the computer, all that is necessary is that he should fill out certain forms that clearly indicate what kinds of data are required and how their consistency can be controlled.

The use of the terminal for interactive work normally causes no difficulties either. A short course is quite sufficient for someone familiar with cattle breeding to learn the use of the operational game.

After the construction and testing of the computer programs, the game itself was subjected to trial use. It was first used to simulate the operation of a "school model" of a cattle breeding farm, and after that was applied to models of several large farms.

On the basis of these tests, during which the most difficult version was mainly used, we found that it was complex and time-consuming, even for experts, to give all the data needed for a complete simulation of the functioning of the cattle breeding farm over a one-year period. Nevertheless, the results obtained were realistic and gave rise to useful suggestions for farm management.

REFERENCES

Csaki, Cs. and Mozes, L. (1976). *Agricultural Companies Decision Game.* Tankoenyu Kiado, Budapest. (In Hungarian.)

Somogyi, S. and Kisimre, I. (1981). *A Simulation Model of Cattle Production: A Method for Making Business Decisions.* Institute of Management Sciences, Subotica, Yugoslavia. (In Serbo-Croat.)

NOTES

1. The model can simulate the operation of a farm with 1-10 different categories of cattle (for instance, calves, heifers, cows, etc.).

2. The transformation formulas have a standard form which is built into the model. If they do not suit the user, he can change them by means of these input parameters.

3. The optimization of daily feeds for the various categories of cattle is not done in isolation: all feeds for all categories are optimized simultaneously for the whole period of simulation. The seasonal availability of some kinds of fodder is also taken into consideration.

PART IX

DEVELOPMENT OF OPERATIONAL GAMES

Chapter IX:a

DEVELOPMENT OF THE CONRAIL GAME

Richard D. Duke and Kathryn M. Duke
University of Michigan, Ann Arbor, Michigan (USA)

1. INTRODUCTION

As a discipline, gaming is most effective when considered as a communications mode between the sciences and public policy issues. This interface becomes critical since it affects so much in public life. Specifically, science has much to offer on the resolution of public issues, but is often ignored or improperly applied. Scientists who attempt to assist in this process are confronted with two primary choices in terms of the perception of how public decisions are made. In one instance, decision is viewed as a logical process, and this leads to a series of scientific activities. In this context the classical theory of games and other mathematical approaches appear to be reasonable and productive. Unfortunately, decision in most instances is more a "gestalt" event than a logical process. If one is making a decision concerning the operation of a petroleum refinery perhaps the model of a logical process is legitimate. If one is dealing with a major public issue such as the Conrail case described here, one has to perceive the actions of major politicians concerning this as being part of an overall context or "gestalt" event.

To deal with this concept of decision as a gestalt event in a public context we have evolved a communications theory of gaming/simulation (Duke, 1974, 1981). This theory leads to several notions. One is that games are situation specific. Another is that games must be constructed from a disciplined process. This process can be divided into ten steps. In this chapter we shall identify the ten steps and indicate briefly how they were applied in the Conrail case.

2. TEN STEPS OF GAME DEVELOPMENT

Step 1. Define the Problem

Conrail Corporation was created in 1976 by the US Congress as a private profit-making corporation with the responsibility of taking over the operations of six bankrupt rail lines in the northeastern quadrant of the country. The Regional Rail Reorganization Act charged Conrail with integrating the six railroads into one system to maximize service and to minimize the required public subsidy. Although Conrail was given a large federal grant to cover the initial costs of taking over the railroads, it was hoped that eventually the corporation would become self-sufficient.

After two years and over three billion dollars in public subsidies, however, Conrail managers were unwilling to guarantee that the system (with its route mileage already trimmed by 30%) could ever become profitable, in the prevailing regulatory environment. The Carter administration, for its part, had hinted strongly that Conrail should not assume that additional subsidies would be forthcoming.

Conrail management was, thus, under a great deal of pressure. While the Administration threatened to cut off funds, various state and local politicians were intent on ensuring that money-losing trunk or branch lines affecting their constituencies would not be closed. To exacerbate the situation, Conrail was a member of a regulated industry. Its management, therefore, had little or no control over two crucial factors that managers in unregulated industries manipulate in order to improve profitability: pricing and the level of service.

As part of an overall effort to improve its financial performance, Conrail management developed a new analytical framework for evaluating the operation of the system. Basically, the new technique placed a greater emphasis on the revenue-cost relationships for individual commodities or lines of business (LOBs) than on the profitability of specific segments of rail line, as had been the traditional practice of the industry.

The development of this analytical approach followed the realization that it is not always productive to think in terms of excess capacity in relation to the fixed plant of railroads. Traditionally, railroad managers had assumed that once the plant (i.e., rail lines, terminals) was fixed in place it was desirable to run as much traffic as the plant would accommodate, regardless of how much or little revenues from particular services covered fixed costs.

Managers have now discovered that additional traffic often adds costs beyond those traditionally considered to be variable costs. In other words, costs that were once thought to be fixed are often actually variable. The result is that railroad managers are beginning to realize that it pays to discriminate between customers. The only services to be provided would be those from which revenues cover all true variable costs and, in addition, cover some of the fixed costs.

Building on the novel assumption that the railroad's fixed plant contained less excess capacity than previously believed, Conrail management developed the analytical framework based on LOBs and commissioned an extensive study of the Conrail system using that framework. One particularly significant result of the study was the conclusion that, out of 80 distinct LOBs identified in the study, only nine were making contributions to Conrail's fully allocated fixed costs.

The study broke LOBs into four broad categories based on their profitability, the competitiveness of rail and truck transportation, and the cost of assets necessary to provide the service. Another significant result of the study was that Conrail could continue to service all four categories of LOBs over the then existing system only at the cost of hundreds of millions of dollars a year in public money. However, the study concluded that if it were allowed to drop certain services and lines Conrail could become self-sufficient.

The results of the study and the threat of losing future public subsidies led the Board of Directors of Conrail to conclude that Conrail should move to divest itself of a large number of LOBs and therefore, inevitably, a number of branch or trunk lines. This conclusion, in turn, led the Board to look upon deregulation of Conrail or of the rail industry in general as a positive goal and even as a necessary goal if Conrail was to wean itself from reliance on the public purse.

Step 2. State Why Gaming and Not Other Methods

Within the context outlined above certain members of the Conrail management felt a gaming exercise would be beneficial. The desire for a simulation tool originated within the ranks of Conrail's middle management. These, our clients, articulated several purposes, each catering to a different audience, that they hoped a game could serve.

The first and most important audience for the game would be Conrail's *top level managers*, the Board of Directors and the vice presidents. The clients believed that while the top level management was extremely competent in matters strictly related to the management of a railroad, it was less than fully cognizant and/or appreciative of the political context within which Conrail was forced to operate. The clients were concerned that these people would base their management plans on a configuration of the system (i.e., regulatory environment and service level) that would be ideal from the management perspective but, in view of political exigencies, impossible to achieve. The clients were interested in creating a simulation that would reveal to those top level managers what the political reactions to various systems alternatives would be. The managers, then, could form a consensus on an alternative that, though perhaps less than perfect from a management point of view, would be politically feasible.

The second audience was to be *political actors*. It was assumed by the clients that once the Conrail management, with the benefits of the simulation, had decided on a policy direction, the game could be used to explain to various political decision makers why this policy made sense. The clients were interested in altering decision makers' beliefs about what the legitimate functions of a railroad ought to be. They were also interested in communicating the notion that decisions to drop particular branch lines are not proposed as ends in themselves, but are by-products of decisions to drop particular commodities or services based on the LOB analysis.

Some of the clients expressed a less subjective purpose. They believed that the game should be used to represent to political actors the various options that were available for Conrail's configuration and operation and the extent of regulations. Associated with each option would, of course, be various costs and benefits. Underlying the entire process would be the trade-off between the level of service desired and the willingness to spend public money. It would be up to the politicians themselves to choose the most attractive alternative. The purpose of the game would be merely to present the alternatives in such a fashion that this trade-off would be pronounced, helping the decision makers to discern how the system really works, to be aware of the policy options, and to comprehend the political consequences of each option.

The clients believed that the game could be beneficial in educating *mid-level managers* and state rail officials about how the Conrail system operates and why deregulation would be necessary for Conrail to move toward self-sufficiency. In addition, the game could be used to demonstrate why particular LOBs would be dropped if regulations were to be removed.

Finally, top management had a very short time between the time it resolved to look at the deregulation question and the time that it expected Congress to act. There was simply not sufficient time to justify more elaborate or rigorous scientific methods. Further, it was assumed that the problem was understood and the real question was to communicate the character of the problem to someone outside the railroad industry. Therefore, one of the primary functions of gaming, namely to try to transmit knowledge to some new group, appeared valid. Thus, the gaming team was called in and was told that the company had resolved that deregulation was good and that the game was essentially to be a propaganda tool to convince Congress to proceed with deregulation.

Step 3. Specifications for Game Design

The first job of the game design team was to prepare a document that treated several hundred variables by defining the particulars of what the client was trying to achieve and the environment in which the game would be operated. These specifications included constraints on the use of computers, the time horizon, the objectives in terms of communication, and the nature of the economic model to be conveyed.

Step 4. Systems Study

Having obtained a written agreement on the specifications describing the objectives of the game, the team undertook a complete, if hurried, systems study. This is an attempt to put into one schematic diagram all of the information that might be available concerning the character of the system that we are dealing with. The lines of business, the kinds of freight transported, the characteristics of the competing rail, truck, sea and air industries, the applicable concepts of fixed and variable costs, and the network itself were all represented. In order to define this rudimentary analytical schema, depicting the costing and pricing mechanisms of the economic system within which Conrail operated, we had to obtain information (both conceptual and empirical) from each of the Conrail vice presidents. The information was incorporated by the game designers into the tentative abstract schema, which was then presented to the same individuals who had provided the information.

Step 5. Selection of Systems Components for the Game

In this step the game design team worked with the Conrail team. Using the specifications as a guide we selected the items from the systems study that had to be included in the game itself. In effect we were making a model of a model.

Given the purpose of the game it was evident that the game had to include some element that would dramatize the effects of various managerial and regulatory options on Conrail's customers. In other words, if Conrail management were allowed to drop certain unprofitable commodities or services, what kinds of shippers would be hurt, how many, and how badly? Would entire branch lines be closed down? What would be the impact on particular political jurisdictions?

Furthermore, it was essential that the game communicate the link between levels of services provided and the amount of public subsidy required. The Conrail management's contention was that unless the regulatory restrictions on its decisions concerning pricing and service provision were loosened, Conrail would continue to require public money to subsidize services for which revenues received did not cover costs incurred. Thus, the game had to provide players with an intuitive grasp of the relationship between costs and revenues and the impact of regulatory restrictions on this relationship.

In short, the game had to be designed to illustrate the market processes affecting Conrail's profitability and the differing effects on various political constituencies of the options available for restructuring the overall market system.

Step 6. Systems Component/Gaming Element Matrix

Having completed step 5, which was the selection of the components of the system that we wished to represent in the game, we then went through a deliberate process of showing how each of these components would be reflected as a gaming element. There are at least 13 gaming elements. The gaming elements are as follows: 1, scenario; 2, pulse; 3, steps of play; 4, psycho-sequence; 5, roles including gamed roles, pseudo roles, and simulated or robot roles; 6, rules; 7, models; 8, decision structure and linkages; 9, accounting system; 10, indicators; 11, symbology; 12, paraphernalia; and 13, referee or game operator (further details are given by Duke, 1974, 1981).

The system component/gaming element matrix is a deliberate procedure whereby one establishes each systems component that is to be represented as some specific element or elements of a proposed game.

Step 7. Concept Report

The Concept Report is a blueprint for the design of the game. It is produced by essentially summarizing each column of the gaming element matrix. In this way everything that had to be represented in the system, and that has thus been transferred to the gaming element matrix, can now be summarized in a logical report. For example, the scenario items can now be assembled in a logical way. The Concept Report becomes the first logical statement of what the game format might be.

Some of the most salient concepts that the Conrail game sought to elucidate include: the range of Conrail's customers and the complexity of its services; the difficulty of accurately determining fixed and variable costs corresponding to specific movements; the implications of different pricing methods (generic versus customer-specific discrete pricing); the competitive nature of Conrail's markets; the feasibility of increasing revenues through price increases or elimination of fixed costs; and the total cost to the region of transportation under regulation compared with the total cost to the region under deregulation.

Step 8. Game Design Process

This is a fairly straightforward process in which the game is designed using an interactive procedure that attempts to emphasize the gaming elements one by one. During this stage teamwork is required, and the repertoire of games previously played is very useful for thinking through what this particular exercise might look like.

We arrived at a game with the players taking four types of role: (1) customers (shippers); (2) Conrail managers; (3) competing railroad managers; and (4) competing truck managers.

Through simulation of three phases representing different market conditions, transportation consumers (shippers) act out their roles in each round by choosing the most economical mode for shipping their commodities. At the same time, players in the roles of managers of the competing transportation modes are given opportunities to improve their profitability by reducing costs and increasing revenues.

The first phase--the status quo--conveys the reasons for Conrail's deficit operations. The second phase--corrective initiatives under the present regulatory environment--demonstrates the limitations to achieving greater profitability under regulation. The third phase--corrective initiatives under a deregulated system--allows players to explore the consequences of pricing and service decisions based exclusively on market conditions.

Step 9. Test and Evaluate

During this stage the "rule of ten" is met. This means that the game is played at least ten times with the appropriate group, with suitable modifications being made after each run. The results are always evaluated against the specifications developed in Step 3. The results from these early runs were dramatic in this case, requiring a rewrite of Steps 3 and 4. The purpose shifted from an *external* propaganda tool to an *internal* policy tool. This is described in more detail in the "Results" which follow. After final modification the artwork and printing are done professionally before final use.

Step 10. Field Use

At this stage the gaming simulation for Conrail was turned over to the corporation, where it was formally run by all the senior vice presidents before final approval and then by the Board of Directors.

Subsequently it has been used extensively in two modes. The first is within the organization and is a way of transmitting to middle management the concept of how the organization would deal with the new deregulated environment. The second is external and is a way of showing members of Congress, state governors, and people in competing transportation modes what the new model for Conrail would be.

3. THE RESULTS

The game was, as mentioned, designed to fulfill the three purposes articulated by the clients before the design process was initiated: 1, to educate top Conrail managers about the political consequences of alternative models for the Conrail system; 2, to educate political actors about the economic realities of operating a railroad; and 3, to educate mid-level Conrail managers about both the political and the economic implications of the LOB-style system analysis. During the design phase however, it became clear that the most valuable benefit of the game had not been foreseen. Furthermore, this resulted not from actual playing of the game, but merely from efforts to develop a consensus on the appropriate systems-analytical framework on which to base the game.

What made the Conrail game so challenging to create was that the development of the game itself modified the perception of the problem for which the game was intended. Thus, the definition of the problem changed substantially over time.

The plasticity of the problem definition could have caused a lot of doubt. However, because of the manner in which design proceeded it was possible to use progressive insights into the problem to good advantage throughout the development of the game. This would probably not have happened had we not adhered very systematically to fundamental game design principles.

The results were surprising. When the managers, as a group, were presented with the schema that had been pieced together from bits of information provided by each of them individually (step 4), the overall scheme was not acceptable to any of them. The vice presidents did not agree among themselves--either on basic concepts or on particular supporting data. For many of those involved this came as a great surprise. They were surprised to find that their colleagues had divergent views about basic elements of the Conrail "system".

At this point it became clear that no progress could be made until the vice presidents were able to agree about how Conrail actually operated and the mechanisms affecting the corporation's performance. Consequently, the first few months of the design phase were devoted to working with the group of vice presidents. We would solicit information from each member of the group; this information would be processed and abstracted into a model. The model would then be presented to the group. The group, inevitably, would break into heated arguments over specific aspects of the model. Through several iterations of this process the model was refined to a point where all could agree that it was a fairly accurate representation of the Conrail "system."

This process proved very valuable to Conrail's management. By forcing individuals to communicate with each other about specific elements of the system, a more elaborate, comprehensive, and consistent model of the system was developed. The most significant fact about the model, however, was not its greater complexity, or even its increased accuracy, but that all of the managers now shared very similar concepts of the underlying system.

The effect of this newly shared conceptual model was a quantum leap in communications. One result of this more efficient and effective discussion was the discovery that there were untapped opportunities within the system for improving profitability that could be pursued immediately and that were not dependent on regulatory reform for their success. Another result was that the managers' ideas of what type of deregulation legislation would be appropriate were substantially modified. The managers were quick to take advantage of their new-found insight. Before the game was ever played, policies had been initiated that would eventually lead to significant improvements in Conrail's profitability.

In some respects, then, the game was a success before it had even been completed. The designers, by forcing the clients to refine their "conceptual map" of the problem, had room to maneuver as the perception of the problem began to shift. When the clients first approached the game designers, they thought they knew two things: how the Conrail "system" operated; and what deregulation would mean, and that they were in favor of it. It became evident very early, however, that these were untenable assumptions. The focus of the game design process had to shift gears rather dramatically and rapidly. That this was possible was very fortunate since perhaps the primary value of the entire process was derived from the initial effort to develop the fundamental model for the subsequent game. Once the model had been developed, the game itself was devised very quickly.

REFERENCES

Duke, R.D. (1974). *Gaming: The Future's Language*. Sage Publications, Beverly Hills, California.

Duke, R.D. and Greenblat, C.S. (1981). *Principles and Practices of Gaming/Simulation*. Sage Publications, Beverly Hills, California.

Chapter IX:b

A METHOD FOR DEVELOPING MANAGEMENT SIMULATION GAMES

Vladimir M. Yefimov
Moscow State University, Moscow (USSR)

Vladimir F. Komarov
*Institute of Economics and Industrial Organization, Siberian Branch
of the USSR Academy of Sciences, Novosibirsk (USSR)*

1. INTRODUCTION

Management simulation games are finding increasingly frequent application for studying organizational processes, where an "organization" can be a plant, a corporation, a branch of industry, a region of a country, a country, a group of countries, or even the world. Designing a management simulation game is at present an isolated activity on the part of individuals, and its quality and efficiency much depend on their skills, experience, and talent. Moreover, various research teams document their designs poorly, making it difficult for other potential users to systematize and use them.

This chapter sets out a procedure for designing management simulation games on the basis of a set of documents.[1] Each document describes a management simulation game (or part thereof) at a certain phase of its development. The documents of the initial phases of the design give a fuzzy description of the elements of the game and the documents of the final phase constitute detailed blueprints. Breaking the design process down into the preparation of separate documents permits the appropriate allocation of work among the designers. These documents stimulate fruitful interactions in the design process among clients and developers and among different developers themselves.

Each document (or part thereof) prepared at the final phase of the design process can be addressed to a particular participant in a gaming simulation experiment (a game administrator, a player, an expert, a computer operator, etc.). The documents must permit such experiments to be carried out in accordance with the intentions of the author but without his direct involvement. The proposed method consists of filling in the documents sequentially. This method raises the quality of the final product and lowers its costs.

2. SOME DEFINITIONS[2]

The peculiarity of this approach to the management simulation game is its consideration of the game as an activity. The main characteristic of a game as an activity is its duality. The duality of the behavior of a player in a gaming simulation experiment is manifested in two types of activity: the gaming activity itself and the activity relevant to the management simulation game. The gaming activity is connected with the functioning of the players as representatives of the members of a simulated organization. The activity relevant to the game includes, for example, discussions about the problem studied in the gaming simulation experiment before, during, and after playing the game; or answering questionnaires about the gaming activity. The activity relevant to the game is the major activity in the gaming simulation experiment. The gaming activity serves as an empirical basis and framework for the development of the activity relevant to the game. If the gaming activity is carried out by players only, the activity relevant to the game is carried out both by players and experimenters, including technical staff with the experts subordinate to them.

During the game design process constructors of the game inevitably are forced to separate it into components. We shall now make a hierarchical decomposition of a management simulation game. The first level of decomposition divides a game into three parts: (1) the experimental situation, (2) the participants, and (3) material on the problem area (the problem studied).

1. The *experimental situation* consists of (a) the scenario, (b) the setting of the game, and (c) the game regulations.

(a) The central part of the *scenario* is the description of roles. A gaming role represents a certain real role or number of roles in the gaming simulation experiment. The participant in the gaming simulation experiment who performs a certain gaming role is a player. The experiment may be successful only if the players show the duality of behavior in the necessary proportion; this depends on the extent of penetration of a player into the gaming role and his/her motivation for the attainment of the objective of the game. The set of gaming roles constitutes the formal structure of a gaming organization, whereas the players in the experiment form a "laboratory culture" with the nonformal structure of a gaming organization. The contents of the set of gaming roles are reflected in the rules of the game, which thus fix the formal structure. Beside the description of the roles, these rules include "techniques", "decrees", "statutes", and other official records defining the activity of the whole team of players as members of the simulated organization.

In addition, the scenario includes the history of the simulated organization. The history brings a player to a certain time in the past, present, or future.

(b) The *setting of the game* consists of the simulation model of the environment and the information system of the game. The model includes formalized procedures for modeling the response of the environment to the decisions of the players. The information system makes the players aware of the results of their activity, offers opportunities, imposes constraints on their interaction, and to some degree represents the information system of the simulated organization.

(c) The *game regulations* are formed by the game schedule and the instructions for the participants.

The *schedule* covers both the game as a whole and its individual periods. A period is a recurrent part of the gaming simulation experiment, and the whole game is the totality of all periods together with pre- and post-game phases. The vital element of the schedule is the time in which the game is played: it can be discrete or continuous. As a rule, the gaming time is considerably shorter than real calendar time. This is one of the advantages of a laboratory experiment. The schedule defines the time allowed for the gaming activity and the activity relevant to the game for each gaming theme. One or several themes may be examined in a single game during the same or different periods.

The *instructions* for the participants, as defined below, show technical means for and constraints on performing operations in the experiment.

2. The *participants* in the gaming experiments are (a) experimenters, (b) players, and (c) experts.

(a) The group of *experimenters* includes the chief experimenter (game administrator), assistants, and attendants (messengers, computer operators, programmers, or calculators). The chief experimenter specifies the objective of the game and ensures its attainment in the experiment.

(b) *Players* have motivations that may facilitate or impede this attainment. Therefore, the players must be briefed so that they are suitably motivated.

(c) *Experts* are knowledgeable and experienced people whose function is to model the responses of, for example, the environment to the decisions of the players and to generate disturbances. Experts constitute "free" parts of the simulation model of the environment.

3. *Material on the problem area* has a different character for different types of simulation game. For teaching games, the material can be manuals on the topic simulated in the experiment. For operational games the material includes information on the decision alternatives which are simulated in the experiment. Material for research games consists of the descriptions of hypotheses to be tested in the experiment. The material must also define the objective of the gaming simulation experiment and the role of each participant in its attainment.

3. THE SEQUENCE OF DESIGNING A MANAGEMENT SIMULATION GAME

The analysis of attempts at designing and developing complex man-machine systems leads us to recommend the following four phases in the design of management simulation games:

1. Conceptual,
2. Definitional,
3. Developmental,
4. Operational.

For certain problem systems of relative simplicity and short duration, the definitional and developmental phases can be combined. In addition, implementation of certain phases may take place simultaneously.

1. The objective of the *conceptual phase* is to formulate the conception of the game and requirements to be imposed on its functional subsystems. In order to formulate the game conceptually the system to be modeled has to be explored. During this exploration it is necessary to identify the problem area and justify the need for the game; to identify the parameters and interrelationships that need to be represented in the game; to formulate the game objective; and to outline the experimental situation.

The set of requirements imposed on the game, i.e., the specifications, are formulated as a result of an analysis of the system to be modeled.

The procedures of the conceptual phase depend on the complexity of the game. In the general case they include:

(a) a statement of general objectives;

(b) identification of essential components and their interrelationships in the system to be examined;

(c) making organizational and technical preparation for the exploration of the system;

(d) exploring the system;

(e) analysis and preparation of the results of the exploration;

(f) research (working out the game conception);

(g) development of the principal requirements imposed on the game and formulation of its specifications;

(h) a tentative estimation of the cost-efficiency of the game;

(i) coordination and approval of the specifications.

2. The procedures of the *definitional phase* are aimed at identifying both design alternatives for the management simulation game and the conditions for application of the game. The definitional phase includes the following procedures:

(a) selection and justification of design alternatives with regard to particular subsystems of the simulation game;

(b) development of the required documentation;

(c) examination, coordination, and authorization of the material obtained in the definitional phase.

Selection and justification of design alternatives for subsystems involve:

(a) analysis of the parameters of and requirements imposed on the game design obtained in the conceptual phase;

(b) revision (if necessary) of the exploratory material;

(c) a study of literature and other sources containing available designs for a particular subsystem of the simulation game;

(d) exploration of various alternatives of the game structure and the choice of the best one (with an explanation of this choice);

(e) design of data processing, specifications for computer programs, structure of data base, and choice of equipment and facilities.

3. The purpose of the *developmental phase* is to generate a set of documents containing information that is sufficient for producing a complete collection of material on the game for running gaming simulation experiments in full compliance with the conceptual and definitional requirements. The developmental phase includes the following procedures:

(a) designs for particular subsystems of the simulation game are clarified and set out in detail;

(b) game software is prepared and debugged;

(c) manuals are prepared for players, administrators, experts, data-processing operators, and other participants.

The process of clarifying and specifying design alternatives includes the further analysis of parameters and requirements specified in the definitional phase, as well as the development of the final versions of scenarios, algorithms, and other game components. The development and debugging of the software includes making, testing, and describing programs.

4. The *operational phase* (installation stage) is more than merely a closing phase in the construction of the game. It is recommended even for existing games if the users are not the original game designers: in this latter case the users must prepare all game material and thoroughly study the game. To check the manageability of the complete set of material it is advisable to carry out a trial run. In the operational phase the following procedures are performed:

(a) preparation of game material;

(b) organizational and technical preparation of the gaming simulation experiment;

(c) trial run;

(d) analysis and documentation of the trial output;

(e) correction and modification of operating material.

The task of making the game material depends on the structure and substance of a specific game. This task includes preparation and duplication of different gaming forms, preparation of boards, wall sheets, tables, nomograms, etc.

The organizational and technical preparation of the experiment includes the selection of players, experts, and experimenters as well as the provision of rooms and computer services. In addition, it is necessary to attend to the required formal routines (order for carrying out the experiment, directions on the participation of experts, schedule time of the computer center, tenancy agreements, etc.). Making the experiment program is a necessity.

The trial run of the game differs from its regular running: game regulations can be violated, the gaming activity interrupted, certain periods "replayed", etc. In this way, the game is debugged. During the trial run, thorough observations (using prepared forms) of individual game subsystems are made. Thus, software capabilities, efficiency of visual aids, sufficiency of instruction material, the load on experts and operators, etc., are separately tested.

During the analysis of the output of the trial run, all deviations from the developed regulations are studied and the comments of participants on how to improve the gaming procedures are analyzed. The results of the analysis are documented in the experiment report. Suggestions on the improvement of operating material leading to corrections in the design are an essential part of the report.

4. THE SET OF DOCUMENTS

4.1. Overview

Special documentation is prepared for the design and operation of every management simulation game. We distinguish between conceptual, definitional, developmental, and operational documentation.

An overview of the sets of documents that we recommend for various phases is given in Table 1. The numbers associated with each document in this section correspond to those used in Table 1.

4.2. Documents for the Conceptual Phase

Three documents are recommended for the conceptual phase:
- Description of the Simulated System
- Justification of the Requirements on the Management Simulation Game
- Specifications of the Game.

In some cases it may be necessary to extend this list to include such documents as Report of System Exploration, Estimate of Cost-Efficiency, Research Report, etc.

Table 1. Recommended sets of documentation of a game.

Type of document	Phase			
	Conceptual	Definitional	Developmental	Operational
1. Description of the simulated system	R^{α}			
2. Justification of the requirements on the management simulation game	R			
3. Specifications of the game	R			
4. Scenario		R		
5. Description of the setting of the game		R		
6. Description of algorithms		R		
7. Overview of the game			R	
8. Administrator's manual			R	
9. Player's manual			R	
10. Instructions on running the setting of the game			R	
11. Material on the problem area			R	
12. Experiment program				R
13. Experimental analysis report				R

$^{\alpha}$R = recommended.

1. The *Description of the Simulated System*, which contains the analysis of the system to be modeled in the game, can be divided into:

(a) introduction (justification of the design of the game and its objectives, methodology, material used);

(b) game objectives (hypotheses and statements to be studied);

(c) description of the system (purpose, structure, characteristics, and analysis of the conditions in which the system functions);

(d) appendices (schemes, forms of documents, reference and calculation material, etc.).

2. The *Justification of the Requirements on the Management Simulation Game* is a result of the analysis of opportunities obtainable through gaming simulation for resolving certain problems of the functioning of the system. The following sections are recommended:

(a) conception of the game (principal scheme of the game or a diagram of functional interactions indicating the model of the environment, subsystems and roles of the simulated system, and a description of the playing themes);

(b) scenario (general characteristics of the simulated system, initial conditions, history, rules of the game);

(c) setting of the game (general solutions concerning the information system of the game and the model of the environment);

(d) game regulations (justification of the requirements on the game schedule and instructions for the participants);

(e) experimenters (teams and requirements);

(f) players (gaming roles and requirements on their performance);

(g) experts (their place in the game and the team, and requirements on their skills);

(h) material on the problem area (requirements);

(i) cost-efficiency estimation (calculation of expenditures on designing and running the game; estimation of economic, social, or educational effects).

3. The *Specifications of the Game*[3] contain requirements on the game to be constructed and include the following components:

(a) general (grounds for design objective of the game);

(b) requirements on the functional subsystems (scenario, game setting, regulations, experimenters, players, experts, material on the problem area);

(c) requirements on supporting subsystems (software and hardware);

(d) jobs and executors (client, developer, financial sources, the form of presenting the outcome to the client);

(e) phases of the process (indicating dates of completion);

(f)   specifications (to be obtained as a result of the design);

(g)   tentative cost-efficiency estimates (limited to calculated outcome and qualitative analysis);

(h)   appendices (cost estimates, network schedule of designing, etc.).

4.3. Documents for the Definitional Phase

The output of the *definitional phase* is a set of documents including:

- Scenario
- Description of the Setting of the Game
- Description of Algorithms

4. The design document *Scenario* is at the same time an operating document. For this reason, it must be addressed to both the game designer and the players. It contains game rules and describes gaming organization and structure.

5. The *Description of the Setting of the Game* contains selected alternatives with regard to the information system of the game and the model of the environment and serves as an initial base for their design and implementation. The following structure of the document is recommended:

(a)   graphic model of information flows in the game;

(b)   model of the environment;

(c)   composition of algorithmic modules of the setting of the game;

(d)   data base;

(e)   classification;

(f)   forms of gaming documents;

(g)   requirements on software;

(h)   requirements on hardware.

6. The *Description of Algorithms* is written separately for each algorithmic module of the setting of the game. This document defines the objective of data processing and describes input and output data and the sequence and techniques of calculation, or other data-processing procedures. The purpose of the document is to design the specification for computer programs or a calculator's guide (in the case of non-computer games). In the general case this document can be divided into:

(a)   purpose (conception);

(b)   data (list and characteristics);

(c)   output (listing, form of arranging, dimensionality);

(d)   solution approach;

(e)   algorithm (computation sequence and formulas).

4.4. Documents for the Developmental Phase

The developmental phase documentation includes:
- Overview of the Game
- Administrator's Manual
- Player's Manual
- Instructions on Running the Setting of the Game
- Material on the Problem Area

7. The *Overview of the Game* is intended for wide circulation of details of the game so that a potential user can decide whether or not he is interested in the game. This document can be broken down into:

(a) introduction (game objectives, the opportunities it offers, information about the authors);

(b) general information about management games;

(c) game objectives in detail;

(d) characteristics of the game and its play;

(e) theoretical assumptions;

(f) recommendations on how to use the manuals.

8. The *Administrator's Manual*, for aiding game directors and experimenters, may have the following sections:

(a) setting up the game;

(b) forming the game material;

(c) selecting and briefing the players;

(d) selecting and briefing the experts;

(e) selecting and briefing the technical staff;

(f) running the experiment;

(g) debriefing;

(h) report on the analysis results;

(i) appendices (computational tables, sketches of the gaming material).

Each of the items contains instructions for performing a set of jobs. It is recommended that these instructions define the list of jobs and give methods for carrying them out.

9. The *Player's Manual* includes as many items as the number of roles. In some cases it is reasonable that the instructions common to all players (e.g., on filling in gaming forms) form a special item. Each player's manual is built according to the following scheme:

(a) definition of the role (name of gaming position, the significance of this position in the gaming organization, etc.);

(b) rights and duties of the position;

(c) interactions with other players;

(d) interactions with experimenters and experts;

(e) summary list of actions in all specific game phases (during the preparation phase, in each game period, when passing to another gaming theme, etc.).

10. The *Instructions on Running the Setting of the Game*, which define the methods for operating the information system of the game and the model of the environment, can include:

(a) description of the setting of the game (description of the information system of the game and the model of the environment);

(b) information model of the game;

(c) data base;

(d) description of programs and algorithms;

(e) instructions on data gathering and processing;

(f) computer program patterns;

(g) appendices (program listings, tables, forms, etc.).

11. The *Material on the Problem Area* entirely depends on the type of game.

4.5. Documents for the Operational Phase

The whole process of staging the simulation gaming experiment can be resolved into four phases:

• preparation of the experiment:

• design of the experiment program:

• running of the game:

• reporting on the experiment.

In the general case, *preparation of the experiment* includes:

(a) organization of computer use;

(b) duplication of game documentation forms;

(c) duplication of instructions and aid material;

(d) preparation of card indexes, tables, graphs, etc.;

(e) drawing up and duplication of abstracts of lectures and other material on the problem area;

(f) development and approval of the experiment program;

(g) selection of players and assignment of roles;

(h) selection and training of experimenters (including programmers or calculators);

(i) preparation of rooms for running the game;

(j) trial run of the game.

To fulfill these operations it is necessary to form a group of experimenters with the administrator as its head. To check the setting up, it is reasonable to make a schedule including dates and names of persons in charge of particular operations. This schedule must be sanctioned by the head of the organization where the experiment is staged.

12. The *Experiment Program*, which defines the objectives of the specific gaming experiment, the methods for obtaining the results, and the game schedule, can have the following sections:

(a) general (date and location of the experiment);

(b) objectives of the experiment;

(c) approach to the investigation of the problem area;

(d) participants (list and functions of each);

(e) schedule.

The program must be approved by the head of the organization where the experiment is run. It is desirable to duplicate this document so that each participant may have it at his disposal.

During the *running of the game* experimenters perform four major jobs: ·

(a) briefing the participants;

(b) training the players;

(c) controlling the course of the experiment;

(d) gathering data on the problem studied.

During the experiment, great attention has to be paid to synchronization of the work of different groups of participants. This task is facilitated by the schedule and other organizing documents. To be able to attend quickly to problems arising and to enhance efficiency it is advisable to hold short discussions for the experimenters. These may take place between gaming rounds or at the end of each gaming day.

In the general case, the gathering of data during the experiment is carried out by observing the behavior of the players (recorded in the experiment journal), by questionnaire survey, or by use of debriefing material.

13. The *Experiment Analysis Report* includes:

(a) introduction (general characteristics of the game);

(b) report on the gaming activity;

(c) report on the activity relevant to the game;

(d) conclusions concerning the relevance of the gaming method to solving this class of problems;

(e) results of the gaming simulation experiment;

(f) appendices (shorthand record of the discussion, suggestions from participants, etc.).

REFERENCES

Duke, R.D. (1974). *Gaming: The Future's Language*. Sage, Beverly Hills, California.

Fennessey, G.M. (1973). Simulation games and guidelines: a framework for writing the user's manual. *Simulation and Games*, 4: 205-220.

Yefimov, V.M. (1978). Towards a theory of management simulation games. In K.K. Waltuch (Ed.), *Dynamic and Probabilistic Optimization of the Economy*. Nauka, Novosibirsk, pp. 132-174. (In Russian.)

Yefimov, V.M. (1979). On the nature of management simulation games. *Review of Econometrics*, 15:403-416. (In Russian.)

Yefimov, V.M. and Komarov, V.F. (1980). *Introduction to Management Simulation Games*. Nauka, Moscow. (In Russian.)

NOTES

1. A detailed description of this method is given in chapter 3 of the book by Yefimov and Komarov (1980). In developing this method, the authors were much influenced by the work of Fennessey (1973) and Duke (1974). The rich experience gained in the development of management information systems was used as well.

2. More detailed descriptions of the concepts used are given by Yefimov (1978, 1979) and Yefimov and Komarov (1980).

3. This document partly overlaps the previous one, but specifies requirements on the components of the game without justifying them.

PART X

SIZE AND REALISM OF OPERATIONAL GAMES

Chapter X:a

SMALL OPERATIONAL GAMES—ADVANTAGES AND DRAWBACKS

Ingolf Stahl
*International Institute for Applied Systems Analysis,
Laxenburg (Austria)*

1. INTRODUCTION

This chapter deals with small operational games.[1] We shall in particular examine those operational games that in Chapter III:a were called "operational research games" as well as other operational games with closely similar goals. In Chapter III:a we noted that operational research games deal in particular with one or more of the following specific tasks:

1. Model testing;
2. Producing general forecasts;
3. Answering "what if" questions.

Since some pure research games also have these purposes, it should be explained that here we limit ourselves to operational or operational research games that distinguish themselves from ordinary research games by the following characteristics:[2]

1. *Purpose.* The aim is to aid decision making or planning.
2. *Players.* The players should be "decision maker similar" but not necessarily the final decision makers themselves. (This is discussed in greater detail later in the chapter.)
3. *Data and Structure of the Game.* The data and game structure are those of a model of some real decision situation.

Before proceeding further, we must also define the concept "small". The size of a game can be measured in numerous ways, including the following:

1. Time required for playing the game;
2. Number of players involved in the game;
3. Resources used for constructing the game;
4. Total size of the game model on the computer (in the case of a computerized game);

5. Total size of game "paraphernalia" (size of board, size of manuals, etc.);

6. Total size of the whole gaming activity.

We do not intend to pick one specific criterion from this list, particularly since many of these dimensions are so closely interrelated. However, we primarily have points 1 and 2 (and to a lesser extent point 3) in mind, regarding the others as somewhat less immediately relevant. In particular, point 6 is not necessarily directly related to the size of the game: in specific situations with a *given* total amount to be spent on the gaming activity, the choice is often between using a small game many times or a large game just a few times. Point 4 may in some cases be of interest, while point 5 is relatively insignificant. Therefore our main emphases in our examination of "smallness" will be on points 1 and 2, followed by point 3, with a short discussion of point 4.

2. WHY SMALL GAMES?

Having discussed which type of operational games we are studying and what we mean by "small", we can now discuss the advantages of keeping such games small. The point of reference here is mainly that stated above, namely a situation with a given total budget for gaming activity. Should one, in such a situation, choose a small game to be played many times or a large game to be played once or, at best, only a few times?

The advantages of choosing a small game will be presented under six separate headings, covering the following ideas:

1. Advantages of repeated play;
2. Higher likelihood of involving real decision makers;
3. Testing small models;
4. Higher motivation of players;
5. Start small--get started fast;
6. Using small and cheap computers.

2.1. Why Repeated Playing of the Game?

The advantages of repeated playing of games can be divided into five topics:

A. Greater chance of drawing significant conclusions;
B. Experimental design for answering "what if" questions;
C. Introduction of one complication at a time;
D. Development of the game through constructive criticism;
E. Development of robot players.

A. Greater Chance of Drawing Significant Conclusions

The effects on the degree to which *significant* conclusions can be drawn when repeating a game arise from basic statistics. We shall give here only one very simple example. If a game is played, e.g., only three times, and each time the same result is obtained, this is *not* enough to infer, with what is commonly regarded as sufficient probability, that the result is not due to random causes. In the very simplest case, with the total population of all games such that a certain result "A" is just as likely as "not A", then the outcome of three "As" in a row will statistically occur on one occasion out of every eight. To be able to draw any kind of conclusions in a similar case that "A" is more likely than "not A", with at least 95% probability that one is correct, one would need at least five runs of the game. However, even five game runs is generally too low, even for situations of the simple type discussed above. It is fairly seldom that one encounters five straight "As" in a row, i.e., that *all* experiments point in one direction. Often some group of players will, for more or less circumstantial reasons, happen to play in a way contrary to the other players. Hence, as a good rule of thumb, if one wants to be able to draw any statistically significant conclusions,[3] one should have at least 10 game runs (for example, see Siegel and Fouraker, 1960).

B. Experimental Design for Answering "What if" Questions

Gaming for answering "what if" questions, i.e., questions of the type "what happens to factor C if we change from value A to value B", involves the use of the game for experimentation. One can, for example, have two groups of game runs; in one group a given set of values would be specified for an important parameter in the game (e.g., one particular information scenario, one mode of information exchange, one form of payoff function); in the other group of game runs, a different set of values for this important parameter would be given. With everything else being the same (except for the game players), it is possible to study whether there is any difference in behavior which can be attributed to the difference in the critical parameter.

At least two separate groups of game runs are required in order to vary the parameter, and within each group a number of repeated plays must be run to offset random effects. Roughly the same kind of reasoning then applies as discussed above regarding statistically significant conclusions. While the total number of game runs will be higher in this two-group case, it is generally not twice as high[4] as in the earlier one-group case. In some cases one might even want to have more than two different experimental arrangements, obviously increasing the number of game runs even further.

C. Introduction of One Complication at a Time

Playing a small game several times, allowing for certain variations in the institutional set-up of the game between various groups of runs, is one way to cover a more complex reality and thus compensate for simpler modeling compared to that used in larger games. By introducing one complication (or factor) at a time, one can investigate whether this complication really matters or not. The advantage of using several slightly different versions of the same small game, rather than one more complex game, is connected with the question of the mental model of the real situation held by the players; this will be discussed further in Section 2.3.

D. Development of the Game Through Constructive Criticism

In most cases it is very difficult for a game constructor to develop a reasonably well functioning game on his own, without testing it by actually playing it a fairly large number of times. Duke suggests a "rule of 10", implying that one should have a game played at least 10 times before it is "released to the public" (Duke, 1975, p.167, and Chapter IX:a of this volume, step 9). During these tests of the game, it should be possible to discover the weaknesses of the game, both by observing with care the actual playing of the game and by obtaining constructive criticism from the players in *post mortem* sessions. Hence a game must be played a fair number of times during the development phase.

E. Development of Robot Players

Robot players are artificial players that have exact instructions on how to play in every conceivable situation. Today almost all robots in games are handled by computers, but in principal a human could perform the role of a robot by following exactly a comprehensive set of instructions. A computer program playing the role of a robot should preferably pass the so-called Turing test, which may be formulated as follows: A human shall not be able to say whether the role played by the robot is played by a robot or another human (Turing, 1963; Hoggatt et al., 1978).

There are several reasons for introducing robots into a game:

a. Robots provide a practical way of making a small game in terms of human players into a fairly large game with many players. As discussed below, it is in many cases difficult to find enough suitable players. In this situation robots can be programmed into the computer to play some roles, in particular the roles of those players that individually might not be so important for the outcome of the game (Shubik, 1975, p.238).

b. Robots provide a way of minimizing random variations due to differences in players and their playing styles. Since the robots can be made to play in the same way in, for example, both of two experimental set-ups, any variability will then be due to either the difference in experimental design or the remaining *human* players. One can think of the behavior of each human player as a kind of random variable that depends, *inter alia*, on the randomness of the *other* players. For example, if one human player plays in a very strange manner he will affect the other human players and perhaps also induce them to behave in a strange manner. The random character of the playing of a game will then grow with the number of *human* players involved in the game, assuming the *total* number of players (human and robot) is constant.

c. To test the normative value of a model, one might proceed by having certain players--robots--who act in accordance with the normative model. One can then investigate whether their behavior will have enough impact to induce the *human* players to also act in accordance with the normative model. This is one of many possible ways of testing the normative value of a model in a game (for further discussion, see Chapter VIII:b). The important idea here is that one can test whether people who in some way become informed about a certain theory will understand the idea behind it and then *act* in accordance with it.

d. Robots provide a route towards a pure simulation model. Simulation that does not involve humans has, in many cases, great cost advantages: one does not have to involve a large number of human participants, and one can concentrate computer power on *calculations*, rather than providing on-line input/output to the human players. Therefore one can often run a great number of "game simulations" at relatively low cost.

Having explained the benefits of *using* robots in games, we must point out that the *development* of robots itself requires repeated game playing. Experience with experimental gaming and computer simulations to replicate the outcome of gaming experiments has shown that it is often virtually impossible to specify any reasonable behavioral equations for the players, even in very simple types of games, without first having studied a certain number of actual runs of the game. When one has run the game a great number of times, one is able to specify these behavioral equations based on how the real players have played in the various sessions. This implies that, for the simulation of systems involving several players, gaming involving only human players should precede gaming with robots. It also stresses the need to play the game several times, in order to get a clearer idea about the relevant behavioral equations for *robot* players. The number of times one has to play the game with human players only is dependent on many factors, *inter alia*, what specific type of robot one wants to construct.

Here we shall give a very simple example, from a bidding game we constructed and used in teaching business administration (see Stahl, 1982). For this game we constructed robots with behavioral equations of the following type. Player J determines his price in period T, using the following equation:

$$P_{J,T} = P_{J,T-1} + \alpha(S_{J,T} - S_{J,T-1}) + \beta(\bar{P} - P_{J,T-1}) + \delta C_{T-1}$$

where P = price, S = stocks, $\bar{P}$ = average price, and C = total capacity.

On the basis of 20 games, each having 6-9 periods with only human players, we determined the coefficients α, β, and δ using linear regression and obtained reasonably high correlation coefficients. These equations were then used in a new game with both human players and robots.

2.2. Small Games and Real Decision Makers

In this section we will present two working hypotheses:

a. In order to obtain the most valuable conclusions as regards an operational research game, it is preferable to involve real decision makers rather than students.

b. Real decision makers are generally more likely to take part in a small game than in a large game.

However, before embarking on a detailed examination of these two hypotheses, let us first establish who we regard here as "real" decision makers.

In operational gaming, when dealing with a specific decision and planning problem, one can in many cases identify a "real" decision maker as the person who ultimately has to make the decision in question. However, for many games one cannot possibly involve exclusively the real decision makers. As an example, take a marketing game, where one wants to study the reaction of one's competitors to a certain change in strategy. In this case it is obviously impossible (or at least inadvisable!) to ask one's real competitors to participate. However, it is very important to use people with similar backgrounds, similar ways of thinking, etc., to simulate the real competitors. In line with this we shall here define the term "real decision maker" much more broadly, as a person who, through his background and experience as well as his knowledge of the role of the "real" real decision maker, is likely to be able to play the role in fairly much the same way as the "real" real decision maker would.[5]

Why Do We Want Real Decision Makers?

After having defined *real* decision makers fairly broadly, we note that the main alternative to using such persons in a game is generally to use university students. The advantage of having students as players is of course that they can often be ordered by their professor (who is the experimenter or game constructor) to participate in the game, even if it is time consuming. Thus the length of the game is generally not a very critical problem as regards student players. The disadvantage is that students, due to their age, lack of experience, and incomplete knowledge about the problem at hand, are often likely to find difficulty in playing their assigned roles in the operational research game.

From our own experience we have noted a considerable discrepancy between the behaviors of students and professional water planners as regards a game concerning cost allocation in water projects (see Chapter VIII:b and Stahl, 1980). While the planners focused on coalition formation and discussion of general division principles, and felt little time pressure, the students focused on division of the costs of a given coalition, spent more time on calculating divisions, and felt more time pressure. The students also appeared to behave in a more random fashion. Finally, and perhaps most importantly, real decision makers appear more aware of certain social norms or accepted implicit rules of the game that must be followed: for example, the principle of "good faith bargaining", implying that if party A has at a certain time said that B shall have X in payoff, then A cannot at a later time say that B shall have less than X.

Another such accepted practice is "not to fight for the last cent". In contrast to theoretical assumptions, many parties would, in reality, not go to extremes to achieve that solution which gives the highest payoff. In particular we note that the party having the strongest strategic position frequently will, when reaching the final agreement, make some minor concession to the weaker party in order to promote some longer term "good-will". Real decision makers acting in a specific game would tend to regard this game as belonging to a larger "super game", i.e., a series of games, most of which are unknown or unspecified.

Against this background it is our opinion that it is generally quite worthwhile to make extra efforts to get real decision makers rather than students to play.

Why Are Real Decision Makers More Likely to Take Part in a Small Game?

The main reason that real decision makers are reluctant to take part in a *large* game is no doubt lack of time. Unlike the students, most busy executives in business or government cannot be expected to spend several days on a game unless they are absolutely sure that they will get something substantial out of it.

Another factor that makes businessmen reluctant to take part in a game during business hours appears to be the connotation of lack of seriousness connected with the words "games" and "game playing". However, the same people, who are unwilling to play during office hours, are often prepared to play in the evening, for example for three hours after a dinner. It is then not regarded as "improper" to be involved in such a "frivolous" activity as game playing. From our experience we have found it difficult to get qualified people to play even for a day, during regular office hours, even when the game dealt with issues that were of interest to the players. We have, on the other hand, been quite successful in getting highly qualified people[6] to play games in the evening.

Based on this experience we can set up one concrete definition of a small game: that it should be playable in an evening, i.e., that it should take at most 3-4 hours to play. We have found that for a game of this size one can fairly easily get the desired persons to play. If the game is any larger in terms of playing time it would require daytime playing or playing over several evenings. Both of these would, no doubt, cut down participation. The problems with daytime playing have already been mentioned. As regards playing over more than one evening, there is the problem that it will often be difficult for the players to find an evening when they would all be free to convene again.

2.3. Testing Small Models

Most real problems are quite complex. However, the mental pictures people have of various complex problems are much simpler. In order to mentally grasp a problem a person has to make some kind of model of it, focusing on a small number of factors that he regards as significant. This model is generally verbal and only very seldom mathematical. Just like a more formal model, this mental model that a person has can be divided into two parts: the *institutional* assumptions regarding, for example, who the actors are, what the payoffs are, what information is available or can be obtained, etc., and the *behavioral* assumptions regarding how the actors will behave and how they think (see also Chapter III:a). The mental model hence includes, first of all, a small set of institutional assumptions dealing with what the person perceives as the most important aspects of the complex situation. Furthermore, the mental model contains behavioral assumptions about how the most important actors will behave.

Gaming can be seen as a way of testing certain behavioral assumptions one has for a given set of institutional assumptions. It should be stressed that we cannot test for behavior in the real situation, but only for behavior in the model defined by the institutional assumptions (see Chapter VIII:b). To test the hypotheses that a person has about how people will behave when confronting the institutional assumptions of his mental model, one should therefore have a game that replicates these institutional assumptions. Hence, if the person has a small and simple set of institutional assumptions in his mental model of the game situation, the game itself should also be based on a small and simple set of institutional assumptions.[7]

To make the discussion more concrete, let us give an example. A corporation is involved in a competitive market and wants to test some hypotheses about the response of its competitors to a change in its marketing strategy. Even if there are a score of competing corporations in the market, only four of them really matter according to our corporation's management. Similarly, although the total product range contains some fifty items, management regards only two of these to be of real importance. In their mental model of the game situation, the institutional assumptions of the corporation's management concern just four competitors and two products, although in the real world there are twenty competitors and fifty products. Since the management's hypotheses regarding the behavior of its competitors are based on this smaller simplified set of institutional assumptions, an appropriate game to test these hypotheses should also deal with this smaller set of four competitors and two products and not with the larger set of twenty competitors and fifty products.

2.4. Motivation of Players

The following hypothesis, arising from experience with educational gaming, concerns not only operational games, but any kind of games.

Our hypothesis is that players are generally more motivated to play well in a small game of a couple of hours' duration than in a large game taking several days. In educational gaming, it is quite common to have games played over several days, sometimes stretched out over several weeks. It is also a fairly common observation that, over time, many players get bored of the game and drop out or at least minimize their involvement. We do not claim that three to four hours of playing constitutes any rigid upper limit; however, we do believe that, if one does not constantly introduce new elements into the game, a substantial percentage of players will find the game boring after it has been played for any longer period without starting again.

Small games also have the motivational advantage of rules that are easy to learn and that allow the participants to start playing after only a short introduction. The motivation factor, combined with the deliberate focus on the most essential aspects, appear to be important reasons why some small games have been so effective in operational games for demonstration purposes.

2.5. Start Small - Get Started Fast

Even if one ultimately aims at developing a large game, there can be advantages in starting with a small game and successively building it into a larger game. By starting with a small game requiring a smaller development effort, one can make progress faster and get a faster feedback on one's initial hypotheses. It is quite possible that conclusions can already be drawn on the basis of the smaller game leading to a decision that there is no reason to extend the game further. If it is decided to proceed to build a larger game, the feedback obtained from playing the smaller game can often be useful by indicating in which specific areas one should extend the game, for example, in areas where the players have regarded the smaller game as too simplistic.

2.6. Use of Small Computers

A large number of games are already computerized and the share of computer-supported games is probably increasing. The cost of computer support is generally reduced drastically if it is possible to get the game onto a microcomputer. It is particularly desirable to adapt the game for a microcomputer in widespread use, since this increases the portability or transferability of the game greatly. For the cheapest computers with 8-bit processors, this limits the size of the computer program to roughly 40,000 characters of code (e.g., in BASIC),[8] thus putting another practical limitation on the size of the game. With the advent of the newer microcomputers (with 16-bit processors) this size will increase, but since 8-bit computers are at the same time going down in price, it is reasonable to assume that computing costs for a game that is "small" in the sense used here will continue to be noticeably lower than those of a larger game.

For very small games (<2000 characters), very low cost and extreme portability is obtained by using pocket computers. I have two games (one on cost allocation, one a business game) on a pocket computer (costing $300 including a printer) which can easily be transported (see Stahl, 1982).

3. DISADVANTAGES OF SMALL GAMES

Since my own experience in this field has led to a marked preference for smaller games, this section is noticeably shorter than the preceding sections. Nevertheless, two main disadvantages of smaller games can be identified: those of the games *being* too simple or *appearing* too simple.

3.1. The Game Actually is Too Simple

One can first raise the objection that it is impossible to capture all the most relevant factors of many specific game situations in a small game (i.e., one defined as playable in three to four hours). One might, for example, first write down the simplest possible set of institutional assumptions, in the sense that reducing the set further would make the game meaningless. If this minimum basic set of institutional assumptions is too large to be covered by a small game (as defined above), then this obviously speaks heavily against using such a game. The problem of excessively simplistic institutional assumptions will itself probably fall into one of the following categories:

A. *Number of Players.* This category can be subdivided into two questions, concerning the number of teams and the number of players per team.

    (a) By having too few *teams* in certain types of games, there is the risk of making the game unsuitable for investigating the issue of interest. Take, for example, the question of whether or not there will be cooperation in a game. By having, for example, only three or four teams in a game that represents a real situation with a dozen players, one may bias the game too much towards cooperative behavior. It would probably be more appropriate to have at least six teams in this case.[9] The problem of the total number of players can, in some small games, be relieved by the use of robot players, as discussed above.

    (b) By having several *players* in each team, it is possible to represent to some extent the various "subgames" that take place within the main game. Consider, for example, a game focused on potential cooperation between various nations as regards a specific issue, such as energy policy. If the teams represent nations, one cannot, with only one player per team, represent different interests within each country.

B. *Number of Decisions.* For those games where decisions are repeated one can distinguish between the number of rounds and the number of decisions in each round.

(a) By having too few *rounds*, one runs the risk of stopping the game before it gets "interesting", for example, before it starts to portray cyclical behavior.

(b) By having too few *decisions* in each round, there is the risk of excluding decisions that are truly crucial to the problem.

C. *Time for Deliberation on Each Decision.* In a small game played very rapidly, the reduction of time for each decision may be too great, leading to less "rational" behavior than would have been observed if more time had been allowed. This disadvantage can, however, be partly overcome by providing the players with a decision aid, as described in Chapter XI:a.

D. *Information Disseminated to Players.* In a small game one is likely to cut down on the amount of information presented to the players, for example, on the effects of earlier decisions, and only to inform the players about one or two broad payoff factors. In games dealing with situations of multicriteria decision making this more or less arbitrary aggregation of payoff criteria can seriously decrease the game's operational research value. Also, the amount of information on the organizational environment of the game situation, usually distributed prior to the start of the game, may have to be cut down in a short game.

E. *Exchange of Verbal Messages Between Players.* When a small game has to be played rapidly there may not be time for much exchange of verbal messages between the teams. This might cut down the amount of interteam bargaining and lead to less cooperative behavior than might otherwise have been the case.

F. *Focus on Rigid Rules.* The short playing time allowed in a small game may lead the game constructor to prefer a rigid-rule game, i.e., one with all the rules given, even in cases when a free-form game, allowing the players themselves to influence the rules of the game, would really have been more suitable. The determination of rules in free-form games is generally fairly time consuming but the process can be speeded up somewhat by using the man-computer dialogue system presented in Chapter XI:b.

G. *Special Needs for Complexity.* It should finally be stressed that for some purposes it is important that the game is complex; examples include games for testing methods, like decision aids and management information systems, designed to help decision makers deal with complex situations.

3.2. The Game Appears to be Too Simple

Even if the game constructor, according to the criteria discussed above, considers a certain small game to be of sufficient complexity to answer the questions posed, one cannot rule out the possibility that the *players* themselves may regard the game as unrealistically simplistic. They may then not take the game seriously and their play in the game might be affected by this. In such cases it might be better to increase the complexity of the game to a level that would induce the players to accept it. Since the game constructor may not be able to determine in advance how much complexity one should include for this reason, one could argue, however, that the best course of action is to start with a relatively small game, increasing its complexity only as one gets feedback from the players.

The advocates of larger games may argue that one needs a fairly complex game with outward credibility in order to attract the most desirable types of players. As regards the time-factor, if the game appeared to be really important to the players, then they would find the time for it. These arguments possibly hold true for operational games in the strict sense, i.e., those where the games deal directly with specific decisions. They are, however, less likely to hold for operational research games, i.e., those where the games do not focus on specific decisions, but rather on certain types of decision problems.

REFERENCES

Duke, R. (1975). Specifications for game design. In C. Greenblat and R. Duke (Eds.), *Gaming-Simulation: Rationale, Design and Applications*. Halstead Press, New York.

Hoggatt, A.C., Brandstätter, H., and Blatman, P. (1978). Robots as instrumental functions in the study of bargaining behavior. In H. Sauermann (Ed.), *Bargaining Behavior. Contributions to Experimental Economics 7*. J.C.B. Mohr, Tübingen.

Rapoport, A. (1981). 'Realism' and 'relevance' in gaming simulations. *Human Ecology*, 9(2):137-150.

Selten, R. (1973). A simple model of imperfect competition, where 4 are few and 6 are many. *International Journal of Game Theory*, 2:141-201.

Shubik, M. (1975). *Games for Society, Business and War: Towards a Theory of Gaming*. Elsevier, New York.

Siegel, S. (1956). *Nonparametric Statistics for the Behavioral Sciences*. McGraw-Hill, New York.

Siegel, S. and Fouraker, L. (1960). *Bargaining and Group Decision Making*. McGraw-Hill, New York.

Stahl, I. (1980). *Cost Allocation in Water Resources: Two Gaming Experiments with Doctoral Students*. WP-80-134. International Institute for Applied Systems Analysis, Laxenburg, Austria.

Stahl, I. (1982). *Six Small Games for Research and Education*. Internal Discussion Paper. International Institute for Applied Systems Analysis, Laxenburg, Austria.

Turing, A.M. (1963). Computing machinery and intelligence. In E.E. Feigenbaum and J. Feldman (Eds.), *Computer and Thought*. McGraw-Hill, New York, pp. 11-38.

NOTES

1. The chapter owes much to the ideas of Rapoport (1981); however, Rapoport focused mainly on experimental games without any operational purpose.

2. For further details see Chapter III:a, Section 7.

3. One can, of course, to some extent dispute the use of statistical methods as regards this type of gaming activity. It is very often not possible to choose gaming groups in a truly random fashion.

4. Compare for example the Fisher exact-probability test with the earlier binomial test. No conclusions on the 0.05 significance level can be drawn with the Fisher exact-probability test with less than six game runs, with three runs for each of the two experimental designs (see Siegel, 1956).

5. Hence, we shall in this section, for the sake of simplicity, also include players that we have elsewhere called "decision maker similar" in the set of "real decision makers".

6. For instance, the majority leader of a parliament representing several million people.

7. We can in this connection refer to Figure 2 in Chapter VIII:b. The "theory" we want to test is the "mental model" of the decision maker. In order to test R_5, i.e., to what extent players behave according to the theory (= the mental model) we require that $R_4 \sim 1$, i.e., that the institutional assumptions (IA_T) of the mental model correspond to those of the game (IA_G).

8. This is roughly the maximum size of programs in BASIC that one can get on to an 8-bit computer with a maximum memory of 64 kbyte.

9. This idea is based on game-theoretical investigations of simple games where four players lead to cooperative and six to noncooperative behavior (see Selten, 1973).

THE PURSUIT OF REALISM: THE INTERPRETATION OF GAMING RESULTS USING THE METHOD OF DYNAMIC SIMILARITY

M.A.P. Willmer

Manchester Business School, Manchester (UK)

1. INTRODUCTION

Operational gaming has for many years been an important tool in the exploration of complex problems connected with military, governmental, and industrial problems. It has been used not only as a teaching device but also as a means of selecting personnel, as a way of familiarizing personnel with the operations of complex systems, as a method of demonstrating new ideas, as well as for general research purposes. As far as problem-solving research is concerned, operational gaming has been used to assist in the development of decision models and to evaluate several possible solutions to the problems that have been modeled. In this way the outcomes of alternative courses of action can be compared and new decision strategies discovered.

Gaming can be viewed as a form of controlled experimentation, the experimental situation being constructed as an iconic or analog model of real conditions about which information is required. It is well known that designers of operational games lean towards excessive elaboration in order to achieve the appearance of reality. Perhaps one reason for this attitude is that they are sensitive to that most common of criticisms of the gaming approach: the results obtained cannot be used to tell us about the real world because they are only games. In their own defense, therefore, game designers strive to ensure that their creations contain the "essence of reality". This goal can be very elusive, however, and it is easy to believe that just one more development will lead to this essence being captured. Thus in some cases development follows development, and the construction costs mount, without any worthwhile benefits accruing.

Despite the criticism of operational gaming that the results are only game results, the method is the only way in which some types of activity and human decision making can be explored. That a game requires some degree of realism is undoubtedly true, but the actual amount will depend to a large extent on the purposes for which it is designed and used. Whether a game is designed with educational, operational, experimental, or research objectives in mind, the literature provides scant guidance concerning the level of realism required in order to make inferences about real behavior.

Similar problems have been encountered by scientists and engineers who have developed their own approach to the question of how accurately they should copy reality in their experiments. Their work has led to the development of a concept called dynamic similarity. This chapter explores the possibility of extending the concept to operational gaming situations in the management science area.

2. COMPARISON WITH PHYSICAL LABORATORY EXPERIMENTS

In the physical sciences an understanding of the way some natural phenomena occur is gained by the use of iconic models, usually with a change of scale. The models represent reality and, by manipulating them under real or iconically represented conditions, simulations can be constructed which generate a motion picture of the phenomena under investigation. Thus in aeronautic engineering, scale models of aircraft are put into wind-tunnels where air is blown over them in order to generate information about the pressures on the aircraft and the nature of the air flow. Such experiments are much cheaper to run than the construction and flight testing of full-scale experimental aircraft. Similarly, model ships have been tested in hydraulic tanks to give data about the hydrodynamic properties of the flows obtained.

The research scientists and engineers involved have not attempted to make their models perfect replicas of the full-scale with respect to every possible aspect of the situation under consideration. For instance, model aircraft are often made of wood, rather than being complex metal constructions.

In deciding in any given situation what factors should be modeled seriously and what factors are unimportant, some knowledge of the nature of the phenomenon under investigation is necessary. If an important factor is omitted, data from model experiments are likely to be grossly misleading. Thus in the case of a wind-tunnel experiment in which the structural properties of the model are important, one would not expect a model aerofoil made of a solid hardwood to give results applicable to the full-scale version of flexible tubular construction.

When investigating the nature of some types of physical phenomena, the number of quantities involved is sometimes so large that it is impossible to write down the equations connecting them, let alone solve them. However, by using the method of dimensional analysis it is possible to derive in formal terms the relationship that must exist between some of these quantities, thus reducing the number of parameters involved.

Consider, for instance, the motion of a body in a fluid; the main physical quantities are: (1) resistance, (2) velocity of the body, (3) density of the fluid, (4) viscosity of the fluid, and (5) compressibility of the fluid.

At medium speeds the compressibility of the fluid can be ignored so that the resistance on the body can be written as a function of the remaining four quantities. Each of these quantities is measured in terms of different dimensions: velocity is length divided by time, density is mass divided by length cubed, etc. By considering the force acting on a typical body and by expressing the above quantities, which all affect the magnitude of the force, in terms of their dimensions, it can be shown that two or more geometrically similar situations can only be regarded as "dynamically similar" if a certain nondimensional number, called the Reynolds number, is the same in each case. Keeping the Reynolds number constant implies that changes in any one parameter must be balanced by changes in others. For example, all other factors being equal, if one were carrying out an experiment on a model of a body that was 1/100 of full-scale, tests would need to be carried out in a fluid 100 times more dense in order to obtain dynamically similar flows.

If one were examining flows near the speed of sound the effect of the compressibility of the fluid could not be ignored. In this case dimensional analysis would have indicated two important nondimensional variables: these are referred to as the Reynolds number (mentioned above) and the Mach number. Hence two flows of this type are dynamically similar when both the Reynolds number and the Mach number are the same in each case. The effects of variations in these nondimensional numbers can be considerable, as a result of fundamental differences in the behavior of the fluid. Thus, from the point of view of using the model data for full-scale design purposes, it is important to know whether the differences in the appropriate nondimensional numbers indicate a major difference of fluid flow.

3. EXPERIMENTS INVOLVING HUMANS

In the management sciences we are interested in the interaction between human beings and the environment in which they operate. Experiments carried out with *one* active decision maker and with the environment represented by some artificial construction based on real life are known as simulations. The decision maker can be viewed as analogous to the model and the artificial environment as analogous to the laboratory conditions of physical science experiments.

In some cases the artificial construction may be a simplified mock-up of a real situation, but more frequently it is simply a computer program. To provide a background for the following discussion two examples will be presented, one of each of these two types.

An example of the first type of simulation is the air traffic control simulator originally developed at London Airport around 20 years ago. Its purpose was to investigate the effects on inbound and outbound traffic movements of changes in the air traffic control arrangements in the London area. Civil air traffic in the London area flows mainly along airways under the direction of controllers at London Airport. Each airway is divided into sectors, each of which is controlled by an air traffic controller. From time to time new ideas about how the pattern of airways should be arranged or new operating procedures would be suggested by various civil aviation organizations. At the time no formulas were available for estimating what the effects of such changes would be on the delays to aircraft, the volume of traffic dealt with, etc.

It was to give insight into such questions that the simulator was used whenever some new idea had gained sufficient popularity with those in charge. The simulator consisted of a room fitted out to represent accurately the operating environment of a typical air traffic controller in charge of a sector of an airway. Each participant was given the layout of a new sector under consideration and appropriate video screens, telephones, microphones, etc. Alternatively, if new procedures were to be investigated, the layout would be similar to that of a sector in operation. The calls from ingoing and outgoing aircraft were obtained by having a group of housewives, playing the roles of pilots, in another room. They were trained to respond in the same way as normal commercial airline pilots. In this way each participant was able to perform his usual operational task as though he were controlling a real sector.

In contrast to this type of simulation, where the participant interacts with human beings, there are others in which the computer is used to represent all the sociotechnical aspects of relevance with respect to the operational environment under consideration. An example of this type of simulation is concerned with the behavior of police officers (Willmer, 1972). A Chief Constable has just returned from a course on modern business methods and seems infatuated with the idea of measuring his force's efficiency in quantitative terms. He has noted that the present clear-up rate for crimes committed in a particular area is only 35%, which compares unfavorably with the clear-up rate of 45% in the adjacent police district. The chief believes the difference to be positive proof of the operational inefficiency of the officer in charge and has given him the following ultimatum in no uncertain terms. If his clear-up rate is not up to 45% within a year, he will be transferred to a dead-end office job at headquarters. It is assumed that the officer in charge has already tried, albeit unsuccessfully, to persuade his chief that there are good grounds for believing that the other force's high clear-up rate is not a true indicator of efficiency.

Each simulated month the participant, representing the officer concerned, is asked questions about how he will deal with:

1. Crimes that look as though they will be impossible to solve but where an opportunity exists for not officially recording them;

2. Crimes that appear to be solved but which on close inspection might reveal that no crime had in fact been committed; and

3. Opportunities for good police work which could lead to more unsolvable crimes being recorded, crimes which in the normal course of events would stay unrecorded.

At the end of each simulated month the participant is given data relating to his performance.

When the 12-month task is completed the participant is asked to perform a similar task, but this time the measure of his performance is based on the reduction in the uncertainty about crime in the district resulting from his detective work. At the beginning of the year he is given the degree of uncertainty and told to achieve a new target figure by the end of the year. He is asked the same questions as in the first task and is given immediate feedback regarding his performance.

The objective of the experiments using simulation was to compare and contrast the effects of two different methods of performance appraisal on the behavior of the participants. Here the participant can again be viewed as the "model" being tested, with the computer program, which determines the number of crime reports, arrests, etc., resulting from the decisions of the participant, representing the environment.

4. APPLICATION OF THE DYNAMIC SIMILARITY CONCEPT TO SIMULATIONS

Instead of considering the forces acting on the scale model under test, as in the case of a physical science experiment, attention should be focused on the participant during a simulation exercise. In a well designed and well run trial, where the participants take the exercise seriously, it is possible to view the decision maker as a body being acted upon by a force. Drawing a parallel with the Newtonian definition of mechanical force--every body continues in its state of rest or uniform, straight-line motion unless acted on by an external force--one can postulate that a person's state of mind will remain unaltered unless acted on by a "psychological force". By analogy with the mechanics example it will be assumed that the ingredients of this force are:

1. Time;
2. Level of mental stress within the participant; and
3. Degree of complexity of the task under consideration.

When applying the method of dimensional analysis to the air traffic control simulation, the first step is to determine those quantities which are likely to have a significant effect on the psychological force acting on the participant. For the purposes of this paper it will be assumed that the degree of complexity C will be important. Other quantities to be included are:

V The rate of change of complexity with time. As the complexity grows so one can expect the pressure on the participant to increase and vice versa.

S The stress level.

Q The rate of change of stress with respect to changes in complexity. This quantity is likely to be important because the participant will be aware that the safety of people depends on his decisions.

Using dimensional analysis it is shown in Appendix A that the psychological force is a function of the nondimensional parameter (S / CQ).

In contrast, the assumption is made that the level of complexity in the police simulation case does not have a major effect on the psychological force although its rate of change with time is still significant. Furthermore, since the time dimension T is considerably shorter in the case of the simulations, it will be considered as an important quantity in the force equation. Analysis now shows (see Appendix A) that the psychological force is a function of the nondimensional parameter (QVT / S).

Continuing with the analogy with the physical sciences it can be seen how extraordinarily fortunate scientists and engineers are in being able to carry out experiments not only to demonstrate the relevance of nondimensional parameters such as the Reynolds number, but also to show regions where changes in the values of these parameters are important. These experiments have shown that significant effects due to changes in the nondimensional parameters indicate some major changes in flow behavior. In the management sciences, if it were possible to carry out sufficient experiments and research to be able to obtain the relationships between the nondimensional parameters and various important quantities, we might be able to determine the points at which there are fundamental changes in human behavior. Furthermore, in those regions where the effect of the nondimensional parameters are unimportant, simulation results could be used to predict actual behavior with confidence.

At the present time such developments are limited by a lack of freedom to experiment. However, a first step towards increasing our understanding of nondimensional parameter effects is to develop a databank containing details of results of simulation experiments and the results obtained when any ensuing recommendations have been implemented in practice.

As far as the air traffic control simulation experiences are concerned, it was observed that when a new sector arrangement is introduced into operational service the actual flow of traffic is about 75% of that obtained in the simulation tests. These simulations are designed so that the level of complexity C and its rate of change over time V are the same as in reality. Unfortunately, very few other data of this nature seem to exist (McPherson, 1981).

5. EXTENSION TO AN OPERATIONAL GAME

When considering the development of an operational game to represent a problem in which there are two or more decision makers, there are two approaches that may be followed.

First, one may adopt the conventional approach of building the environment around the decision makers so that they can interact both between themselves and with the environment in a way similar to real life. This situation can be viewed as analogous to the physical science experiments of putting two or more models in a fluid at the same time to examine the effects that they have on each other. In such experiments, what should be taken as the characteristic value of a length, etc., is often a matter for discussion. Until such discussions are satisfactorily resolved the values of the appropriate nondimensional parameters cannot be determined, and hence the concept of dynamic similarity cannot be employed.

The effects of this uncertainty are likely to be more important in cases where it is the interactions between the decision makers themselves rather than with the environment that is the major concern of the experiments. In such cases as these the alternative approach of replacing human beings with robots, designed to operate in as lifelike a fashion as possible, has many advantages. This is the approach that I have been using in connection with my own research into the superior/subordinate interface problems within organizations and societies.

Powerful people have difficulty in obtaining the truth from their subordinates. Subordinates have a strong tendency to tell their leader what they think he wants to hear. The greater the leader's power the greater the chance that he will be isolated from reality. Nevertheless, to be effective and to be able to make correct decisions he needs to know the truth about matters of importance. In contrast, the subordinate's aim is often merely to be thought well of by his superior; thus the objectives of the superior and his subordinates are different, a difference which has many implications for the management control process in an organization.

To investigate the conflict of objectives at the superior/subordinate interface I constructed a game of a production situation involving two principal decision makers:

1.   The subordinate, the manager of a factory, who has direct control over the workforce and the machines, together with a large measure of control over the information sent to headquarters relating to the activities at the factory.

2.   The managing director of the group, who owns the factory and who has the authority to nominate the main objectives, lead a target negotiation process, and reward or penalize the performance of his subordinate.

In running the factory, which produces goods called "clunks", the manager has to make decisions regarding the allocation of men to machines, the use of maintenance men for production, the allocation of overtime, the percentage of production not declared but held over to the following month, and the use of subcontracting money to boost production. There are a number of company rules governing the way the men, money, and machines should be used. However, it is assumed that the managing director, remote from the factory, takes very little interest in the day-to-day details of factory management. Thus the manager may violate these company rules without fear of immediate exposure unless he decides to bring rule violations personally to the notice of the managing director. The effect of rule violations, as far as the production of clunks is concerned, depends on which rules are broken and by how much; violations can also have both short- and long-term effects on the state of the factory in succeeding months.

The development of this game, entitled *So You Think That You Would Make a Managing Director*, started by asking people attending courses at the Manchester Business School to act as the managers of a factory reporting to a boss with only limited control capability. In these experiments a number of different robots were used and participants were told that their objective was to be well thought of by their boss. At the start of the exercise they were told the managing director's main objective and each month the following sequence of events was followed:

1.   A target was negotiated between subordinate and superior. The managing director stated the number of clunks that he wanted manufactured. The subordinate was asked for his view, after which the managing director announced the final target.

2.   The manager was asked to make a number of decisions about the operations of the factory. The recorded production figure for the month was then given.

3.   The manager was asked how many rules he had broken; his response depended on the extent he wished to be either honest or a tactical liar.

4.   The manager was given his superior's rating of his performance.

At this stage the behavior of the managing director was based entirely on assumptions about human beings generally. When sufficient data had been collected a second computer program was developed but this time it was designed for participants to act as the managing director. In this program the computer acted as a robot manager based on an analysis of the data previously collected. Another set of experiments was carried out in which participants were asked to supervise two factory managers, who would act in a way similar to production managers from a number of multinational companies. It was now the participants' turn to select the main objective each month (they could choose between asking for increased production, closeness to the agreed target, or honesty of information about rule violations), lead the target negotiation process, and reward or penalize their subordinates depending on their assessment of the latter's performance. In this set of experiments participants were told that the objective was both to increase the production and at the same time to have an accurate appreciation of the rules being broken at each factory. The results of these early experiments are described in Willmer and Berry (1976).

This process of data collection, analysis, and program modification has continued. As this development proceeds so the contribution of *assumptions* about human behavior are diminished. More recent results are described in Willmer (1978, 1980).

Obviously this process could continue almost indefinitely and the question therefore arises as to when should we consider robots to be sufficiently realistic. From the point of view of dynamic similarity, consideration should be given first to the basic quantities involved. As far as time is concerned, this dimension is considerably decreased for both sides of the interface. At the managing director level, decisions which in the real case are taken once per month become decisions every few minutes. This shortening effect will probably not be so severe at the subordinate level although it will still be very significant, the time reduction being of the order of days to minutes. From the complexity point of view, the managing director's task is of the same order of magnitude as a real-life case in which the boss takes a very detached and only superficial interest in his company. On the other hand, at the subordinate level the degree of complexity confronting the factory manager is very much less than that which faces his real-life counterpart. With regard to stress the simulation levels are bound to be lower for both roles.

Remember that it is only when there are no significant effects due to variations in the appropriate nondimensional parameters that we can use simulation data as a guide to real behavior. Further, when the effects of the nondimensional parameters are significant there is a change in the nature of the activity under consideration. For example, in connection with a simulation of a steel production process it was noted: "We built a mock deck for an arc furnace and drove the dials from a computer to give changes in power input as the steel making in three furnaces progressed. This could be influenced by changing the transformer tappings and therefore the power input to the furnaces...[We found] a complete switch of decision making logic when the pace of decision requirement was increased" (Tocher, 1981).

There is, therefore, a clear need for a thorough search of the gaming literature for data relating to experiments in which levels of stress, complexity, and time have been varied. If there are gaps in this information then consideration should be given to ways of filling them. In the above game the computer could be programmed to react more slowly and various types of prizes could be given to the winners, thus varying the time and stress dimensions. Similarly, a renewed and more intensive search should be carried out to find data on cases where simulations have been compared to their real-life equivalents. In this way it may be possible to build up an understanding of which of the other quantities are important so that we may be in a position to determine the nondimensional parameters required to ensure dynamic similarity.

APPENDIX A

Assume that the psychological force F is a function of

V the rate of change of complexity with time,

C the degree of complexity,

S the stress level,

Q the rate of change of stress with respect to changes in complexity,

so that $F \propto (CS / T^2)$ and $\propto C^a V^b S^c Q^d$ where a, b, c, d, are numbers to be determined, and T denotes time. Since the dimensions of V are C / T and those of Q are S / C a comparison of dimensions gives

$$a = -c$$
$$b = 2$$
$$d = 1-c$$

so that the force can be written as

$$F = QV^2 \, \Phi(S / CQ)$$

In a similar way, if the components of the force are assumed to be $T, S, Q,$ and V it can be shown that

$$F = (SV / T) \, \Phi \, (QVT / S).$$

REFERENCES

Burniston-Brown, G. (1952). *Science: Its Methods and its Philosophy*. George Allen and Unwin, London.

Huntley, H.E. (1952). *Dimensional Analysis*. McDonald, London.

Lucas, F.L. (1938). *The Delights of Dictatorship*. Heffer and Sons, Cambridge.

Reynolds, O. (1883). *Philosophical Transactions*, 174:935.

Richardson, E.G. (1961). *Dynamics of Real Fluids*. Edward Arnold, London.

Willmer, M.A.P. (1972). *Entropy and the Reduction of Distorted Information in Social Systems. Part II*. Working Paper No. 4. Manchester Business School, Manchester.

Willmer, M.A.P. (1978). *System Uncertainty and Leadership Strategy*. Proceedings of the Meeting on Cybernetics and Systems Research, 4th, Linz.

Willmer, M.A.P. (1980). *Subordinate Behavior and Management Control*. Proceedings of the European Meeting on Cybernetics and Systems Research, 5th, Vienna.

Willmer, M.A.P. and Berry, A.J. (1976). *Managerial Performance and System Uncertainty*. Proceedings of the European Meeting on Cybernetics and Systems Research, 3rd, Vienna.

PART XI

SPECIAL METHODS IN OPERATIONAL GAMING

Chapter XI:a

OPERATIONAL RESEARCH METHODS AS DECISION AIDS IN GAMING

Thomas M. Schuenemann
University of Hamburg, Hamburg (FRG)

1. PROBLEMS OF THE DECISION MAKER IN GAMING

In gaming the decision maker analyzes a decision situation and takes actions, i.e., sets decision variables, in order to derive optimum or, at least, feasible solutions. This has to be done periodically with changing decision situations since typical games extend over several periods. To prevent trivial and boring decision situations, multiperiod games should be complex. As in the real world, complexity in gaming is usually secured by *interdependence* between the decision variables, *uncertainty* in the decision situation, and constraints on *decision time*.

1.1. Interdependence

Decision variables are interdependent if there is any direct or indirect mutual relation between them. In complex games typically the majority of the decision variables are interdependent. Interdependences can be functional as well as temporal.

Functional interdependences cover all interdependences between decision variables that exist at the same point in time or, in gaming, during a period that cannot be interrupted by the decision maker. Functional interdependences result from flows of material, monetary funds, energy, and information as well as from their joint influences. For example, in every period the amount of products to be put into stock or to be taken from stock depends on the amount of products to be produced and sold.

Temporal interdependences occur between decision variables from different points of time or periods. In general, the resulting value of any decision variable being set in a specific situation is automatically transferred into the subsequent decision situation; therefore, temporal interdependences exist more or less for every decision variable in multiperiod games. There are various means to intensify such interdependences: the introduction of time lags between the setting of the decision variable and the production of the result, the use of aging processes for equipment and material; and the utilization of environmental changes like seasonal influences.

A decision maker without suitable decision aids usually tries to solve problems in small, sequential steps. When interdependences between decision variables are weak or negligible this method will result in useful solutions, but when there are significant interdependences such a method will generally lead to inferior or unacceptable solutions. Functional interdependences require simultaneous treatment of all interdependent decision variables of the period concerned. Temporal interdependences magnify the effort required for solution: not one but several periods must be considered simultaneously. Thus, a decision maker trying to cope with interdependent decision variables will probably be overworked and frustrated as a consequence. This problem can be avoided by providing suitable decision aids.

1.2. Uncertainty

In gaming the decision maker is regularly confronted with the problem of uncertainty. He is usually uncertain about the reaction of the game model, e.g., the influence of marketing activities and price upon the demand for a certain product. Uncertainty is intensified if stochastic influences are used in the game mechanisms. In competitive games the decision maker is unsure about the actions of competitors. In general, uncertainty forces the decision maker to consider different outcomes of the same action.

The decision maker can cope with uncertainty by various means. A common method is to calculate alternatives for different possible situations and to select the alternative that yields the best results for a given risk. Another method is, for instance, sensitivity analysis, which informs the decision maker about the stability of a solution when input data are modified. In any case, methods for coping with uncertainty require considerable efforts of calculation. If the decision maker is not provided with adequate decision aids he will most probably calculate only one solution for the most probable situation and apply it, regardless of its value.

1.3. Decision Time

One of the advantages of gaming is the time contraction, i.e., the possibility to simulate the behavior of systems in a short time, a task that would take much longer in the real world. On the other hand, this time contraction also puts constraints on the decision time available. Therefore, the decision maker usually has a fixed amount of time for analyzing the situation, estimating data, and setting the decision variables. Because of external constraints, the decision time cannot be prolonged in most cases.

If the decision maker does not use any decision aid he will often spend a considerable amount of his decision time in manual calculations, thus reducing his time for strategic planning and problem solving. Particularly in complex games with interdependences and uncertainties, the limited amount of decision time forces the decision maker to adopt a "muddling through" problem-solving approach. This can be changed substantially if he is supplied with suitable decision aids that free him from time-consuming manual calculations and thus give him more time for planning.

2. OPERATIONAL RESEARCH TECHNIQUES AND GAMING

Operational research has developed general and specific methods and algorithms for the solution of a vast number of different problems. The applicability of a particular technique for gaming depends on certain properties required of the decision aid.

2.1. Properties Required of a Decision Aid in Gaming

A vital property that determines the applicability of any decision aid is its *problem-matching accuracy*, i.e., the correspondence between the external problem and its representation in the internal model solved by the decision aid. The internal model usually lacks certain details of the external, real-world problem. Therefore, a decision maker cannot apply the solution of the decision aid directly to the real world problem. Bearing in mind the difference between the external problem and the internal model, the decision maker has to adjust the solution accordingly. In gaming the "real world" is the game model. As the game already is an abstract representation it will very often be possible to represent it entirely in the internal model of the decision aid. The decision maker is then able to apply the solution of the decision aid without further adjustment. This is not a suitable procedure if the decision maker has to be trained to solve problems; it is advisable then to deliberately produce a difference between the external problem and the internal model, especially if the decision aid is able to solve major parts of the game model.

A property of special importance in gaming is the *time requirement* of the decision aid. As already mentioned, the decision maker has only a limited amount of decision time. Since a decision maker in gaming generally cannot switch to other activities while the decision aids solve his problem, the solution times of decision aids suitable for gaming should be low, preferably of the order of minutes.

Similarly, the *input requirements* of the decision aid have to be low and not time-consuming. As any input is prone to error, plausibility checks are compulsory. The correction of errors should be easy and quick. In gaming there are no special requirements for the output from decision aids, except that shortage of time warrants that it be minimized.

For complex games and generally for decision situations with uncertainty the decision maker uses the same decision aid several times with different data. Such reiterations should be possible without much effort. Therefore, in successive runs the decision maker should submit only the altered data items to the decision aid. The *reiteration capability* of a decision aid depends mainly on the time it requires to solve the problem.

In gaming, decision aids should be applied rather than developed. The decision maker should therefore be provided with a decision aid already fitted for application to the particular game. This usually requires the *availability of an algorithm and an internal model* of the part of the game to be solved by the decision aid. In consequence, the decision maker provides only the input data and uses the decision aid more or less as a black box.

2.2. Computer Support

Manual decision aids, including those based on standard printed forms, cannot cope with all of the requirements mentioned above, since they usually take up too much time and lack any reiteration capability. In complex games, computer support has to be considered as the basic requirement for adequate decision aids. In most cases this requirement can easily be met, since the majority of the games are computer-supported themselves.

In contrast to manual aids, more *elaborate algorithms* can be applied by the decision maker if the decision aid is supported by a computer. The results are not subject to the errors of manual calculation. In some cases, even standard algorithms available from the program library of the computer system concerned can be used.

Another major advantage of a computer-supported decision aid is the possibility of sharing the *same data base* with the game. For gaming purposes the data base contains all information on the actual period. Information on past periods is usually also available, making it easy to apply statistical decision aids, e.g., forecasting and extrapolation methods. Thus a major amount of the necessary data for a decision aid can be automatically provided, releasing the decision maker from data input efforts. Furthermore, automatically provided data are not subject to input errors.

In gaming the usefulness of a computer-supported decision aid will be greatly enhanced if the decision maker applies it in *dialogue* mode. In general, the interactive application of a decision aid saves time, but on the other hand, decision makers usually have no experience in operating computers. Therefore, a user-friendly dialogue is indispensable. In gaming, user friendliness focuses on the input and output facilities of the decision aid: the overall handling should be simple, efficient, uniform, and secure. This can be achieved, for example, by providing special screen formats for data entry and using the menu technique for selecting the desired output as well as for program control. If the results are to be used later—especially in case of reiteration—a hard-copy or printer output should also be provided.

2.3. Linear Programming

Linear programming (LP) is one of the oldest[1] and commonest operational research techniques discussed in theory and applied in practice. Because of its properties regarding problem size and solution capability it is generally accepted as a decision aid for various real world problems, e.g., those covering production and distribution planning in the petrochemical industries and the mixture of feed in animal nutrition. In LP the real-world problem is converted to a linear model that is solved by means of standard algorithms, e.g., the simplex method. As these algorithms are generally available and independent of the problem to be solved, the decision maker has only to supply the linear model and the necessary data.

To evaluate the benefits of LP as a decision aid in gaming, the general characteristics and requirements of the method have to be analyzed. These depend on the elements and their relations in linear models. Elements are the data to be provided by the decision maker and the decision variables to be set by the algorithm. Data and decision variables constitute the constraints that determine the feasible solutions and the objective function to be minimized or maximized according to the problem concerned. General characteristics and requirements of LP are the *linearity* of the relations in the model, the restriction of the decision variables to *real values*, and the *constancy of data*. Additionally, *model size* has to be considered.

Linear models imply an additive connection between the variables; multiplicative connections are permitted only between decision variables and data. Although this assumption holds for many real-world problems, nonlinearities exist and have to be represented occasionally in linear models. A typical nonlinearity in management games is the joint influence of the decision variables "stored quantity" and "time of storage" on the result variable "warehousing expenses". In such cases, the nonlinear relation concerned has to be linearized by suitable approximations, producing a more or less essential difference between the game model and the linear model.

In real-world problems as well as in gaming some decision variables are restricted to integer values only. A typical integer variable is the number of ships to be sent on a certain route or the number of hospitals to be built in a certain region. Some decisions, e.g., the choice of a plant location, or decisions implying fixed costs or benefits, e.g., the fixed charge to be paid if any nonzero amount of an item is to be produced, can be represented in a model only if integer variables, or in some cases binary variables, are available. The use of such variables is not permitted in ordinary LP, since common algorithms are restricted to real variables only. The use of special integer algorithms leads to enormous solution requirements even for relatively small models. Therefore, in gaming the decision maker usually has to dispense with the availability of integer variables.

The data supplied by the decision maker have to be constants. Therefore, data should not depend on other variables: e.g., if the demand for a certain product is dependent on its price, different data items have to be used. Similarly functions cannot be represented directly; they have to be approximated by several values. Data are regarded as deterministic. Special algorithms, e.g., chance-constrained programming, can cope with uncertainty, but since they are time-consuming they are again less suitable for gaming.

The model size depends on the quantity of functional and temporal interdependences represented in the model and--in multiperiod games-- on the number of periods to be covered. The size of the model influences the input and solution time requirements. Although LP fares better than integer and nonlinear programming when models grow, small models are favored also for LP. Therefore, adequate procedures have to be employed to reduce the size of linear models, while affecting their usability as little as possible.

These problems usually impair the problem-matching ability of LP depending on the extent of nonlinearities, integer exigencies, functional dependences, and stochastic influences, etc. Although special algorithms are basically available, their enormous solution requirements usually prohibit their application for gaming purposes. In some cases, making alternative runs with different values for the data items concerned can alleviate these problems. Nevertheless, these characteristics and requirements of LP have to be borne in mind. It is a comforting fact, however, that in gaming a certain inequality between game model and linear model is desirable, as mentioned above (Section 2.1.).

3. THE TRIMDI SYSTEM

The TRIMDI System (TRaining in Integrated Management Decisions in Industry) is a combination of a complex management game and a corresponding decision aid, linear programming. Both are computer supported. The system has been in constant use in university education and management training since 1973 at the University of Hamburg. Its main objectives are: to increase perceptions regarding business interrelationships; to reduce the gap between methods taught in university and those applicable in business; to improve problem definitions and solution capabilities as well as the ability to work in groups.

3.1. The Management Game

The management game usually is employed by four or five groups, each having four participants on average. Twelve periods are normally played. Each group representing one enterprise is involved in highly interdependent activities concerning purchasing, production, warehousing, investment, marketing, and financing. All enterprises have the same history. Figure 1 shows the material flow of the game model. The game is described in Scheer and Schuenemann (1978a).

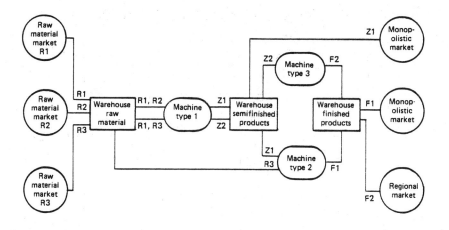

Figure 1. The TRIMDI game model.

The decisions to be made in each period are listed in Table 1. Functional interdependences result from the flow of materials and the problems of distributing limited financial funds for different purposes, e.g., investment versus sales promotion activities. Temporal interdependences are enforced by means of time lags for purchasing and investment, limited storage stability for raw material and products, and seasonal influences on the demand for the products. Uncertainty is caused not by stochastic elements in the game but by the incomplete knowledge of the market mechanisms for purchasing and marketing as well as the lack of information on the marketing activities of other enterprises.

As the full size of the management game can easily over-stretch a new participant's capability, only a self-contained, small subset of the game is introduced in the first period. This subset is gradually extended in the following periods. Therefore, the decision maker spends more and more time just on coping with the growing complexity of the game. Usually after having dealt with the full game for one or two periods, the decision maker calls for a powerful decision aid to relieve him from time-consuming manual calculations. At this point, LP is introduced.

3.2. The Decision Aid

The decision maker is supplied with a computer-supported decision aid containing a matrix generator that produces a custom-made linear model, access to the data base program, and a simplex algorithm with reinversion property. The handling of the decision aid is made easy by

Table 1. Decisions in the TRIMDI management game.

Activity	Decisions on
Purchasing	Quantity of raw material (3 kinds) Terms of delivery (prompt, 1-period delay, negotiations with other groups)
Investment	Extension of warehouses (raw material, semi-finished products, finished products) Replacement and extension of production capacities (3 machine types)
Production	Quantity to be produced (2 semi-finished products, 2 finished products)
Marketing	Price, sales promotion expenses, quantity of products to be offered (1 semi-finished product, 2 finished products) on different types of markets (monopolistic, oligopolistic, regional) Purchase of a market report
Financing	Raising and granting loans and funds

the dialogue mode. The decision maker uses only one command for data entry and only one command for the algorithm.

The majority of the data are automatically taken from the data base of the game model, e.g., interest rates as well as the available stocks of raw material and products. The decision maker supplies data concerning the future development of prices for raw material, the amount of money to be spent on decisions not covered by the game, e.g., marketing decisions and the cost of the market report. Only the marketing data are compulsory.

The marketing data comprise prices, sales promotion expenses, and the quantities of products offered for sale. In the linear model it is assumed that the given sales promotion expenses are paid in any case and the given price is valid for every product sold. The solution algorithm is prevented from setting the decision variable "sold quantity" higher than the given quantity for sale. To allow different combinations of the offered quantity and the sales promotion expenses in one run, the decision maker can enter a factor for each product representing the sales promotion expenses to be spent on one additional unit of the product concerned. As the marketing data have to be estimated by the decision maker, this relaxation--limited to a certain percentage of the original quantity to be offered--can cope to a certain extent with the imminent uncertainty of marketing data. To investigate the influence of different prices, alternative runs have to be made.

The size of the model varies according to the circumstances of the enterprise, e.g., the number of machines already invested, and the data supplied by the decision maker, e.g., the additional market constraints caused by the relaxations mentioned above. However, the main influence on size is the number of periods to be considered. The decision maker can generate models ranging from one to four periods in length. A small number of periods results in a small model requiring less solution time. To cover long-range decisions and temporal interdependences several periods have to be considered simultaneously; e.g., the extension of warehouses requiring two periods necessitates at the very least a three-period model. To reduce the solution time for multiperiod models, the model structure has to be simplified. To affect the problem-matching capability as little as possible, only later periods are simplified, e.g., by using only one decision variable for one machine type regardless of the age and intensities, and by dispensing with negotiations for raw material. In this way, a four-period model consisting of, e.g., 425 decision variables and 240 constraints is reduced to 208 decision variables and 161 constraints.

Apart from the inaccuracy caused by the simplifications of later periods, the linear model matches the game model fairly well. Only the fixed costs linked to the purchase of raw materials and the transportation costs for the regional markets cannot be represented. In order to influence the solvency planning in the model, the decision maker may supply the fixed costs as data.

The use of decision variables with real values for integer purposes is necessary for the investment in machines. This is not a major problem because the decision maker can decide whether this variable is a genuine decision variable to be set in the model or a data item to be set by him. Therefore, the decision maker, having obtained real value proposals in the first runs of the decision aid, may choose different integer values for the investment in machines and supply them as input data in subsequent runs.

3.3. Experience With the System

The TRIMDI System has, as mentioned above, been in use since 1973. The following remarks are based on a questionnaire given to twenty groups of players in different games during the years 1977-1982. All games covered twelve periods.

In the first seven periods the groups developed and applied manual decision aids. Nearly every group used its own sheet of calculation. Statistical methods, e.g., regression and correlation, were used to estimate the mechanisms of raw material and product markets. Special algorithms for production and solvency planning were applied. Although the groups reported improvements in their decisions, the manual decision aids were used generally only once or twice because of the calculation effort required.

LP was applied after the seventh period. The differences in planning time and results after the computer-supported decision aid was introduced are shown in Table 2.

Table 2. Comparison between manual and computer-supported decision aids.

Parameter	Decision aid	
	Manual	Computer-supported
Planning time per period (minutes)	192	218
Planning time per plan (minutes)	136	34
Number of plans per period	1.4	6.4
Number of meetings per period	1.1	1.6

Computer-supported planning reduced the planning time per plan by 75%. In consequence, four times as many plans were evaluated in each period. The prolongation of planning time per period and the increased number of meetings in each period were probably due to the higher motivation of the groups.

As shown in Table 3, data on quantities to be offered, prices, and sales promotion expenses were entered by all groups. As mentioned above, the decision aid proposes real values for the investment in machines. All but one group adjusted these decisions in subsequent runs by setting the respective input data with integer values. Factors for the increase of demand and price estimations for raw material were entered by the majority. These data provide higher flexibility in the market decisions for the decision aid as well as better problem-matching accuracy.

The groups reported that differences between alternative runs in one period were generally due to modifications of market and investment input data. In 48% of the cases only the last run was used as a decision basis while in 36% of the cases *all* runs were used. As shown in Table 4, compared with the first solution the last run revealed minor or major differences in 80% of the cases. This indicates the significance of the reiteration capability of the decision aid. The input proposal was employed with negligible alterations in 47% of the cases; major alterations being necessary in only 3% of the cases. Furthermore, the applicability of the decision aid is demonstrated by the correspondence between the results from the decision aid and the results of the game: negligible or minor differences occurred in 78% of the cases. Without exception, estimation errors, concerning especially the input data for marketing activities, were held responsible for the differences encountered by the groups, rather than deficiencies in the decision aid itself.

Table 3. Utilization of input data for the decision aid.

Input data	Number of groups	
	Data entered	Data modified
Quantity of products to be offered	20	16
Price of products	20	16
Sales promotion expenses	20	17
Investment in machines	19	13
Factor for the increase of demand	15	8
Fixed costs (purchasing, transport, market report)	10	5
Price estimation for raw material	12	4

Table 4. Differences encountered in the application of solutions.

Items compared	Extent of differences (%)		
	Negligible	Minor	Major
Structure of the first and structure of the last solution from the decision aid	20	55	25
Input proposal of the decision aid and actual input to the game	47	50	3
Results from the decision aid and results of the game	53	25	22

The degrees of relevance of the decision variables to the game solutions are displayed in Table 5. As the dominant objective in the game is to achieve a maximum profit, the groups regarded profit/loss as the most relevant criterion. The almost identical priorities of production, marketing, and financing results indicates the similar degree of difficulty for these decisions in the game and the general applicability of the decision aid for these planning activities. Purchasing and investment decisions received lower priorities, basically because their main influence falls into subsequent periods and the groups favored short-term decisions.

Table 5. Relevance of the decision variables to the solutions.

Decision variables	Relevance priority	
	First	Other
Profit/loss	16	3
Production	1	12
Marketing	3	9
Financing		11
Purchasing		8
Investment		6

Table 6 shows the advantages ascribed to the decision aid by the groups. All groups rated the reduction of the manual calculation as the dominant advantage. In consequence, given more time for operational and strategic planning, the groups regarded a better general view as being another major advantage of the decision aid. The increase of motivation and the improvement of decisions were considered advantages, too. Being a decision aid for a self-contained game model, its ability to indicate new problems was not regarded as a major advantage.

Table 6. Advantages of the decision aid.

Advantage	Average score[a]
Reduces manual calculation	2.7
Provides better general view	2.1
Increases motivation	1.7
Improves decisions	1.5
Detects new problems	1.3

[a]Scale: 0 = no advantage; 1 = small; 2 = medium; 3 = big advantage.

Looking at Table 7, we see that the groups assessed the disadvantages of the decision aid as generally lower than the advantages. The increase of estimation errors was considered the dominant disadvantage but, in spite of that, was rated as being of less than medium importance. As mentioned above, estimation errors were the main source of differences between the results from the decision aid and those of the game. The groups reported that in many cases their first estimations had been more realistic than those in subsequent runs. Obviously the possibility of easily modifying estimations can lead to a sort of self-deception, as subsequent runs with less realistic data apparently yielded better solutions and were consequently adopted. This seems to be a general problem in the application of decision aids in dialogue mode, especially if the decision aid does not comment on the usefulness of the estimated data.

Table 7. Disadvantages of the decision aid.

Disadvantage	Average score[a]
Increase of estimation errors	1.6
Emphasis on the game character	1.2
Discrepancies between game model and linear model	1.2
Inflexibility	1.0
Increase of decision time	0.5
Reduction of long-range planning	0.5
Diminution of the player's proficiency	0.4

[a]Scale: 0 = no disadvantage; 1 = small; 2 = medium; 3 = big disadvantage.

The remaining disadvantages were considered generally to be of low or negligible importance. The game character of the decision situation is emphasized only minimally by the decision aid. The problem-matching accuracy is sufficient, as the discrepancies between the game model and the linear model, as well as the inflexibility caused by the preformulation of the linear model, are not considered major disadvantages. The increase of decision time pointed out already (Table 2) obviously is compensated for by the increase of motivation. Finally, the long-range planning activities of the groups were not limited by the application of the decision aid.

Other experiences reported earlier illustrated the superiority of LP as a decision aid for the management game (Scheer and Schuenemann, 1978a,b). For identical game situations and periods the same groups made independent parallel runs using manual decision aids and the computer-supported decision aid. To evaluate the impact of long-term decisions, e.g., the investment in warehouses and machines, several periods were played successively. Two tendencies were observed: decisions based on solutions from the computer-supported decision aid had short-term as well as long-term results of significantly higher quality than those based on manual calculations. On the other hand, groups that calculated more solutions with alternative input data in one period had better results than those making fewer runs. These tendencies have also been confirmed elsewhere in this volume, demonstrating the overall usefulness and benefits of decision aids in gaming.

REFERENCES

Scheer, A.W. and Schuenemann, T.M. (1978a). TRIMDI--Ein Planspiel-konzept zum Einsatz von LP-Entscheidungsmodellen. *Schriften zur Unternehmensfuehrung, Wiesbaden,* 25:151-167.
Scheer, A.W. and Schuenemann, T.M. (1978b). Interaktiver Einsatz von LP-Planungsmodellen in einem Unternehmensplanspiel. In I. Kupka (Ed.), *Techniken des Dialogues.* Munich/Vienna, pp. 133-146.

NOTE

1. According to George Dantzig, the method goes back to Joseph (in Genesis), who, on hearing the dream of the Pharoah, advised him to save the grain from the seven "fat years" for the coming seven "lean years". This was the first case of "lean year programming" *(Editor's comment.)*

INTERACTIVE MAN-COMPUTER DIALOGUES FOR DETERMINING
THE PAYOFF FUNCTION OF A GAME

Ingolf Stahl
International Institute for Applied Systems Analysis,
Laxenburg (Austria)

1. INTRODUCTION

In Chapter III:a, Section 7, we discussed the difference between free-form and rigid-rule games. We defined a rigid-rule game as one in which all the institutional assumptions of the model of the game situation are given by the game constructor. In a free-form game, some institutional assumptions can be determined by the players. In particular, this refers to the rules of the game defining not only the decisions that players are allowed but also what payoffs are related to a certain set of decisions. This latter relationship takes the form of a payoff function that often works in two steps: first relating the particular combination of decisions to a specific state of the system, then relating this state of the system to a value result, i.e., a positive or negative payoff.

In a free-form game the players may be able to change the state of the system resulting from a certain set of decisions (including the random decisions of nature) or the value result associated with this state of the system. Such possibilities of changing the payoff function have the prime advantage of making the game more realistic, especially in cases when players actually know more facts relevant to the institutional assumptions than does the game constructor.

It is often assumed that free-form games have to be very "soft" games of a discussion type and, in contrast, that all computer games must be of the rigid type, with the payoff functions exactly defined by the game constructor. We shall, however, present here a method - interactive man-computer dialogues - by which the players themselves can in a fairly simple manner change the payoff functions of a computerized game.

2. THE CO_2 + COAL GAME

In this chapter we shall take some examples from a game concerned with CO_2 emissions and coal trade, developed at IIASA.[1] The game focuses on the problem of the potentially negative impact on climate of rising levels of CO_2 in the atmosphere caused by the probable increase in the use of fossil fuels (mainly coal) in the next century. The game deals with national decisions on mining, burning, and trading in coal during the next fifty years. The roles of some twenty countries are played by a mixture of human players and robots. The major countries, played by humans, can also cooperate to restrict the burning of coal and thus the emission of CO_2.

Three computer dialogues have been developed for collecting data and forecasts for each of the countries in the game:

1. A coal mining costs dialogue.[2]

2. A benefits of burning coal dialogue, focusing on the costs (including conservation costs) of alternative energy sources which one would have to utilize if one burnt less coal.

3. A CO_2-impacts module, dealing firstly with global impacts, and secondly with impacts on each country, of increased CO_2 levels.

3. OVERVIEW OF THE METHOD

Before going into specific details, we shall first present a brief overview of the most important aspects of the dialogue method.

In many games, such as the CO_2 + Coal game referred to above, the total payoff function is a very complicated function of many variables. The interactive dialogue will divide the total payoff function into many subfunctions, each of *one* variable, and step-by-step obtain the parameters for each such subfunction.

Examining how this is actually done we must first distinguish between the *functional form* and the *parameters* of the (sub)function. $f(x) = ae^{bx}$ and $f(x) = a + bx$ are two examples of functional forms for a function $f(x)$, each allowing for two parameters a and b. While the game constructor himself has to decide on the functional form of the subfunctions and hence of the whole payoff function, he can allow the players to change the *parameters* of the function. To a limited extent he can also even allow a limited degree of choice concerning the functional form, by using (sub)functions of the type $\alpha ae^{bx} + (1-\alpha)(a + bx)$. By setting the parameter α to be 0 or 1, the player can in this case choose between an exponential and a linear function.

To input these parameters a man-computer dialogue is used. It is often unreasonable to ask a player directly about the value of a parameter,[3] particularly in cases when the parameters (or coefficients) are used to let the function approximate other types of functions.[4] Instead, one asks about the value of $y = f(x)$ for various values of x. In the case of a function of two parameters one would ask about the values of y for two values of x. With, for example, the equations $y_1 = a + bx_1$ and $y_2 = a + bx_2$, the parameters a and b can be uniquely determined. For three parameters, three values of y would have to be given, etc. As will be discussed below, it might also be appropriate to allow the player to specify some values of x.

In order to make this method more concrete, let us assume that we want to determine the development of productivity in coal mining over time in a certain country. The computer might then ask for the production per man-shift in two years, t_1 and t_2. If we assumed an exponential development of production we would, with the two production levels y_1 and y_2, determine the parameters a and b from the relations $y_1 = ae^{bt_1}$ and $y_2 = ae^{bt_2}$. In some cases it might be appropriate to let t_1 be the present year,[5] and to let the player himself decide on a suitable year for t_2, possibly a year in the past for which he has data about y.

An important aspect of the method is that the computer, when asking for a certain value of y, will at the same time also *suggest* a value. The idea behind this is that it is not always certain that the player knows the data requested. The player can then accept or reject the data which the computer already has regarding this parameter, input earlier by another player or by the game constructor. In the case described above, the computer would first suggest y_1, the production per man-shift for year t_1. The player can accept this value y_1, or, if he has a better idea, input some other value. After the player has next stated t_2, the computer will, on the basis of the values of the parameters a and b, calculate a tentative value for y_2. The computer presents this to the player who can choose to input this or some other value for y_2.

The player thus determines some values of y that imply certain values of the parameters. The question is next, whether the player is willing to also accept those other values for y that are implied by the parameter values just determined. In the case described above, the question is whether the player would accept the implied values of production for other years than t_1 and t_2. In order to check this, the computer presents a projected level of production per man-shift, based on the parameters just determined, for certain years (e.g., every fifth or tenth year) from the present year until some predetermined year in the future. The player then scrutinizes this projection. In reply to the computer's question of whether the projection is reasonably realistic, the player can, by answering no, get a chance to input new y values. In this way he can continue until he is satisfied with the projection and hence the underlying parameters. In some cases he will also, as mentioned above, have a chance to switch to another functional form.

We have just described the determination of the parameters of *one* of the many subfunctions building up to form the total payoff function. This buildup of the payoff function follows a hierarchical structure. Projections are given not only for each separate relation or subfunction, but also at more and more aggregate levels of the payoff function. For example, in the coal mining cost dialogue of the $CO_2 \div$ Coal game, there is, at the most aggregate level, a projection of total mining costs. On the level below this, projections are given for costs in *old* and *new* mines. As regards costs in, e.g., old mines, projections are given of wage costs and nonwage costs. As regards wage costs, there are, in turn, projections for wage rates and productivity. As regards productivity, the projections concern, on the lowest level, changes in productivity due to working more difficult seams and changes due to technological development. At each stage, one does not proceed further to a *higher* level without having first approved the projections given thus far for all lower levels.

4. WHO ARE THE USERS OF THE DIALOGUE SYSTEM?

We can distinguish three main categories of users of the dialogue system:

1. *Players in a game.* The most suitable use of the dialogues is in a short session prior to the playing of the actual game. It is, however, also possible to interrupt the game playing to allow players to change the payoff functions.

2. *Experts who are not participating in the game.* Although the main function of the dialogue system is to allow input from the actual players of the game, one can also use the system for getting input from experts, independent of the game playing. The use of such experts is of particular interest as regards those parts of the payoff function for which neither the players nor the game constructor have much information.

3. *The game constructor himself.* The constructor can also use the dialogue system when inputting the parameters of the payoff function.

5. WHAT ARE THE MAIN BENEFITS OF THE DIALOGUE SYSTEM?

We shall suggest six major groups of benefits that can be obtained by using a dialogue system.

5.1. Obtaining Valid Data and Forecasts

In an operational game it is of particular importance to have data and forecasts that are as valid as possible. It is, however, often very difficult for just one or two game constructors to gather the data necessary for specifying the correct form of the payoff functions. This is especially true for games where conditions in many different countries are represented and where the subject matter of the game is related to several scientific disciplines, such as in the CO_2 and Coal game. In these cases it is difficult enough to obtain sufficient data on past and present conditions in the different countries from the literature, but it is even harder to find published forecasts of future relationships. It is usually a better idea to collect the necessary data and forecasts from a large number of sources, if possible from different countries and with different disciplinary backgrounds.

More specifically, as regards collecting these data and forecasts for the payoff function of the game, the dialogue system appears to have the following six advantages:

a. It is *convenient.* The use of a terminal, possibly with a game assistant to help with the input of the answers, is fast and convenient.

b.   It focuses on easily *understandable* questions. As mentioned earlier, the computer asks for specific values of variables that are more understandable than relatively strange parameters. It then provides projections of different parts of the payoff function on different levels. Thus, the dialogue method makes it easier for the player to better understand the concrete meaning of the payoff function. This understanding can be even further improved when the dialogue is related to the playing of the game, and in particular if the dialogues are repeated after the playing of the game.

c.   It *motivates* the players to answer correctly. The running of the dialogues in connection with the playing of the game also increases the motivation of the players to do their best in answering the questions, since they perceive that the game will be more realistic if they provide the most correct answers possible.

d.   It helps to *focus* the players on giving the kind of answers that one really wants. The use of the man-computer dialogue has, compared to a "man-man" dialogue, the advantage that one gets only the type of answers that one wants, i.e., quantitative estimates, not qualitative opinions. When using a "man-man" dialogue for the collection of data from experts, we have encountered the following problem: The experts want to give only qualitative opinions, sometimes of a methodological character, and in some cases these are not even related to the specific question. If a human were to behave like the computer, essentially insisting on a certain kind of answer, he would be considered very rude, and, therefore, probably not be as successful as the computer in performing this task (Stahl, 1980).

e.   It allows the data to be *recorded* in a fast and convenient manner. Only by using a computer for the dialogue can one rapidly transform the answers into parameters for immediate use in the computer game. Since it is generally only possible to get the players to attend for the playing of a game, it is important that the results from the dialogues should be rapidly available to influence the payoff function of the game.

f.   Data from the "best" *experts* can be recorded. The dialogue method allows the entire set of parameters to be recorded as a computer file under an individual name (for example, the name of the expert) at the end of the dialogue process. Having recorded many such files on the same subject, one can, by scrutinizing the expertise of the various players, choose the most suitable parameter for a standard file (to be used, e.g., as a basis for the suggested values during a dialogue).

5.2. Aiding the Preparation of Forecasts

An important problem for any game dealing with future events, such as operational games for futures research, is that the payoff function will be based on forecasts or rather "intelligent guesses" about future relationships. Such guesses are generally difficult to make, particularly if one has not previously thought through the problems at length. The guesswork is facilitated, however, by the dialogue system. This provides, at different levels, projections of what the inputs made thus far imply and then allows for new answers if the projections appear unreasonable. The player can thus test a great many arrangements of the parameters.

5.3. Making the Assumptions of the Game Transparent

Even if a player does not change any of the parameters and just accepts the suggested answers to the questions posed by the dialogue, it can still be very worthwhile for him to run through the dialogue. This will in a straightforward way make him aware of the data assumptions behind the payoff function. The projections will also give him some idea about the functional form of the functions used. The dialogue will thus enable him to understand better how the game functions.[6]

In many cases there is the problem that the players are unwilling to take the game seriously, because it is a black box in the sense that the assumptions behind the payoff functions are hidden. This can lead the players to regard certain reactions of the payoff function as arbitrary. By providing more transparency, the dialogues will help the players to understand why the payoff function reacts in a certain way and the game will then appear less arbitrary.

Increased game transparency also facilitates a constructive critique of the total game structure. The *post mortem* discussion at the end of the game will then be more fruitful, both for the operational purpose of the gaming session and for the further refinement of the game.

5.4. Giving the Model Face Validity

Transparency is, however, not always enough to make players take a game seriously. If a player regards a specific assumption, now made transparent, to be unrealistic, his reaction might in fact become even more unfavorable. It is then important that he has a chance to change the assumption. Possibilities of changing the parameters are provided by the dialogue method. The experience of both understanding the assumptions and having had a chance to change those payoff assumptions that appear unrealistic appears to increase the "face validity" of the game and thus increases the player's degree of seriousness when playing the game.

5.5. Aiding Scenario Generation

When one wants to use the game as a scenario generation tool the use of the dialogue method can be very helpful. The scenario method usually aims at the construction of a number of scenarios that are fairly different with regard to the assumptions used.[7] By interactive use of dialogues one can find suitably different sets of institutional assumptions. Furthermore, the description of a scenario usually requires a fairly extensive and explicit verbal description of the assumptions behind each scenario. These verbal descriptions can then, to a considerable extent, rely on the questions and answers in the dialogue. This makes for a much more "understandable" scenario than would be obtained by merely stating the values of the parameters directly (Stahl and Ausubel, 1983).

5.6. Aiding the Game Constructor

Finally, it should be mentioned that the computer dialogue method can be very helpful to the game constructor while he is gradually building up the game. When making choices as to the general form of the payoff assumptions, the use of preliminary versions of computer dialogues proved very helpful, for example, in the CO_2 + Coal game.

6. HOW MANY QUESTIONS SHOULD THE DIALOGUE CONTAIN?

Having discussed at some length the benefits of the dialogue method, we shall proceed to answer some more specific questions regarding the size of the dialogue (this section), the type of data (Section 7), the wording of questions (Section 8), the number of parameters (Section 9), the determination of the domain of the subfunctions (Section 10), the construction of projections (Section 11), and the use of the computer (Section 12).

The first question concerns the appropriate size for a dialogue. This is, of course, dependent on the time available for running the dialogue and the number of parameters one wants to include in the payoff function. From our experience it appears that one can, in 15-30 minutes, run through a dialogue with around 30 questions, allowing for considerable feedback in the form of different projections. It also appears that, for most persons, 30 minutes is about the maximum useful time for running the dialogue without a pause;[8] if one goes on much longer one risks losing the player's attention. In addition, it seems that such a dialogue should not contain more than about 30 questions.[9]

If considerably more questions are required to establish the parameters of the payoff function of the game, several computer dialogues would probably be needed. It is then appropriate to let different dialogues focus on different themes, in particular with reference to different persons' expertise. Players with one kind of expertise should use one dialogue, while players with a different expertise use another. For example, in the CO_2 + Coal game we have one dialogue on coal mining costs, one on alternative energies, and one on CO_2 impacts, each suitable for players with different types of expertise.

7. WHICH TYPE OF DATA SHOULD THE DIALOGUES INVOLVE?

The type of data used in the dialogues depends first of all on what type of data one needs in the game: this, in turn, is mainly dependent on the subject of the game. One important question is how uncertain the data can be and still be meaningful enough for use in the game and as a basis for questions in the dialogue. Although, as mentioned above, the dialogue can help the players in making guesses, it is our experience that it is wise to avoid guesses about data in cases where different, equally well-informed players are likely to be orders of magnitude apart in their guesses.[10] If this happens, the players will then tend not to accept each other's payoff functions and the game's "face validity" will decrease.

Secondly, it is important that the dialogue does not ask for unreasonable data. Sometimes, one can let the computer deduce, on the basis of the answer to a given question, that it would be meaningless to proceed to another similar question.[11]

Finally, when the game, like our example, concerns many countries it appears more appropriate to ask about per capita figures rather than total figures, for example, for energy consumption. This is because it is then easier to make international comparisons, since per capita figures generally do not differ so much between countries of similar types. The actual total consumption is then computed using the country's population, which one probably requested anyway. Likewise, instead of asking for the value of total agricultural production, one should ask about agriculture's share of GNP.

8. HOW SHOULD THE QUESTIONS IN THE DIALOGUE BE WORDED?

Since an important function of an operational game is to provide an interface between analysts and decision makers, the actual wording of the questions in the man-computer dialogue becomes an important issue. Only if the questions are easily understood by the players is it possible to use the dialogues for making the assumptions of the game explicit. Scientists and laymen often do not use the same terms. For the computer dialogue it is necessary to avoid any terms or concepts that, although in general scientific usage, could be confusing to the layman.[12]

Another problem in this connection is to what extent hypothetical questions can be used. Since we are asking about one relationship at a time, we have to rely greatly on the *ceteris paribus* assumption, and this, in turn, is often hypothetical. In some cases certain simplifications of the questions, although increasing the layman's understanding, may make scientists feel less comfortable. There is a delicate balance to be struck here, particularly if some players have a certain scientific background and others do not.

Finally, a technical point on the wording of questions. Using text string variables one can allow the players to select not only values, but also the "names" of certain values. By allowing these names to be also used in the printout of the game results one can allow the players further flexibility in shaping the game.[13]

9. HOW MANY PARAMETERS SHOULD EACH SUBFUNCTION CONTAIN?

We now turn to a question regarding the functional form of the sub-functions or relationships: how many parameters should one allow for each relationship? This is, of course, highly dependent on the relationship that one wants to approximate. There is obviously a tradeoff between, on the one hand, the simplicity of few parameters, leading to fewer questions and greater transparency, and on the other hand, the greater realism of many parameters.

For example, for the CO_2 + Coal game we tried to get by with as few parameters as possible, and used only two parameters for most relationships. For certain relationships in the CO_2-impacts dialogue we used the special quadratic function $y = ax + bx^2$. In the case of constant marginal effect, $b = 0$; if the marginal effect is decreasing, $b < 0$; if it is increasing, $b > 0$. The function is thus able to provide a very rough approximation of linear, logarithmic, and exponential relationships. However, as we used this dialogue, we found that for some of the functions b is often set close to 0. We were then able to simplify the dialogue by redefining these functions as simply ax.

In this connection it should be mentioned that although the combined function $\alpha a r e^{bx} + (1-\alpha)(a+bx)$ presented earlier has three parameters, the parameter α can be established in most cases without any extra question. Having first set $\alpha = 1$, one first asks for two values, y_1 and y_2, establishing a and b. The first projection is thus based on the exponential function. Only if a person discards this projection does the computer ask whether the person would rather have a linear relationship. If the answer then is yes, α is set to 0.

10. HOW TO DETERMINE THE DOMAIN OF THE SUBFUNCTIONS

One important problem encountered when establishing the parameters of a relation or subfunction concerns the choice of values of the independent variable x. As mentioned in Section 3, for each parameter one needs to state a dependent value y for a given value of x. The choice of the values of x will for many subfunctions determine within which limits the function provides reasonable values. For example, if we have a function with two parameters, established by the two pairs (x_1,y_1), (x_2,y_2) with $x_1 < x_2$, it is possible that the function will appear unreasonable for x values considerably smaller than x_1 and considerably higher than x_2, even though the projected values of y lying *between* y_1 and y_2 have appeared reasonable.

One possible solution would be to always allow the player to state both x_1 and x_2. He could then adjust these values until he is satisfied with the projections. A problem is, however, that the player might not know between which values x_1 and x_2 will vary during the game. Secondly, it may become too time-consuming to ask the player to supply all x values; the dialogue is speeded up if as many x values as possible are given by the computer.

When x denotes time, it is appropriate to have x_1 as the initial time. The player can then decide on x_2. This time can, as mentioned, be an earlier year, so that the player can base his forecast on historical data. We then obtain a projection, ranging from the present year up to a year not far away from the time when the game might end. In the CO_2 + Coal game, projections are given from 1982 up to 2030. In the beginning of the dialogues associated with this game it is stated that it is more important to have a good forecast for the years 2000-2010 than for the years towards the end of the game. Hence, if the player does not, for example, regard the forecast for 2010 as reasonable, he can input a new value pair (y_2, x_2), now with $x_2 = 2010$.

When the independent variable is not time, but some other variable, like the level of CO_2 in the atmosphere, it might be more appropriate for the computer to supply all the x values. Since the CO_2 level is not likely to decrease, x_1 in the CO_2 + Coal game is set as the present CO_2 level, while x_2 is set at 2.5 times this level. Since one does not envisage that the game will proceed so far that this level is exceeded, one avoids the problem of projected levels for $x > x_2$ that are unrealistic.

Finally, it should be mentioned that a dialogue based on simple functional forms, although giving reasonable projections for say 1982-2010, may lead to some less reasonable projections for 2010-2030. Instead of going over to more complicated functional forms, which would decrease the transparency to the player and increase programming problems, one can proceed as follows. One runs the dialogue first for the period 1982-2010 and saves this in one file to be used when the period 1982-2010 is simulated in the game. One then runs the dialogue again for 2010-2030, (possibly after the simulated time in the game has reached 2010), saving these new parameters in another file for the simulation in the game of the 2010-2030 period. In cases where some variable other than time, such as CO_2 level, is critical, one can perform a similar division, depending on when this variable reaches a critical level as regards the reasonability of the parameters.

11. PROJECTIONS FOR TESTING PARAMETERS

Regarding the projections of the functions, we shall mention here three ways of making it easier for the player to judge whether or not the implicitly input parameters are reasonable.

First, in order to allow the players to scrutinize a certain relationship more closely it is often appropriate to print out not only the independent and dependent variables, but also a third variable, which in turn has a pre-established relationship with the independent variable.[14]

Second, in some cases the projections are most suitably presented graphically. The ease with which this can be done is, however, dependent on the available computer system. If one must rely just on print out of numerical values in tabular form, it is important to remember not to confuse the players with unnecessary decimals.

Third, the player can give the computer special information for the sole purpose of improving these projections. For example, when making a projection of the development over time of total and average costs in coal mining, the computer needs to base this development on some rate of growth of production. It would be much less interesting to get a projection of these costs only under the assumption of no production increase. This "forecast" of future increase in production is, however, not used in the actual game, but only for the projection.

12. COMPUTER ASPECTS OF THE DIALOGUE METHOD

We shall finally discuss some details of specific computer and programming aspects of the dialogue method.

The input of data by players of the game is preferably made through computer terminals directly linked to the computer that handles the whole game. An alternative is to make the input into a microcomputer with a floppy-disk drive and after the dialogue to move the disk to the (micro)computer handling the game. When it comes to obtaining data from various experts in other countries who are not taking part in the game, the use of disks is worth investigating, particularly since they can be sent by mail. A faster alternative is to run dialogues using teleconferencing and thus get the data immediately into the central data base.

Regardless of which programming language one uses it is important to build up the dialogue program in modules or subroutines. Some such subroutines, e.g., for projections, can be used many times in a dialogue. In the case of a game with more than one dialogue, certain subroutines might also be used for more than one dialogue.

As regards the choice of computer language, the demand for structuring the program into well-defined modules points to a programming language suitable for structural programming, such as PASCAL (and, although somewhat less suitable, FORTRAN 77). On the other hand, the need for flexible testing of the dialogue in many steps might indicate an interpretative language like BASIC or APL. If one wishes to use inexpensive microcomputers, BASIC is preferable. If one wants to be able to move the program to many different computers, standard FORTRAN is preferable.[15]

REFERENCES

Leontief, W. (1982). Academic economics. *Science*, 217:104.
Schneider, S. and Chen, R. (1980). Carbon dioxide warming and coastline flooding: a problem review and exploratory climatic impact assessment. *Annual Review of Energy*, 5:107-140.
Stahl, I. (1980). *An Interactive Model for Determining Coal Costs for a CO_2 Game*. WP-80-154. International Institute for Applied Systems Analysis, Laxenburg, Austria.

Stahl, I. and Ausubel, J. (1981). Estimating the future input of fossil fuel CO_2 into the atmosphere by simulation gaming. In R.A. Fazzolare and C.B. Smith (Eds.), *Beyond the Energy Crisis: Opportunity and Challenge.* Pergamon Press, Oxford.

Stahl, I. and Ausubel, J. (1983). A gaming approach to scenarios of CO_2-emissions and the role of coal. *Climate Change*, forthcoming.

NOTES

1. For further details see Stahl and Ausubel (1981).

2. This dialogue is described in detail in Stahl (1980).

3. See for example Leontief (1982).

4. Take for example the function $y = ax + bx^2$ used in the CO_2 + Coal game for relations between global warming and warming in specific countries, as discussed further in Section 9.

5. Or the most recent year for which a complete set of statistics is available; this year is generally kept as a constant reference point throughout the dialogue procedure.

6. For the sake of making the model assumptions more transparent, it may be appropriate to ask not only about relationships in the future, which are subject to uncertainty, but sometimes also about fairly certain facts, just in order to draw the players' attention to the facts on which the payoff function is based.

7. See, e.g., Chapter VII:c in this volume.

8. If, however, one only runs through a dialogue to make the assumptions transparent, without aiming at changing the parameters, then 30 minutes is probably sufficient for a couple of dialogues.

9. We refer here to questions concerning specific data, i.e., we exclude questions of the YES/NO-type and questions of the most suitable years for data (i.e., t_2 in Section 3).

10. We have, for example, in the CO_2 + Coal game, avoided asking about the value of flooded property at the end of the next century in the event of a sea-level rise due to the collapse of the West Antarctic Ice Sheet; this contrasts with the approach used in other studies (e.g., Schneider and Chen, 1980).

11. In the CO_2 + Coal game the computer asks, for example, what Antarctic warming is necessary for the probability of a West Antarctic Icesheet collapse to be 0.1, 0.5, or 0.9. If the Antarctic warming deemed necessary for a 0.1 probability is very high (implying that one regards the collapse as unlikely) the computer will not bother about asking for the warming connected with the 0.5 and 0.9 probabilities.

12. As an example from the CO_2 + Coal game, a doubling of the CO_2 level

is usually calculated by scientists on the basis of a hypothetical preindustrial level. For a layman it appears more natural to think of a doubling from the present level. The CO_2 level is usually given by scientists in ppm (parts per million); for laymen it is easier, in a game dealing with decisions to burn megatons of coal, to also use megatons to define the CO_2 level.

13. For example, in the CO_2 + Coal game we allow the players to choose the name (be it "tourism", "fishing", etc.) for any secondary sector of the economy affected by climate change.

14. For example, in projecting the relationship between the probability of a West Antarctic Icesheet (WIS) collapse and Antarctic warming, it seemed appropriate to also give the corresponding global warming, since many people appear to relate the WIS collapse directly to global warming.

15. For the CO_2 + Coal game we used first FORTRAN 77 (on a VAX-780) and then BASIC (for APPLE microcomputers) to make the game truly portable.

PART XII

THE PROSPECTS FOR OPERATIONAL
GAMING: A SUMMARY

Chapter XII

THE PROSPECTS FOR OPERATIONAL GAMING: A SUMMARY

Ingolf Stahl
International Institute for Applied Systems Analysis,
Laxenburg (Austria)

1. INTRODUCTION

To conclude and summarize this volume we present here an examination of the prospects for operational gaming. This summary is based on discussions at the three meetings on gaming held at IIASA (in 1978, 1980, and 1981) and at the meetings of the International Simulation and Gaming Association (ISAGA) over the last few years. Many of these discussions, as well as the summary itself, were themselves inspired by earlier versions of various chapters in this book.

2. BENEFITS OF GAMING

A good starting point is to try to summarize the benefits of gaming. During the 1978 IIASA workshop on gaming, various statements regarding the different benefits to be derived from gaming were collected. Some had the air of slogans. These statements are presented below, without comments and without any serious attempt to put them in a logical order.

1. Gaming is a pre-science of clarifying concepts.
2. Gaming is a suitable brain-storming device.
3. Gaming is a heuristic device for thought experiments.
4. Gaming is the only science which uses humans not only as an end but also as a means.
5. A great benefit of gaming lies in the self-instruction of the game constructor.
6. The running of a game with experienced players is a good device for teaching the teachers.
7. Gaming is a device for two-way learning.
8. Gaming opens lines of communication between the players.
9. Gaming aids communication between the analyst and decision makers with regard to problem clarification.
10. Gaming can be seen as a means for communication between analysts.

11. Gaming changes the nature of feedback loops among information preparers and information users.

12. Gaming exposes deep biases in large-scale models.

13. Gaming is the only way of transmitting the "gestalt" of the problem.

14. Gaming is the only way of pretesting the behavioral assumptions in decision models; it puts them to the "acid test".

15. Gaming facilitates the understanding of goal setting, the link between analysis and planning.

16. Gaming is an important research tool for studying the effects of the variation of policy variables.

17. Gaming is important, not only in determining the "right" policies, but also for determining what the "right" players should look like.

18. Gaming catches the attention of the players and is more efficient for transferring ideas and data than a written report.

3. WHY HAS OPERATIONAL GAMING NOT BEEN USED MORE EXTENSIVELY?

The many advantages of gaming, reflected in the list above, were contrasted, at the 1978 IIASA workshop, with the conclusion that the participants could report very few applications of operational gaming outside of the military sphere. Later surveys, made by the IIASA Gaming Task in collaboration with Richard Duke (see Chapter I), have shown that the use of operational gaming seems to be somewhat wider than the 1978 workshop participants believed. This might be partly due to the fact that details of many operational games have not been published. It is still true, however, that civilian operational gaming has not reached the position that military operational gaming has, for example in terms of the money spent on each. Also there seems to us to be a very great discrepancy between what operational gaming *could* do in the civilian sector and its present rather restricted scope. Therefore, the discussion at the 1978 workshop on the reasons for this discrepancy is of some interest.

The following three reasons were given by participants with business experience for the very limited use of operational gaming in large corporations:

1. Some top managers regard gaming as a nonserious activity and balk at the very idea of letting gaming influence their decisions.

2. Top managers think that there is nothing new that they could learn from a gaming exercise.

3. Top managers regard games as too simple and hence too unrealistic to depict complex reality well.

Closely connected with these objections was the feeling that many gaming exercises had the "weakness" of inducing behavior among the participants which was felt to be too competitive. The confrontation implied in many game situations is unappealing to some decision makers.

The problem of gaming implementation can, however, also be explained to some extent by factors well known from studies on the implementation of other operations research or systems analysis methods. In particular, there is the problem of the *outside* consultants, who do not know the actual problem or decision-making structure of the corporation or organization studied. Outside consultants also often run into the problem that data are confidential. For similar reasons, the use of "outside players", such as students, is often impossible, making the testing of the game more difficult.

It was further noted that the "sponsorship" of gaming models is generally limited to that of the model constructor who, naturally, wishes to sell his game. Instances of top civilian managers requesting gaming appear to be rare. This problem of gaming in the civilian sector was considered by many workshop participants to be connected with the fact that operational gaming is a very new and little-known idea, so that there are virtually no "in-house" experts: very few people working within corporations have experience of gaming or game construction. This contrasts strongly with the military sphere where gaming has a century-long tradition in several countries and where many "in-house" experts are available.

Another reason for gaming being more successful in the military sphere than in the civilian sector is the *time* factor. In peace-time, top-level military personnel have considerable time for long-term planning activities such as gaming, whereas people on the civilian side are in a sense constantly "at war" and generally are forced to tend towards short-term "muddling through" solutions.

In this connection the importance of getting the "correct" players was stressed. A very busy top-level executive cannot be easily replaced in an operational game by a very junior employee (who has the time to play) because the junior staff member has very dissimilar experience and perspectives.

The duration factor was considered important in another respect. Much top-level military gaming is focused on long-term, e.g., five-year planning, where gaming is used partly as a discussion device, in which different branches of the armed forces bargain over their share of a fairly fixed "cake". The outcome of this bargaining can, in some countries, determine the relative sizes of these branches, within fairly narrow limits, for the next five years. In private corporations, long-term planning could seldom be binding to this extent. The existence of a market within which the corporation can expand (or contract) lessens the importance of this type of intraorganizational bargaining and hence also the importance of gaming as a bargaining device for allocation *within* bureaucracies.

4. HOW TO INCREASE THE USE OF OPERATIONAL GAMING

Faced with this large discrepancy between the many benefits of gaming (as outlined in the 18 points in Section 2) and the fairly negative experience as regards the actual use of gaming in the civilian sector (discussed in Section 3), the question naturally arises as to how the practical use of operational gaming can be promoted.

On the basis of the chapters in this book, as well as the discussions at the various meetings mentioned above, we can outline the following possible approaches:

a. Focus on the Most Suitable Situations

Operational gaming is more likely to meet with success if efforts are made to apply it to the problems for which it is best suited. There are some reasons to believe that an emphasis on tactical rather than strategic problems and on middle-management rather than top-management problems would increase the chances of implementation. Also, gaming is more likely to be adopted in situations where a well-understood process is modeled, the players have a clear objective, and real players are playing their own roles.

b. Disseminate Information about Operational Gaming

Although the literature on gaming in general is quite extensive, there are very few reports on practical nonmilitary uses of operational gaming and this material is hardly known at all among decision makers. It therefore seems especially important to gather all available information on uses of operational gaming in practice and to disseminate this information in such a way that it reaches the largest possible audience of decision makers.

c. Strive to Overcome Negative Attitudes

More widespread implementation of gaming methods cannot, however, be achieved by merely disseminating more information. A change in attitudes may also be required. As noted in the preceding section, "gaming" has the connotation of being a less-than-serious activity. In some cases it may be more appropriate to use the alternative term "multiperson interactive simulation". Furthermore, in many cases, it is important *not to oversell* the idea of gaming. Gaming should not be presented as the *only* tool in the analysis of a problem. Rather, it should be presented as an important complement to other tools of systems analysis, such as optimization, simulation, econometrics, etc., since it can reveal critical aspects inaccessible to these other methods. Furthermore, it might help to "warm the managers up" for gaming by presenting some very simple games before the more complicated ones.

d. Reduce the Costs of Obtaining a Suitable Game.

The cost of building a new operational game can be very substantial and this cost may be important for many smaller and middle-sized corporations that now avoid the use of gaming. The costs can be reduced by (1) increasing the possibilities of using an existing game and (2) cutting down the actual development costs for a new game.

The possibilities of using an existing game can be increased in several ways: (a) Setting up better and more comprehensive computer files about existing games. In this connection the project within the CMEA countries on a joint file of all available games is of interest (see Chapter IV:a). (b) The possibilities of modifying an existing game are greatly increased if this game is constructed in a suitable way from the beginning, e.g., in a modular fashion (see Chapter V:a). The construction of "frame games", which with small changes can serve for many purposes, is an important step towards lowering the cost of suitable games.

The costs of building a new game from scratch can mainly be reduced by work on more formalized methods for constructing games, such as those presented in Part IX. Further research on the development of such methods, more published reports on this work, and an increase in the amount of university courses on game development methods are all needed. Particular phases of game development can be improved by using specific methods; for example, the costs of collecting data for a game can be cut by using man-computer dialogue methods (see Chapter XI:b).

e. Reduce the Cost of Operating the Game

The expense or lack of computer resources with suitable software[1] was previously a problem for the running of games in many organizations. With the advent of portable microcomputers with substantial memory capacities, this difficulty will probably decrease, particularly if future game development focuses on microcomputers.

f. Reduce the Cost of Playing the Game

As noted above, one of the factors restricting the implementation of operational gaming in the civilian sphere is the greater difficulty in this sector to get top personnel with time for game playing. Since the cost of their time is very high, the total cost of playing for a long time can easily become prohibitive. Hence small games, playable in an evening, would (as discussed in Chapter X:a) probably stand a better chance of being implemented, provided that they have sufficient outward credibility to satisfy the potential players. Hence, there appears to be a need for research on the question of how, in a small game, one can achieve reasonably realistic modeling (for example, along the lines of the methodology outlined in Chapter X:b).

The cost of playing the game is dependent not only on the length of the game, but also on the number of human players involved. This number can be reduced using devices such as robot players. Further development in this area could therefore also contribute to lowering the total cost of playing a game.

5. INTERNATIONAL COOPERATION

For many of the approaches mentioned above for promoting the practical use of operational gaming, it appears that international cooperation would be helpful. This would involve, among other things, obtaining information on actual uses of operational gaming, establishing files on games suitable for use in other situations (possibly after modification), developing frame games, developing methodologies for game construction, teaching game development methodology, etc.

In the Western countries the International Simulation and Gaming Association (ISAGA) has held annual meetings since 1970.[2] Within the CMEA, as described in Chapter IV:a, there have been annual meetings of gamers from the socialist countries since 1974. Thanks to the IIASA Gaming Task, the first general meeting between the ISAGA and CMEA gamers will take place in June 1983 in Sofia, in collaboration with Bulgaria's National Committee for Applied Systems Analysis and Management. It is hoped that this meeting will be the first in a series that could lead to further fruitful international collaboration in the field of operational gaming.

NOTES

1. Even if an organization had a computer, it very often did not have a compiler or interpreter for a programming language suitable for games.

2. For further information about ISAGA contact Jan Klabbers, General Secretary of the ISAGA, University of Utrecht, The Netherlands.